Tort Law in Germany

Tort Law in Germany

Fourth Edition

Oliver Rieckers
Simon Gerdemann
Andreas Seidel

This book was originally published as a monograph in the International Encyclopaedia of Laws/Tort Law.

Founding Editor: Roger Blanpain
General Editor: Frank Hendrickx
Volume Editor: Britt Weyts

Wolters Kluwer

Published by:
Kluwer Law International B.V.
PO Box 316
2400 AH Alphen aan den Rijn
The Netherlands
E-mail: lrs-sales@wolterskluwer.com
Website: www.wolterskluwer.com/en/solutions/kluwerlawinternational

Sold and distributed by:
Wolters Kluwer Legal & Regulatory U.S.
920 Links Avenue
Landisville, PA 17538
United States of America
E-mail: customer.service@wolterskluwer.com

ISBN 978-94-035-0028-7

e-Book: ISBN 978-94-035-0038-6
web-PDF: ISBN 978-94-035-0048-5

This title is available on www.kluwerlawonline.com

The Authors

Dr Oliver Rieckers studied Law at the University of Göttingen, Germany, and at the University of Chicago. He worked as an assistant to Professor Dr Gerald Spindler from 1998 to 2002. Since 2005, Dr Rieckers has been working as an attorney in Düsseldorf, Germany. He is a lecturer at the University of Frankfurt, Germany, and has published various book contributions and articles in German and international law reviews concerning tort law as well as German and US corporate and securities law.

Dr Simon Gerdemann studied Law at the University of Göttingen, Germany, and the University of California, Berkeley, where he completed his PhD in Comparative US and German Law in 2017. After working for an international law firm and in the German Federal Parliament, he became a postdoctoral fellow (Habilitand) at the Institute for Business and Media Law at the University of Göttingen and a principal investigator for the German Research Foundation in 2022. He has published various books and papers in German and international law journals and served as an expert advisor to the German legislator.

The Authors

Dr Andreas Seidel studied Law at the University of Göttingen, Germany, and at the Catholic University of Leuven, Belgium. He worked as an assistant to Professor Dr Gerald Spindler from 2017 to 2020. After his legal clerkship, he started in 2022 as a postdoctoral fellow (Habilitand) and academic councillor (akademischer Rat auf Zeit) at the Institute for Business and Media Law at the University of Göttingen. He has published various book contributions and articles in German and international law reviews concerning civil law in general, tort law in particular, as well as corporate and competition law.

Table of Contents

List of Abbreviations

AcP	Archiv für die civilistische Praxis
AG	Amtsgericht (*Local Court*)
AtG	Atomgesetz (*Atomic Energy Act*)
BB	Betriebs-Berater
BBergG	Bundesberggesetz (*Federal Mining Act*)
BDSG	Bundesdatenschutzgesetz (*Federal Data Protection Act*)
BeckOGK	Beck-online Großkommentar (*beck-online Grand Commentary*)
BeckOK	Beck'scher Online-Kommentar (*Beck's Online Commentary*)
BGB	Bürgerliches Gesetzbuch (*Civil Code*)
BGH	Bundesgerichtshof (*Federal Supreme Court*)
BGHZ	Entscheidungen des Bundesgerichtshofes in Zivilsachen (*Decisions of the Federal Supreme Court*)
BImSchG	Bundesimmissionsschutzgesetz (*Federal Emissions Control Act*)
BVerfG	Bundesverfassungsgericht (*Federal Constitutional Court*)
BVerfGE	Entscheidungen des Bundesverfassungsgerichts (*Decisions of the Federal Constitutional Court*)
DAR	Deutsches Autorecht
DB	Der Betrieb
DVBl	Deutsches Verwaltungsblatt
EU	European Union
FamRZ	Zeitschrift für das gesamte Familienrecht
GDP	Gross Domestic Product
GenTG	Gentechnikgesetz (*Genetic Engineering Act*)
GPSG	Gesetz über technische Arbeitsmittel und Verbraucherprodukte (*Act on Technical Work Equipment and Consumer Products*)
GSG	Gerätesicherheitsgesetz (*Act on Safety of Technical Equipment*)

GVG	Gerichtsverfassungsgesetz (*Judicature Act*)
HPflG	Haftpflichtgesetz (*Strict Liability Act*)
JA	Juristische Arbeitsblätter
JuS	Juristische Schulung
JZ	Juristenzeitung
KG	Kammergericht (*in fact: Appellate Court for Berlin)*
KUG	Kunsturhebergesetz (*Act on Artistic Creations*)
LG	Landgericht (*District Court*)
LM	Nachschlagewerk des Bundesgerichtshofs, von Fritz Lindenmaier & Philipp Möhring (*Reference Book of the Federal Supreme Court, by Fritz Lindenmaier & Philipp Möhring*)
LuftVG	Luftverkehrsgesetz (*Air Traffic Act*)
MDR	Monatsschrift für Deutsches Recht
MedR	Medizinrecht
NJW	Neue Juristische Wochenschrift
NJW-RR	NJW-Rechtsprechungsreport Zivilrecht
NZBau	Neue Zeitschrift für Baurecht und Vergaberecht
NZG	Neue Zeitschrift für Gesellschaftsrecht
OLG	Oberlandesgericht (*Appellate Court*)
PatG	Patentgesetz (*Patent Act*)
PflVG	Pflichtversicherungsgesetz (*Obligatory Insurance Act*)
ProdHaftG	Produkthaftungsgesetz (*Product Liability Act*)
RdA	Recht der Arbeit
RGRK	Reichsgerichtsrätekommentar (*Commentary by the Judges of the Supreme Court of the German Reich*)
RGZ	Entscheidungen des Reichsgerichts in Zivilsachen (*Decisions of the Supreme Court of the German Reich*)
SGB VII	Sozialgesetzbuch, Siebtes Buch (*Social Security Code, Book* VII)
SGB X	Sozialgesetzbuch, Zehntes Buch (*Social Security Code, Book* X)
SPD	Social Democratic Party
StGB	Strafgesetzbuch (*Criminal Code*)
StPO	Strafprozessordnung (*Code of Criminal Procedure*)
StVG	Straßenverkehrsgesetz (*Road Traffic Act*)
UmweltHG	Umwelthaftungsgesetz (*Environmental Liability Act*)
UrhG	Urheberrechtsgesetz (*Copyright Act*)
VersR	Versicherungsrecht
VVG	Versicherungsvertragsgesetz (*Insurance Act*)

WHG	Wasserhaushaltsgesetz (*Water Resources Act*)
WM	Wertpapiermitteilungen
WpG	Die Wirtschaftsprüfung
ZHR	Zeitschrift für das gesamte Handels- und Wirtschaftsrecht
ZIP	Zeitschrift für Wirtschaftsrecht
ZPO	Zivilprozessordnung (*Code of Civil Procedure*)
ZRP	Zeitschrift für Rechtspolitik

List of Abbreviations

General Introduction

§1. General Background of the Country

I. Geography

1. Europe's most densely populated country, the Federal Republic of Germany, is located in the heart of Europe between the natural borders of the Alps in the south and the Baltic Sea and the North Sea in the north.[1] Since the unification of the two German states on 3 October 1990, Germany has been flanked by nine neighbouring states: the Netherlands, Belgium, Luxembourg, France, Switzerland, Austria, the Czech Republic, Poland, and Denmark.

2. The country covers an area of 357,112 square kilometres. The longest distance from north to south is 876 kilometres, and from west to east is 640 kilometres. As of 2022, Germany had a population of some 84.3 million people. The country boasts of great cultural diversity, with about 20.2 million citizens having foreign origins. Germany has eighty cities with more than 100,000 inhabitants. The German capital is Berlin, with a population of approximately 3.9 million.

3. Germany's landscapes are extremely diverse. Low and high mountain ranges alternate with elevated plains, hilly and mountainous regions, lake lands, and wide, open lowlands. Located off the coast are numerous islands, such as Langeoog, Norderney, Sylt, Föhr, and Helgoland in the North Sea and Fehmarn, Rügen, and Usedom in the Baltic Sea. Germany's highest mountain is the Zugspitze, with at 2,962 metres above sea level.

II. History

4. Germany's name (*Deutschland*) derives from the term Deutsch, which first surfaced in the eighth century and referred to the language spoken in the eastern part of the Franconian realm.[2] Since the eleventh century, the word was used to describe its speakers and their residential areas. The term *Deutschland* was not used before

1. For more details, *see* Statistisches Bundesamt (ed.), *Statistisches Jahrbuch 2019*; information in English is available at the homepage of the Federal Statistical Office at www.destatis.de (accessed 20 Apr. 2023).
2. For a brief summary in English, *see* Fulbrook, *A Concise History of Germany* (3rd ed., 2019); Freckmann & Wegerich, *The German Legal System* 1–28 (1999); and Craig, *Germany 1866–1945* (1980);

the fifteenth century. The transition from the East Franconian to a German empire can be marked by the election of Conrad I in 911. As of the eleventh century, the German empire was called 'Roman Empire', and as of the thirteenth century, it was called 'Holy Roman Empire'. In the fifteenth century, the words 'of the German Nation' were added.

5. In 962, Otto I was crowned Kaiser in Rome. This imperial status, which was similarly exercised by Otto's successors, amounted, in theory, to dominance over the entire Occident and supremacy of the Kaiser over the Papacy. However, a dispute over the investiture of bishops ended with Henry IV doing penance to Pope Gregory VII in 1077 in Canossa, from which time onwards, the Pope and the Kaiser were equal-ranking powers. Around the same time, territorial fragmentation began, and the ecclesiastical and temporal princes became semi-sovereign territorial rulers.

6. In 1356, Charles IV issued the so-called Golden Bull (*Goldene Bulle*), a form of Imperial constitution decreeing that seven prominent princes, the Electors (*Kurfürsten*), were awarded the exclusive right to elect the German king. In the fourteenth century, the economic power of the cities increased. This process was furthered by the forming of leagues, most prominently the Hanseatic League (*Hanse*) that became the leading Baltic power. In 1495, Maximilian I created a new formal organization of the Empire. However, the reforms foundered, and the territorial princes increased their influence.

7. On 31 October 1517, inspired by the critical spirit of the Renaissance and the ideas of Humanism, the Reformation began with the publication of Luther's ninety-five theses against abuses by the Catholic Church. The Reformation aimed to return the Christian religion to the truths of church doctrine as revealed in the Gospels. The consequences went far beyond the religious sphere and had influence, for example, on the Peasants' Revolt in 1525, the first major revolutionary movement in Germany. Politically, the Reformation enabled the territorial princes to increase their powers, with the 1555 Peace of Augsburg bestowing upon them the right to dictate their subjects' religion. From this time forth, Protestants enjoyed the same rights as Catholics, and Germany became 80% Protestant. However, the Catholic Church was able to recapture many areas during the Counter-Reformation (*Gegenreformation*). The differences between the faiths sharpened, leading to the formation of religious parties. Finally, a local conflict in Bohemia started the Thirty Years' War, which lasted from 1618–1648 and left many areas of Germany devastated and depopulated.

8. During the following period, the German territorial states adopted French absolutism that enabled a tight administration and an organized fiscal policy, as well as operational armies. In the eighteenth century, Prussia (under Frederic William I

---

in German *see* Müller in: Brockhaus, *Deutsche Geschichte in Schlaglichtern* (3rd ed., 2007); and Schulze, *Kleine deutsche Geschichte* (6th ed., 2008).

and Frederic the Great) and Austria, after repelling the Turks and acquiring Hungary, rose to European Great Powers. Both of them lay claim to external territories and pursued growing and opposing interests. When the French revolution broke out in 1789, Prussia and Austria attempted to intervene by force. The effort failed and led to a counter-attack of the French revolutionary armies. Finally, the Empire collapsed under the attack of Napoleon's forces, and the left bank of the Rhine was occupied by the French. In 1806, the Confederation of the Rhine (*Rheinbund*) emerged under French protection. Concurrently, the Holy Roman Empire of the German Nation formally ceased to exist with the abdication of Kaiser Franz II.

9. Following the War of Liberation (1813–1815), the 1815 Congress of Vienna (*Wiener Kongress*) rearranged the map of Europe and formed the German Confederation (*Deutscher Bund*), a loose association of sovereign states. However, the French revolution of 1848 provoked an immediate response in Germany. In March 1848, uprisings in all states forced the territorial princes to make concessions. Nevertheless, the National Assembly, which convened in Frankfurt's St. Paul's Church (*Paulskirche*), failed in its attempt to create a nation state based on liberal constitutional principles.

10. The German Confederation was dissolved after Austria had been defeated in the German War of 1866. One year later, the North German Confederation (*Norddeutscher Bund*), which included all German states north of the River Main, was founded. After France's resistance was broken in the 1870–1871 war, the southern states joined the North German Confederation to form the German Reich. On 18 January 1871, King William I of Prussia was proclaimed German Kaiser in a coronation ceremony in Versailles. Otto von Bismarck became Reich Chancellor (*Reichskanzler*). Bismarck attempted to direct the Reich towards a secure position in the new European balance of power by means of a far-sighted alliance policy. At home, Bismarck rejected democratic tendencies and fought the labour movement, the left-wing liberal middle class and political Catholicism. Hence, despite progressive social legislation, Germany largely remained an authoritarian State.

11. Bismarck was dismissed in 1890 by the young and inexperienced Kaiser William II, who attempted to shorten the lead of the other imperialist Great Powers. However, due to competing interests, Germany found itself increasingly isolated. The tensions between the European States led to the outbreak of the Great War, with Germany and Austria facing France, Russia, England, and Italy. The turning point of the war can be marked by the accession of the US in 1917. The military defeat was followed by the German revolution in November 1918 that led to the abdication of Kaiser William II.

12. Following the Great War, a National Assembly convened in Weimar and created a republican constitution. Attempts of radical left-wing groups to drive forward a socialist revolution were repelled. Yet, the initial years of the Weimar Republic were characterized by inflation and social unrest. In the following period, economic recovery led to a certain degree of political pacification. Germany resumed its political role on the international stage with the signing of the Treaty of Locarno in 1925 and the accession to the League of Nations (*Völkerbund*) in 1926.

13. The decline of the Weimar Republic started with the world economic crisis in 1929. Left-wing and right-wing radicals were able to make political profit from the horrendous unemployment rate and economic misery. No more majorities capable of government were to be formed in parliament. In the elections of 1932, the National Socialists under Adolf Hitler's leadership became the strongest political force, although they did not enjoy a majority in the Reichstag. In January 1933, members of the conservative and right-wing factions planned to use Hitler for their own ends by making him Reich Chancellor. Shortly after Hitler's rise to power, the Reichstag passed the so-called Enabling Act (*Ermächtigungsgesetz*) that accorded him almost unlimited political powers. Hitler used these powers to restrict basic rights, rescind the freedom of the press, and ban trade unions as well as political parties. Dissenters were subject to terror and often disappeared without trial in concentration camps. The political persecution went hand in hand with the realization of Hitler's anti-Semitic programme that deprived Jewish citizens of their rights and ultimately led to the systematic murder of an estimated 6 million Jews in the Holocaust.

14. In the first years of National Socialist rule, Hitler's employment and foreign policy, notably the reintegration of the Saarland into the Reich in 1935, the occupation of the demilitarized Rhineland by German troops in 1936 and the annexation of Austria and the Sudetenland in 1938, met with general approval. Hitler, however, wanted more and ordered German troops to occupy Prague in March 1939. Later that year, on 1 September, he invaded Poland and thereby started World War II. After a series of German victories, the turning point came when the US entered the war, and the German army was defeated by Russian forces at Stalingrad in the winter of 1942–1943. Hitler committed suicide on 30 April 1945. A week later, on 8–9 May 1945, World War II came to an end with Germany's unconditional capitulation. The war left 55 million people dead and large parts of Europe devastated. The surviving National Socialist leaders were sentenced for crimes against peace and humanity before the International Military Tribunal in Nuremberg. The US, the United Kingdom, France, and the Soviet Union assumed supreme authority and divided up the territory of the Reich into four occupation zones. Berlin was divided into four sectors.

15. Increasing differences between the Western powers and the Soviet Union brought the four-power administration in the occupation zones and Berlin to an end. During the night of 23 June 1948, all land routes between the Western zones and West Berlin were closed by the Soviet Union. Supplies from the surrounding occupation zone were discontinued. The response of the Western powers was the organization of an airlift (*Luftbrücke*) that maintained supplies to the citizens of West Berlin until May 1949. The division of Germany was sealed on 23 May 1949, with the formal proclamation of the Basic Law (*Grundgesetz*) and the founding of the

Federal Republic of Germany on the territory of the three western occupation zones. The proclamation of the constitution of the German Democratic Republic followed on 7 October 1949.

16. In West Germany, the first Federal Government, led by Federal Chancellor (*Bundeskanzler*) Konrad Adenauer, proceeded with the reintegration of the country into the western community. The Federal Republic of Germany became a member of the North Atlantic Treaty Organization in 1955 and was among the founding members of the European Community in 1957. Economic recovery was fostered by the European Aid and Reconstruction Programme announced by US Secretary of State George C. Marshall in June 1947 (so-called Marshall Plan). Between 1948 and 1952, Marshall Plan funds of some USD 1.4 billion flowed into West Germany. Whereas in the Federal Republic of Germany, a successful social market economy was set up, the Soviet occupation zone went on with a policy of nationalizing industry. On 17 June 1953, Soviet tanks bloodily put down a people's uprising in the German Democratic Republic. Increasing dissatisfaction led to 3.5 million people fleeing from East to West Germany. The flow of refugees came to a halt when a death strip was set up along the border between the two German states, and on 13 August 1961, the Berlin Wall was built.

17. On 12 August 1970, the Federal Republic of Germany and the Soviet Union signed a treaty on the renunciation of force and the permanent nature of the European borders. The treaty was a result of Federal Chancellor Willy Brandt's policy of détente and peace. The relationship between the Federal Republic of Germany and the German Democratic Republic was normalized with the Basic Treaty of 21 December 1971. It was agreed that each German state would establish permanent diplomatic missions in the other. On 18 September 1973, both German states were admitted to the United Nations, and on 1 August 1975, they both signed the Final Act of the Conference on Security and Cooperation in Europe in Helsinki on questions of security and cooperation in Europe.

18. From the mid-1980s onwards, an ever-increasing number of people from the German Democratic Republic were looking for new ways to leave their country. In 1985, new Soviet leader Mikhail Gorbachev supported this desire for freedom with his policy of Perestroika (conversion) and Glasnost (openness). However, the East German regime under Erich Honecker tried to resist Gorbachev's relaxed approach. Nevertheless, further successful disarmament negotiations between East and West led to increasing demands for greater freedom and reform in the German Democratic Republic. In the summer of 1989, the East German regime started to erode when Hungary opened its borders to Austria. This step initiated a mass exodus by enabling thousands of East German citizens to migrate to the Federal Republic of Germany and encouraged ever more people in East German cities, primarily in Leipzig, to participate in mass demonstrations for democracy, freedom of speech, and freedom of travel. As opposed to 1953 in Hungary, 1968 in Prague, and 1980 in Poland, the Soviet Union showed no interest in suppressing the uprising by force.

19. The increasing pressure on the administration led to the announcement of less restrictive travel regulations on the evening of 9 November 1989, prompting the opening of the Berlin Wall. In August 1990, the parliament of the German Democratic Republic (*Volkskammer*) resolved to move forward for the accession to the territory of the Federal Republic of Germany according to Article 23 of the Basic Law. The Unification Treaty (*Einigungsvertrag*) of 31 August 1990 designated that the five newly created federal states Brandenburg, Mecklenburg-Western Pomerania (*Mecklenburg-Vorpommern*), Saxony (*Sachsen*), Saxony-Anhalt (*Sachsen-Anhalt*), and Thuringia (*Thüringen*) become states of the Federal Republic of Germany. On 12 September 1990, the foreign ministers of the Federal Republic of Germany, the German Democratic Republic, Great Britain, France, the US, and the Soviet Union signed the Treaty on the Final Settlement With Respect to Germany (*Vertrag über die abschließende Regelung in Bezug* auf *Deutschland*). The German Democratic Republic formally ceased to exist on 3 October 1990, with the reunification of the two German states. Following the reunification of Germany, on 20 June 1991, the Federal Parliament (*Bundestag*) resolved to move the seat of government from Bonn to Berlin. The final relocation took place in the summer of 1999.

III. Political System

20. The current German constitution is the so-called Basic Law for the Federal Republic of Germany (*Grundgesetz für die Bundesrepublik Deutschland*).[3] Originally enacted in 1949 as the constitution of West Germany, it was intentionally not called 'constitution' to point out that West Germany was considered only a temporary solution until German reunification was achieved. Since the reunification of the two German states was implemented by the German Democratic Republic's accession to the territory of the Federal Republic of Germany in 1990, the Basic Law is still in effect. Amendments with respect to the reunification, however, were made in 1990 and 1994.

21. The Basic Law guarantees enumerated basic rights in accordance with the right of every person to self-fulfilment and the state's commitment to the protection of human dignity. The classical freedoms listed in the Basic Law include freedom of belief; freedom of speech, art, and scholarship; freedom of the press; and the guarantee of property. Others are freedom of assembly and association, the confidentiality of letters and telecommunications, freedom of movement, freedom in the choice of profession, protection from forced labour, the inviolability of the home, and the right to asylum. Moreover, marriage and family are placed under special protection. Alongside these civil liberties, the Basic Law guarantees rights of equality. All persons are equal before the law, and no one may be discriminated against

3. *See* Badura, *Staatsrecht* (7th ed., 2018); for a detailed description of German constitutional law in English, *see* Robbers, *An Introduction to German Law,* Nos 95 et seq. (7th ed. 2019); Foster and Sule, *German Legal System and Laws* (4th ed., 2010); Freckmann and Wegerich, *The German Legal System* 53–104 (1999); and Kau, in: Zekoll and G. Wagner, *Introduction to German Law* (3rd ed., 2018).

or given preferential treatment on the grounds of sex, birth, race, language, national or social origins, faith, religious persuasion, or political opinions. Nor may anybody be discriminated against because of disability. The basic rights are directly applicable as law, and their fundamental essence is inviolable. The legislative body, the executive body, and the judiciary are strictly bound to the basic rights, and every citizen has the right to file a constitutional complaint with the Federal Constitutional Court (*Bundesverfassungsgericht* (BVerfG)) if he feels his basic rights have been impaired by the actions of the state. However, a prerequisite is that he has appealed to the appropriate lower courts without success.

22. In accordance with the Basic Law, the Federal Republic of Germany is a constitutional democratic and social federal State. Germany is a federation that consists of sixteen individual states (*Bundesländer*) with their own sovereignty regarding legislation, administration, and jurisprudence. The Head of State is the Federal President (*Bundespräsident*), who is elected by the Federal Convention by majority vote for a five-year term of office. The Federal Convention is a constitutional body that convenes only for this purpose and consists of the members of the Federal Parliament and an equal number of persons elected by the state parliaments. The Federal President has largely representative functions and may be re-elected only once.

23. The German people are represented in the Federal Parliament (*Bundestag*). Unlike the other constitutional organs, the Federal Parliament is elected directly by the German people for a four-year legislative period. Its function is to pass laws and to elect the Federal Chancellor. Furthermore, it keeps a watch on the government. The preparatory work for all legislation is undertaken in parliamentary committees whose meetings are not regularly open to the public. The sixteen federal states are represented in the Federal Council (*Bundesrat*), which enables the states to participate in legislation and governmental administration. The Federal Council consists of members of the state governments who appoint and recall them. Nevertheless, the Federal Council is a federal body that exercises exclusively federal powers.

24. The government is formed by the Federal Chancellor (*Bundeskanzler*) and the federal ministers. The Federal Chancellor is the head of the Federal Cabinet and decides on the Cabinet's composition as well as on the responsibilities of the individual ministers. He or she determines and is responsible for general policy guidelines. The Federal Chancellor is the only member of the Cabinet elected by parliament, and consequently, it is the Chancellor who is, in the first instance, accountable to the latter. The ministers are appointed and dismissed by the Federal President according to the binding proposals of the Chancellor. The parliament can express its lack of confidence in the Chancellor only by electing a successor by majority vote (*Konstruktives Misstrauensvotum*). The Federal Chancellor has the right to ask parliament for a vote of confidence (*Vertrauensfrage*), and if it is refused, he can ask the Federal President to dissolve the Federal Parliament. This process led to a new election in 2005 when the Federal Parliament refused former Chancellor Gerhard Schröder's vote of confidence. In the following election, the Christian Democratic Union led by Angela Merkel became the strongest political force in the parliament, and Angela Merkel was elected the first female Federal

Chancellor of Germany. Since then, Angela Merkel has reigned in coalitions with the Social Democratic Party (SPD) from 2005 to 2009, with the Liberal Democratic Party from 2009 to 2013 and again with the SPD from 2017 until 2021. Since 2021, Olaf Scholz of the SPD has been Chancellor of Germany in a coalition with the Free Democratic Party (FDP) and Alliance 90/The Greens (Bündnis90/Die Grünen).

25. Adherence to the Basic Law is ensured by the Federal Constitutional Court (BVerfG). The Constitutional Court is located in Karlsruhe and consists of two panels, each with eight judges elected by the Federal Parliament and the Federal Council. The judges serve terms of twelve years and may not be re-elected. The Federal Constitutional Court is embedded in the Basic Law with an extensive scope of jurisdiction. However, it only acts in response to petitions. It rules not only on the infringement of basic rights but also on disputes between the central government and the states or between individual federal institutions. The Constitutional Court examines whether federal and state laws can be reconciled with the Basic Law. A law that is declared null and void by the Constitutional Court may no longer be applied.

26. A fundamental element in the German system of sharing and balancing power is the distribution of authority between central and local state governments. According to Article 70 of the Basic Law, the states have the right to enact legislation as long as the constitution itself does not empower central governments to do so. Based on this principle, federal responsibility for legislation is divided into two categories, namely exclusive and concurrent legislation. Areas that fall exclusively within the scope of federal legislation include defence, foreign affairs, and monetary matters. With respect to concurrent legislation, the states have the right to pass their own laws on matters not governed by federal law. However, the federal legislator may legislate in these areas if it is in the common interest in order to ensure equal conditions or to maintain a uniform legal or economic situation. Since the Federalism reform of 2006, the states may, in some areas of concurrent legislation, enact laws that deviate from federal laws. In other areas of concurrent legislation, such as civil law, criminal law, labour law, and land law, the federal legislator may enact laws even without demonstrating necessity in order to ensure equal conditions or to maintain a uniform legal or economic situation. In these areas, such necessity is generally assumed. A third category of legislation, so-called framework legislation, according to which the federal legislator was only allowed to issue framework regulations but no detailed rules, has been abolished with the 2006 Federalism reform. The states alone are in charge of those fields of legislation the constitution does not place within the sphere of the federal legislator, such as education, cultural policy, and police law.

27. Whereas the federal legislator has broad authority to enact laws, with respect to administration, the areas of responsibility are allocated narrowly. Direct federal administration is basically limited to the armed forces, the border guard, customs, the labour offices, and Foreign Service. The states are in charge of all matters that fall exclusively within state jurisdiction. Furthermore, they are responsible for the implementation of most federal laws and regulations: In some areas, such as building law, state administration implements federal law in its own right and on its own responsibility. In other areas, for example, the construction of national highways, it implements federal law on behalf of the Federal Government.

28. The Basic Law follows the German tradition of local self-government by expressly guaranteeing the right to regulate all affairs of the local community independently within the framework of the law in cities, municipalities, and counties. Specifically, local self-government embraces adult education and youth welfare, electricity, water and gas supply, sewerage, and city planning, as well as local transport, local road construction, the construction and maintenance of schools, theatres and museums, hospitals, sports facilities, and public swimming baths. Basically, the cities and municipalities discharge these tasks independently. As a rule, any monitoring of local self-government by the states is restricted to assessing the legality of the respective actions. Since many such measures are beyond the means of smaller cities and municipalities, they can be assumed by the counties (*Kreise*) as the next highest level of government. The counties have democratically elected bodies and are likewise part of the local self-government system. However, larger cities are independent entities and do not belong to a county.

IV. Economic and Social Values

29. Germany is one of the world's leading industrial nations, with its economy ranking fourth in terms of total economic output.[4] Manufacturing and service industries are the dominant economic activities. Agriculture only accounts for about 0.9% of the Gross Domestic Product (GDP) and occupies less than 1.2% of the workforce.[5] Typical German agricultural products are potatoes, wheat, barley, rye, cabbage, fruit, sugar beets, and dairy products. Furthermore, large numbers of cattle, hogs, and poultry are raised. Manufacturing industries include automobiles, iron and steel, electronics, chemicals, machinery, ships, cement, textiles, food, and beverages. Lignite and hard coal are mined. Germany is one of the world's largest exporters. More than 59% of Germany's trade is conducted with other European Union (EU) countries.[6]

30. The Basic Law does not impose a certain economic system but excludes a purely free market economy by insisting on adherence to the principle of social justice and the welfare state. This balance is secured by the concept of social market economy, which was devised and implemented in West Germany's economic system in the middle of the twentieth century by the first economics minister and later Federal Chancellor, Ludwig Erhard. The concept of social market economy was supposed to

4. *See* Pilz and Ortwein, *Das politische System Deutschlands: Systemintegrierende Einführung in das Regierungs-, Wirtschafts- und Sozialsystem* (4th ed., 2008); and Owen-Smith, *The German Economy* (1994).
5. https://de.statista.com/statistik/daten/studie/323856/umfrage/bruttowertschoepfungsanteil-der-agrarwirtschaft-in-deutschland/; https://de.statista.com/statistik/daten/studie/275637/umfrage/anteil-der-wirtschaftsbereiche-an-der-gesamtbeschaeftigung-in-deutschland/ (accessed 19 Apr. 2023).
6. Statistisches Bundesamt (ed.), *Statistisches Jahrbuch 2019*, 431.

enable the free play of forces on the market by distributing income and profit according to individual achievement, but also to limit the accumulation of market power.

31. The German social system hedges against risks incurred from unemployment, disability, accident, illness, age, and other social conditions. A particular feature is the cooperation of employers and employees, which is expressed in the equal financing of contributions to pensions, medical and long-term care, and unemployment insurance. In addition, the social partnership of employer associations and trade unions is subject to an institutionalized settlement of conflicts. Article 9 of the Basic Law guarantees autonomy in negotiating wages. Hence, employees and employers bear the responsibility for deciding on working conditions in contracts resulting from collective bargaining. The social partnership between unions and employers is supposed to ensure a high degree of social harmony.

32. Since the reunification of the two German states, the Federal Republic of Germany has faced the economic challenge of transforming the former East Germany from a deteriorating command economy dependent on low-quality heavy industrial products to a technologically advanced market economy. As a result, Germany's affluent and technologically powerful economy turned into a relatively weak performance throughout much of the 1990s. Even today, the modernization and integration of the East German economy continue to be a costly long-term problem. Moreover, the ageing population, along with high unemployment, has pushed social security outlays to a level exceeding contributions from workers. Business and income tax cuts introduced in 2001 did not save Germany from the impact of the downturn in international trade, and domestic demand faltered as unemployment began to rise. Therefore, the Federal Government was looking for ways to reform labour law – especially the protection against unlawful dismissal and the social insurance system – to lower ancillary labour costs and boost economic growth. The reforms were bearing fruit. Since 2006, Germany's economy has shown signs of sustained recovery and growth driven by strong domestic demand. The positive development continued until the third quarter of 2008. In the fourth quarter of 2008, Germany was hit by the worldwide financial crisis, which had been triggered by a liquidity shortfall in the US banking system caused by an overvaluation of assets. As a result, the nominal GDP contracted in the second and third quarters of 2008. The overall unemployment rate, which had consistently fallen since 2005, started to rise again. In January 2009, the German government introduced a EUR 50 billion economic stimulus plan in order to prevent a further economic downturn and an additional rise in the unemployment rate. In addition to European measures, Germany implemented a Financial Market Stabilization Fund to stabilize the financial system. The Financial Market Stabilization Fund can guarantee debt securities issued by banks, acquire shares in financial enterprises and thereby increase their equity capital, and, by acquiring a stake, assume banks' risk positions. Caused by the global financial crisis and other defaults among European countries, the European Monetary Union has faced a significant recession, which is still effecting the European economy. The European institutions, in particular the European Central Bank, launched highly controversial programmes in order to maintain financial stability. The European

Stability Mechanism, with a total capacity of EUR 700 billion, pursues the objective to overcome short-term liquidity shortages, e.g., by granting loans or issuing bonds.

33. There was no genuine recession in Germany in the 2010s. Unemployment fell from almost 5 million to just over 2 million, and numerous jobs were created. The German economy grew by an average of 1.5% (apart from the global crisis in 2009/2010). At the same time, the refugee crisis came to a head in 2015/2016. At the end of the 2010s, the ecological crisis also intensified, leading increasingly to severe weather conditions (also in Germany) and accompanied by significant protests for climate justice at the same time.[7]

§2. Legal System

I. Primacy of Legislation and Codification

34. The German Basic Law is based on the separation of powers and strictly adheres to a system of checks and balances with a stringent division of legislative power, administration, and judiciary. Germany's legal system follows a civil law approach based on the idea of legislative supremacy. Therefore, according to the principle of legality codified in Article 20(3) of the Basic Law, the judiciary and administration are bound by the decisions of the legislator. The legislator is principally not obliged to establish specific rules. Even though the Basic Law requires a certain level of protection for tort victims, the Federal Constitutional Court grants the legislator broad discretion.[8] The balancing of interests is not determined by the Basic Law but is a complex political act that can be replaced by a formative judicial act only in case of legislative failure.[9] The rules of tort law codified in sections 823–853 Bürgerliches Gesetzbuch (BGB) and in the accompanying special laws usually suffice to ensure the adequate protection of tort victims.[10] However, the constitutional values have to be kept in mind with respect to the interpretation of these rules and the procedural enforcement of tort law claims.[11]

35. Judges and administrative officers have to proceed in compliance with the law and may, in general, not create legal rules of their own. They are obliged to interpret the statutes in accordance with well-established rules. Although the correct

7. Current overview can be found at Statistisches Bundesamt (ed.), *Statistisches Jahrbuch 2019*, 41 et seq., 455 et seq., 649 et seq.
8. *See Entscheidungen des Bundesverfassungsgerichts* (BverfGE) 85, 191, 212 et seq.; BVerfGE 92, 26, 46; *Bundesverfassungsgericht* (BverfG), *NJW* 1996, 651; BVerfG, *NJW* 1997, 2509; BVerfG, *NJW* 1998, 975, 976; BVerfG, *NJW* 1998, 2961, 2962; BVerfG, *NJW* 1998, 3264, 3265 et seq.; BVerfG, *NJW* 2006, 751, 760.
9. *See* Di Fabio, *Risikoentscheidungen im Rechtsstaat* (1994), 227 et seq., 459; *see also* Dietlein, *Die Lehre von den grundrechtlichen Schutzpflichten* (2. Aufl. 2005), 67 et seq.
10. *See* Horn, in: Handbuch des Staatsrechts, vol. 7, § 149 No. 70 (3rd ed., 2009); Klein, *DVBl.* 1994, 489, 492; J. Hager, in: Staudinger, BGB, Vor § 823 No. 71 (2017); *see also* Wagner, in: Münchener Kommentar zum BGB, Vor § 823 Nos 78 et seq. (8th ed., 2020).
11. *See* BVerfGE 52, 131, 145 et seq.; and BVerfG, *NJW* 2007, 753, 758.

statutory interpretation by the judge can be crucial for the outcome of legal proceedings, German law provides no general provisions dealing with the interpretation and application of statutes. An exception is the explicit prohibition of analogy in the area of criminal law codified in Article 103(2) of the Basic Law. The traditional principles of construction in Germany include historical, grammatical, systematic, and logical interpretation.[12] Hence, the judge has to focus not only on the literal meaning and the context of a provision but also on legislative history and the purpose of a rule. The legislator's intent is documented in explanations of the statutes' drafts and in the parliamentary protocols that are published in the official documents of the Federal Parliament (*Bundestagsdrucksache*).[13] Recently, the economic analysis of law and the comparison of laws have been added to the traditional canons of construction.[14] Nonetheless, these new methods of interpretation have just started to gain acceptance among German scholars and have yet to make their way to the courts.

36. Although the legislator generally intends the enacted rules to be a comprehensive statement of the entire law on the subject addressed, it is possible that gaps in code coverage develop, whether through simple obsolescence or through oversight of the drafters. If this is the case, the judge may supply an answer by an analogous application of suitable rules. He is, however, compelled by the principle of comprehensiveness and legislative supremacy to justify that answer as an interpretation of the code. The Judge-made law does exist not only in areas where the codified law is fragmentary but also in areas where the code merely provides general clauses that have to be interpreted and concretized in order to be operational.

II. Position of the Judiciary

37. According to Article 92 of the Basic Law, the judicial power is vested in the judges. It is to be exercised by the Federal Constitutional Court (BVerfG), by the federal courts provided for in the Basic Law,[15] and by the state courts. Article 95 of the Basic Law establishes five jurisdictional branches: ordinary jurisdiction

12. On the basic principles of interpretation *see* Larenz and Canaris, *Methodenlehre der Rechtswissenschaft* (3rd ed., 1995); Möllers, *Juristische Methodenlehre* (5th ed., 2023); Seidel, *Jura* 2023, 523 et seq.
13. The official documents of the Bundestag can be viewed at https://dip.bundestag.de/ (accessed 19 Apr. 2023).
14. On the economic analysis of law, *see* Cooter and Ulen, *Law and Economics* (6th ed., 2016); Polinsky, *An Introduction to Law and Economics* (5th ed., 2018); and Posner, *Economic Analysis of Law* (9th ed., 2014); on the comparison of laws, *see* Zweigert and Kötz, *Einführung in die Rechtsvergleichung,* (3rd ed., 1996); translated in English: Zweigert and Kötz, *Introduction to comparative law* (3rd ed., 1998).
15. According to Art. 95(1) of the Basic law, the Federation shall establish the Federal Supreme Court (*Bundesgerichtshof* (BGH)), the Federal Administrative Court (*Bundesverwaltungsgericht*), the Federal Finance Court (*Bundesfinanzhof*), the Federal Labour Court (*Bundesarbeitsgericht*), and the Federal Social Court (*Bundessozialgericht*) as Supreme Courts of ordinary, administrative, financial, labour, and social jurisdiction.

(*ordentliche Gerichtsbarkeit*), administrative jurisdiction (*Verwaltungsgerichtsbarkeit*), financial jurisdiction (*Finanzgerichtsbarkeit*), labour jurisdiction (*Arbeitsgerichtsbarkeit*), and social jurisdiction (*Sozialgerichtsbarkeit*). Each jurisdiction has its specific courts, which are equal in rank and independent of each other. Statutory provisions referring to the subject of the litigation allocate each suit exclusively to one of the jurisdictional branches. There is no concurrent jurisdiction between the individual branches.

38. Section 13 of the Judicature Act (*Gerichtsverfassungsgesetz* (GVG)) assigns civil actions to the ordinary jurisdiction, which are executed by the local courts (*Amtsgerichte* (AG)) that are comparable to British county courts or American municipal courts, the district courts (*Landgerichte* (LG)), the Higher Regional Courts (*Oberlandesgerichte* (OLG)), and the Federal Supreme Court (Bundesgerichtshof (BGH)). The local courts are the lowest German civil courts. They have first-instance jurisdiction for a number of specific subject matters and, in principle, for all civil law claims with an amount in controversy of not more than EUR 5,000.[16] The district courts have first-instance jurisdiction in all civil litigation, apart from those matters assigned to the local courts.[17] They also have appellate jurisdiction against most judgments passed by the local courts.[18] Special chambers are established to deal with commercial matters (*Kammern für Handelssachen*).[19] The civil jurisdiction of the Higher Regional Courts includes, *inter alia*, appeals against district court judgments and local court judgments (in parent and child cases and in cases falling within the province of the family courts).[20] As are the local courts and the district courts, the Higher Regional Courts are state courts. The highest-ranking German civil court is the Federal Supreme Court, located in Karlsruhe.[21] The Federal Supreme Court solely decides appeals dealing with questions of law.[22] The court sits in panels-designated Senates. Important decisions of the Federal Supreme Court are published in official reports.[23]

III. Distinction Between Public and Private Law

39. Private law has to be accurately distinguished from public law to determine the applicable substantive law and the competent court: While civil actions based on the Civil Code (BGB) or one of the corresponding special laws are assigned to the ordinary jurisdiction, the administrative courts (*Verwaltungsgerichte*) have jurisdiction over disputes involving public law. Private law is the part of the legal system dealing with the relations between individuals on the basis of equal rights and

16. *See* ss 23–23d *Gerichtsverfassungsgesetz* (GVG).
17. *See* s. 71 GVG.
18. *See* s. 72 GVG.
19. *See* ss 93–114 GVG.
20. *See* s. 119 GVG.
21. *See* s. 123 GVG.
22. *See* s. 133 GVG.
23. Civil law cases are published in the *Entscheidungen des Bundesgerichtshofes in Zivilsachen* ('BGHZ') report.

self-determination. Public law, in contrast, involves the organization of the state and other entities provided with sovereign power. At the same time, it governs the legal relations between these entities and between them and their members.

40. To distinguish private law from public law, German courts used to apply the so-called Subjection Theory (*Subjektionstheorie*): They asked if the connection between the parties can be characterized as a relationship of equivalence (private law) or of subordination (public law).[24] This formula proved insufficient since relationships of subordination – although typical for public law – are also known in the area of private law (e.g., in the field of employment law or in parent and child cases). Likewise, a relationship of equivalence is not excluded under public law (e.g., the relations between states, organs of a public entity, or the parties to a contract under public law).[25] The inaccuracies of the Subjection Theory led to the development of the so-called Special Right Theory (*Sonderrechtstheorie*), according to which a legal relationship is assigned to public law if at least one party is specifically involved in his or her capacity as a bearer of sovereign powers.[26]

IV. Sources of Private Law in General and of Tort Law in Particular

41. The term 'sources of law' relates to the causes for the genesis of legal rules as well as to the law's manifestation characterized by them.[27] Against this background, the law can be divided into codified law and customary law. The origin of customary law requires a persistent routine that has to be accompanied by the involved circles' conviction to act in accordance with existing law by following this routine (so-called opinio *necessitates*).[28] The validity of customary law ends with the enactment of a conflicting statute or with the emergence of opposing customary law.[29] Other than customary law, trade practice (*Handelsbrauch*) and accepted standards (*Verkehrssitte*) do not constitute legal norms.[30] They have, nevertheless, to be taken into account with regard to the construction of legal acts.[31]

24. *See Entscheidungen des Reichsgerichts in Zivilsachen* (RGZ) 167, 281, 284; and BGHZ 14, 222, 227.
25. *See* Grüneberg, in: Grüneberg, BGB, Einleitung No. 2 (82nd ed., 2023); and Papier/Shirvani, in: Münchener Kommentar zum BGB, § 839 No. 199 (8th ed., 2020).
26. *See* BGHZ 102, 280, 283; Grüneberg, in: Grüneberg, BGB, Einleitung No. 2 (82nd ed., 2023); Säcker, in: Münchener Kommentar zum BGB, Einl. No. 3 (9th ed., 2021); and Papier/Shirvani, in: Münchener Kommentar zum BGB, § 839 No. 198 (8th ed., 2020).
27. Grüneberg, in: Grüneberg, BGB, Einleitung No. 17 (82nd ed., 2023); *see also* Säcker, in: Münchener Kommentar zum BGB, Einl. Nos 77 et seq. (9th ed., 2021).
28. *See* BVerfGE 28, 21, 28 et seq.; BVerfGE 22, 114, 122; BVerfG, *NJW* 2009, 1469, 1473; BGHZ 37, 219, 222; and Grüneberg, in: Grüneberg, BGB, Einleitung No. 22 (82nd ed., 2023).
29. *See* BGHZ 1, 369, 379; and BGHZ 37, 219, 224.
30. Grüneberg, in: Grüneberg, BGB, Einleitung No. 23 (82nd ed., 2023).
31. BGH LM (Lindenmaier & Möhring, Nachschlagewerk des Bundesgerichtshofs) § 157 (B) No. 1; Grüneberg, in: Grüneberg, BGB, Einleitung No. 23 (82nd ed., 2023); and Busche, in: Münchener Kommentar zum BGB, § 157 Nos 16 et seq. (9th ed., 2021).

42. The Basic Law can be seen as the highest-ranking source of German private law: The legislator designing private law rules is directly bound by the basic rights codified in Articles 1–19 and the basic institutional principles codified in Articles 20 and 28 of the Basic Law. Even though the influence of constitutional law is more intense in the area of public law, the Basic Law also has a significant impact on the interpretation of tort law rules.[32] However, each individual case requires a careful balancing of the conflicting interests to determine if the application of the existing rules might result in a transgression of the constitutional frame. The most important sources of private law are formal statutes (*formelle Gesetze*) enacted by the Federal Parliament or the state parliament. Formal statutes always need to be promulgated to become effective. On par with formal statutes are state treaties (*Staatsverträge*), provided that they are duly ratified and promulgated.[33] Ranking below parliamentary statutes are regulations (*Rechtsverordnungen*) issued by the Federal Government, a minister, or a state government. Local authorities and non-governmental entities are allowed to issue ordinances (*Satzungen*) as long as they act within the scope of their authority. In addition to the national legal rules, EU Law has become another important source for private law. EU Law can be divided into primary Union Law (i.e., the treaties regarding the founding of the EU, including their amendments as well as general legal principals developed by the European Court of Justice) and secondary Union Law (i.e., EU Regulations and Directives). As regards primary Community Law, certain principles, such as the prohibition of quantitative restrictions on import and export between Member States, have a direct effect and may constitute claims that may be brought to national courts (e.g., government liability claims under section 839 BGB).[34] With regard to secondary Union Law, EU Regulations are generally binding and directly applicable in each Member State of the EU. In contrast, EU Directives do not constitute directly applicable law for the citizens of the Member States. They need to be implemented by the national legislator. Numerous German statutes, such as the German Product Liability Act,[35] are based on EU Directives.[36]

43. Except for certain decisions of the Federal Constitutional Court, the judgments issued by German courts – even those of the Federal Supreme Court – do not have the force of law and cannot affect other cases.[37] Thus, they are not binding on the inferior courts. Nevertheless, lower courts tend to follow the decisions of the Federal Supreme Court and the Higher Regional Courts in similar cases. As a result, these rulings have a considerable impact on the evolution of law, although they are not a primary source of law.

---

32. *See* BVerfGE 7, 198, 203 et seq.; BVerfGE 7, 230, 234 et seq.; BVerfGE 90, 27, 33 et seq.; and BVerfGE 92, 262, 275.
33. *See* Grüneberg, in: Grüneberg, BGB, Einleitung No. 19 (82nd ed., 2023).
34. *See* Grüneberg, in: Grüneberg, BGB, Einleitung No. 27 (82nd ed., 2023).
35. *See* Part III, Ch. 2.
36. *See* Schaub, in: Prütting and Wegen and Weinreich, BGB, Vor §§ 823 ff. No. 28 (17th ed., 2022).
37. Jauernig and Hess, *Zivilprozessrecht*, § 8 V No. 2 (30th ed., 2011); and Wilke, in: Isensee/Kirchhof, Handbuch des Staatsrechts, vol. 5, § 112 No. 32 (3rd ed., 2007).

44. German tort law is codified primarily in sections 823–853 of the Civil Code (BGB).[38] In addition, other miscellaneous provisions of the Civil Code granting claims for damages can be attributed to the area of tort law (e.g., sections 228 sentence 1, 231 BGB). Outside the Civil Code, claims for damages can be based on numerous strict liability statutes, such as the Product Liability Act (*Produkthaftungsgesetz* (ProdHaftG)), the Drug Law (*Arzneimittelgesetz* (AMG)), the Strict Liability Act (*Haftpflichtgesetz* (HPflG)), the Air Traffic Act (*Luftverkehrsgesetz* (LuftVG)), the Atomic Energy Act (*Atomgesetz* or *AtG*), the Federal Mining Act (*Bundesberggesetz* (BBergG)), the Genetic Engineering Act (*Gentechnikgesetz* (GenTG)), the Environmental Liability Act (*Umwelthaftungsgesetz* (UmweltHG)), the Act on Water Resources Management (*Wasserhaushaltsgesetz* (WHG)), the Road Traffic Act (*Straßenverkehrsgesetz* (StVG)), or the Federal Data Protection Act (*Bundesdatenschutzgesetz* (BDSG)). The law of damages is mainly governed by sections 249–254 BGB. Some areas of tort law, such as the product liability act, are heavily influenced by European Directives.

45. The following is an excerpt of the Civil Code's most important German tort law and remedy provisions:

§ 249 BGB Nature and extent of compensation of damages

(1) A person who is liable for damages is to restore the position that would exist if the circumstance obliging them to pay damages had not occurred.
(2) Where damages are payable for injury to a person or damage to a thing, the obligee may demand the required amount of money in lieu of restoration. Where a thing is damaged, the amount of money required under sentence 1 only includes value-added tax if and to the extent that it is actually incurred.

§ 250 BGB Damages in money after the specification of a period of time

The obligee may specify a reasonable time limit for the person liable in damages to undertake restoration and declare that they will reject restoration after the period of time ends. After the end of the period, the obligee may demand damages in money if restoration does not occur in good time; the claim to restoration is excluded.

§ 251 BGB Damages in money without the specification of a period of time

(1) To the extent that restoration is not possible or is not sufficient to compensate the obligee, the person liable for damages is to compensate the obligee in money.
(2) The person liable for damages may compensate the obligee in money if restoration is possible only at a disproportionate expense. Expenses incurred as a result of the curative treatment of an injured animal are not disproportionate merely because they significantly exceed the value of the animal.

38. English translation of the Civil Code can be found at www.gesetze-im-internet.de/englisch_bgb/index.html (accessed 19 Apr. 2023).

§ 252 BGB Lost Profits

The damage to be compensated also comprises the profits lost. Those profits are considered lost in the normal course of events or in special circumstances, particularly due to the measures and precautions taken, and could be expected to be attained as a matter of likelihood.

§ 253 BGB Non-pecuniary Damages

(1) Money may be demanded in compensation for any damage that is not a pecuniary loss only in the cases stipulated by law.
(2) If damages are to be paid for an injury to body, health, freedom or sexual self-determination, then equitable compensation in money also may be demanded for any damage that is not a pecuniary loss.

§ 254 BGB Contributory Negligence

(1) Where fault on the part of the injured person contributed to the occurrence of the damage, liability in damages, as well as the extent of compensation to be provided, depend on the circumstances, in particular on the extent to which the damage was caused mainly by one or the other party.
(2) This also applies if the fault of the injured person is limited to failing to draw the attention of the obligor to the danger of unusually extensive damage, where the obligor neither was aware of the danger nor ought to have been aware of it, or to fail to avert or mitigate the damage. The provision of section 278 applies accordingly.

§ 823 BGB Liability in damages

(1) A person who, intentionally or negligently, unlawfully injures the life, limb, health, freedom, property or some other right of another person is liable to provide compensation to the other party for the damage arising therefrom.
(2) The same duty is incumbent on a person who commits a breach of a statute that is intended to protect another person. If, according to the contents of the statute, it is possible to violate it without fault, then liability to compensation only exists in the case of fault.

§ 824 BGB Endangering credit

(1) A person who untruthfully states or disseminates a fact that is suited to endanger the credit of another person or to cause other disadvantages to their livelihood or advancement is to provide compensation to the other for the damage caused by this even if, although they do not know that the fact is untrue, they ought to have known.
(2) A person who makes a communication and is unaware that it is untrue is not obliged to pay damages if they or the recipient of the communication have a legitimate interest in the communication.

§ 825 BGB Inducing others to sexual acts

A person who induces another person to perform or acquiesce to sexual acts by cunning, duress or abuse of a dependency relationship is under obligation to provide compensation to that person for the resulting damage.

§ 826 BGB Intentional damage inflicted in a manner offending common decency

A person who, in a manner offending common decency, intentionally inflicts damage on another person is liable to the other person to provide compensation for the damage.

§ 827 BGB Exclusion and reduction of responsibility

A person who, in a state of unconsciousness or in a state of pathological mental disturbance precluding the free exercise of will, inflicts damage on another person is not responsible for such damage. If they have temporarily induced a state of this type by imbibing alcoholic beverages or similar means, then they are responsible for damages that they unlawfully cause in this state as if they were at fault for negligence; the responsibility does not ensue if they came into this state without fault.

§ 828 BGB Minors

(1) A person who has not reached the age of seven is not responsible for damage caused to another person.
(2) A person who has reached the age of seven but not the age of 10 is not responsible for damage that they inflict on another party in an accident involving a motor vehicle, a railway or a suspension railway. This does not apply if they intentionally brought about the injury.
(3) A person who has not yet attained the age of 18 is not responsible, to the extent that their responsibility is not excluded under subsection (1) or (2), for damage they inflict on another person if, when committing the damaging act, they do not have the insight required to recognise their responsibility.

§ 829 BGB Liability in damages for reasons of equity

A person who, by reason of sections 827 and 828, is not responsible for damage they caused in the cases specified in sections 823 to 826 nonetheless is to provide compensation for the damage unless it is possible to obtain compensation of damages from a third party with a duty of supervision, to the extent that in light of the situation given, in particular the circumstances of the parties involved, equity requires indemnification and they are not deprived of the resources needed for reasonable maintenance and to discharge their statutory maintenance duties.

§ 830 BGB Joint tortfeasors and persons involved

(1) If more than one person has caused damage by a jointly committed tort, then each of them is responsible for the damage. The same applies if it cannot be established which of several persons involved caused the damage by their act.
(2) Instigators and accessories are equivalent to joint tortfeasors.

§ 831 BGB Liability for vicarious agents

(1) A person who deploys another person to perform a task is liable to provide compensation for the damage that the other unlawfully inflicts on a third party when carrying out the task. Liability in damages does not apply if the principal exercises the care required in business dealings when selecting the person deployed and, to the extent that they are to procure devices or equipment or to manage the business activity, in such procurement or management, or if the damage would have occurred even if this care had been exercised.
(2) The same responsibility is incumbent on a person who assumes the performance of one of the transactions specified in subsection (1) sentence 2 for the principal by contract.

§ 832 BGB Liability of a person with a duty of supervision

(1) A person who is obliged by operation of law to supervise a person requiring supervision because they are a minor or because of their mental or physical condition is liable to provide compensation for the damage that this person unlawfully causes to a third party. Liability in damages does not apply if they comply with their duty to supervise or if the damage would have been caused even in the case of the proper conduct of supervision.
(2) The same responsibility applies to any person who assumes the task of supervision by contract.

§ 833 BGB Liability of animal keeper

If a human being suffers injury to life, limb or health by an animal or if a thing is damaged by an animal, then the person who keeps the animal is liable to provide compensation to the injured person for the damage arising therefrom. Liability in damages does not apply if the damage is caused by a domestic animal intended to serve the profession, gainful employment or subsistence of the keeper of the animal and either the keeper of the animal in supervising the animal has exercised the care required in business dealings or the damage also would have occurred even if such care had been exercised.

§ 834 BGB Liability of animal minder

A person who by contract assumes the supervision of an animal for the keeper of the animal is responsible for the damage inflicted by the animal on a third party in the manner specified in section 833. The responsibility does not apply if they exercise the care required in business dealings in supervision or if the damage also would have occurred even if such care had been exercised.

§ 836 BGB Liability of the owner of a plot of land

(1) If a human being suffers injury to life, limb or health, or if a thing is damaged by the collapse of a building or any other work attached to a plot of land or by parts of the building or work separating therefrom, then the possessor of the plot of land is liable to provide compensation to the injured person for damage resulting from this, to the extent that the collapse or separation is a consequence of defective construction or inadequate upkeep. Liability in damages does not apply if the possessor has exercised the care required in business dealings for the purpose of averting danger.
(2) A previous possessor of the plot of land is responsible for the damage if the collapse or separation occurs within one year after they vacated possession unless, during their period of possession, they exercised the care required in business dealings or a later possessor would have been able to avert the danger by observing such care.
(3) The possessor within the meaning of these provisions is the owner-occupier.

§ 837 BGB Liability of building possessor

If anyone, in the exercise of a right, possesses a building or another structure on the plot of land of another person, then the responsibility specified in section 836 applies to them instead of the possessor of the plot of land.

§ 838 BGB Liability of the person with a duty of upkeep regarding a building

A person who assumes the upkeep of a building or of a work attached to a plot of land for the possessor or is responsible for the upkeep of the building or the work by virtue of a right of use to which they are entitled is responsible in the same way as the possessor for the damage caused by the collapse or the separation of parts of the building.

§ 839 BGB Liability in case of breach of official duty

(1) If an official intentionally or negligently breaches the official duty incumbent upon them in relation to a third party, then they are to provide compensation to the third party for the damage arising therefrom. If the official is at fault only for negligence, then they may be held liable only if the injured person is not able to obtain compensation in another way.
(2) If an official breaches their official duties in a judgment in a legal matter, then they are responsible only for any damage arising therefrom if the breach of duty consists of a criminal offence. This provision does not apply to a refusal, in breach of duty, to perform official tasks or to a delay, in breach of duty, in doing so.

(3) Liability in damages does not apply if the injured person intentionally or negligently has failed to avert the damage by taking recourse to legal remedies.

§ 839a BGB Liability of court-appointed expert

(1) If an expert appointed by the court intentionally or by gross negligence submits an incorrect expert opinion, then they are liable to provide compensation for the damage incurred by a party to the proceedings as a result of a court decision based on this expert opinion.
(2) Section 839 (3) is to be applied accordingly.

§ 840 BGB Liability of more than one person

(1) If more than one person is responsible for damage arising from a tort, then they are jointly and severally liable.
(2) If, besides the person who is obliged to provide compensation for damage caused by another person under sections 831 and 832, the other person is also responsible for the damage, then in their internal relationship, the other is obliged alone, and in the case specified in section 829, the person with a duty of supervision is obliged alone.
(3) If, besides the person who is obliged to provide compensation for damage under sections 833 to 838, a third party is responsible, then in their internal relationship, the third party is obliged alone.

§ 841 BGB Compensation for liability of a public official

If an official, who by virtue of their official duty is to appoint another person for management for a third party or is to supervise such management or participate in it by ratifying legal transactions, is responsible together with the other person, as a result of violating these duties, for the damage caused by the other, then in their internal relationship the other person is obliged alone.

§ 842 BGB Extent of liability in damages in case of injury of a person

Liability to provide compensation for damage resulting from a tort directed against the person extends to the disadvantages the tort produces for the livelihood or advancement of the injured person.

§ 843 BGB Annuity in money or lump sum settlement

(1) If the earning capacity of the injured person is eliminated or reduced as the result of an injury to limb or health or if their needs are increased, then the injured person is to be provided compensation for their damages by payment of an annuity.
(2) The provisions of section 760 apply to the annuity. Whether the person liable for damages is to provide security, the kind of security and for what amount is determined by the circumstances.

(3) In lieu of the annuity, the injured person may demand a lump sum settlement if there is a compelling reason for doing so.
(4) The claim is not excluded by the fact that another person is to provide the injured person with maintenance.

§ 844 BGB Third-party compensation claims in the case of death

(1) In cases in which death is caused, the person liable in damages is to reimburse the costs of a funeral to the person under a duty to bear these costs.
(2) If the person killed, at the time of the injury, stood in a relationship with a third party on the basis of which they were obliged or might become obliged by operation of law to provide maintenance for that person and if as a result of the death the third party has been deprived of their right to maintenance, then the person liable in damages is to provide the third party with compensation for damages by payment of an annuity to the extent that the person killed would have been obliged to maintain for the presumed duration of their life; the provisions of section 843 (2) to (4) apply accordingly. Liability in damages also applies in cases in which the third party at the time of injury had been conceived but not yet born.
(3) The person liable in damages is to pay to the survivor, who had a special relationship of personal closeness to the person killed at the time of the injury, adequate compensation in money for the emotional suffering caused to the survivor. A special relationship of personal closeness is presumed where the survivor was the spouse, the life partner, a parent or a child of the person killed.

§ 845 BGB Compensation claims for lost services

In the case of injury to life, limb or health, as well as in the case of deprivation of liberty, the person liable in damages is to provide compensation to a third party for loss of services by payment of an annuity if, by operation of law, the injured person was under a duty to the third party to render services in the household or business of the latter. The provisions of sections 843 (2) to (4) apply accordingly.

§ 846 BGB Contributory negligence of the injured person

In the cases governed by sections 844 and 845, if fault on the part of the injured person contributed to the genesis of the damage suffered by the third party, then the provisions of section 254 apply to the claim of the third party.

§ 848 BGB Liability for chance in the case of deprivation of a thing

A person who is obliged to return a thing of which they have deprived another person by tort is also responsible for the chance loss, for a chance impossibility of surrender arising for another reason or for chance deterioration of the thing, unless such loss, other impossibility of surrender or deterioration would have occurred even without the deprivation.

§ 849 BGB Interest on the compensation sum

If compensation is to be paid for the value of a thing of which a person has been deprived, or if compensation is to be paid for the reduction in value of a thing as a result of damage, then the injured person may demand interest on the amount to be paid in compensation from the date onwards on which the determination of the value is based.

§ 850 BGB Reimbursement of outlays

If the person obliged to surrender a thing that another person has been deprived of makes outlays on the thing, then in relation to the injured person, they have the rights that a possessor has against the owner for outlays.

§ 851 BGB Compensation payment to unauthorised parties

If the person liable to pay damages for the deprivation of a movable thing or for damage to a movable thing provides compensation to that person in whose possession the thing was at the time when the deprivation or damage occurred, then by so providing compensation they are released, even if a third party was the owner of the thing or had another right in the thing, unless they are aware of the right of the third party or their lack of knowledge is due to gross negligence.

§ 852 BGB Claim to surrender after the end of the limitation period

If by a tort, the person liable to pay compensation obtains something at the cost of the injured person, then even after the claim to compensation for the damage arising from a tort has become statute-barred, they are obliged to surrender the benefit obtained in accordance with the provisions on the surrender of unjust enrichment. This claim becomes statute-barred ten years after it arises, or, notwithstanding the date on which it arises, thirty years after the date on which the act causing the injury was committed or after the other event triggering the loss occurred.

§ 853 BGB Defence of bad faith

If someone obtains a claim against the injured person by committing a tort, the injured person may refuse performance even if the claim to cancellation of the claim has become statute-barred.

§3. Function of the Law of Torts

46. The law of torts has multiple functions: The primary function attributed to the law of torts is the indemnification of the person suffering harm and the satisfaction of the tort victim's need for loss compensation.[39] The compensation can be viewed as the necessary counterpart to the negligent or wilful interference with another person's rights. The victim shall be put in the same position he would have been in had the damage not been inflicted on him. In cases of strict liability for risky activities, this concept is replaced with an overall economic compensatory function.[40] However, it remains doubtful if the indemnification function can be used as a method of interpretation regarding the cause of liability.[41] More likely, it is primarily important with respect to the calculation of damages, as compensation for the infringement of a legally protected interest becomes relevant on this level.[42]

47. Of greater significance with regard to the cause of liability is the second function of tort law, which is the prevention of injurious conduct. Potential tortfeasors shall be deterred from being careless by the threat of liability.[43] The courts have stressed the preventive function of tort law, especially in cases dealing with the violation of personal rights by the yellow press.[44] However, other areas, such as environmental liability, show the limited scope of the preventive function.[45] Although tort law is usually not seen as an instrument to sanction misconduct,[46] the decisions of the Federal Supreme Court concerning the violation of personal rights[47] show that the boundaries between prevention and punishment are not easy to determine. However, the award of punitive damages would be a clear violation of the fundamental principles of German law.[48]

48. The indemnification and preventive functions of tort law are eclipsed by the system of social security and other collective mechanisms to compensate for damages.[49] If a negligent injurer is discharged of the risk of being submitted to severe expenditures in compensating the tort victim, the deterrent effect is significantly mitigated. Nonetheless, the described functions remain important: On the one hand,

39. *See* Wagner, in: Münchener Kommentar zum BGB, Vor § 823 Nos 43–44 et seq. (8th ed., 2020); Spindler, in: beck-online Großkommentar (BeckOGK), BGB, § 823 No. 10 (version 01.02.2023); and Brüggemeier, *Prinzipien des Haftungsrechts*, 3 et seq. (1999); on the guiding legislative concepts of the law of torts in general Picker, *ZfPW* 2015, 385 et seq.
40. *See* J. Hager, in: Staudinger, BGB, Vor § 823 No. 9 (2017).
41. *See* Kötz, Festschrift für Steindorff, 643, 644 (1990).
42. *See* Deutsch, *Allgemeines Haftungsrecht* No. 19 (2nd ed., 1996); and J. Hager, in: Staudinger, BGB, Vor § 823 No. 9 (2017).
43. *See* Kötz, Festschrift für Steindorff, 643, 645 et seq. (1990); J. Hager, in: Staudinger, BGB, Vor § 823 No. 10 (2017); and Wagner, in: Münchener Kommentar zum BGB, Vor § 823 Nos 45 et seq. (8th ed., 2020).
44. *See* BGHZ 128, 1, 15; BGH, *NJW* 1985, 1617, 1619; and Oberlandesgericht (OLG) Hamburg, *NJW* 1996, 2871, 2872.
45. *See* Lübbe-Wolff, *NVwZ* 2001, 481, 485 et seq.; Schwarze, *Präventionsdefizite der Umwelthaftung* (1996); and Balensiefen, *Umwelthaftung*, 33 et seq. (1994).
46. *See* BGHZ 118, 312, 344; Lange and Schiemann, *Schadensersatz*, 12 et seq (3rd ed., 2003); J. Hager, in: Staudinger, BGB, Vor § 823 No. 11 (2017); and Canaris, Festschrift für Deutsch, 85, 107 (1999).
47. BGHZ 128, 1, 15; and BGH, *NJW* 2006, 603 et seq.
48. BVerfG, *NJW* 1973, 1221, 1224; *see* Wagner, *AcP* 206 (2006), 352 et seq.; and Wagner, *ZEuP* 2000, 200 et seq.
49. *See* Wagner, in: Münchener Kommentar zum BGB, Vor § 823 Nos 30–37 (8th ed., 2020); and Brüggemeier, *Prinzipien des Haftungsrechts*, 4 et seq. (1999).

the incentives set by tort law are reflected by the premiums of liability insurance. On the other hand, the insurer regularly has a right of recourse in case of grossly negligent or wilful conduct.[50] Furthermore, despite the existence of collective mechanisms to compensate for damages, tort law is of considerable significance with respect to prohibitive injunctions.

§4. Relationship Between Torts and Criminal Law

49. German law clearly distinguishes between torts and criminal law. German criminal law is codified in the Criminal Code of 1871 (*Strafgesetzbuch* (StGB)). Subsequent to a major revision, the Criminal Code was newly promulgated in 1998. It lists the acts constituting offences and distinguishes between felonies, such as murder, manslaughter or robbery, and misdemeanours, such as theft or criminal mischief. In addition to the Criminal Code, the Code of Criminal Procedure (*Strafprozessordnung* (StPO)), initially promulgated in 1877, provides the rules for criminal actions, which are fundamentally different from the procedural rules for civil actions codified in the Code of Civil Procedure (*Zivilprozessordnung* (ZPO)).

50. As part of public law, the rules of criminal law relate to sanctions imposed by the state. Although crimes often have private victims, they are considered to be offences against the state and society. Principally, the state has an interest in prosecuting criminal offenders beyond the rights or wishes of any private person. Consequently, actions under criminal law are raised by a public prosecutor. Although tortious conduct need not qualify as a wrong for which society seeks criminal sanction, a tort may at the same time qualify as a felony or misdemeanour. Hence, the tortfeasor may become the accused in criminal proceedings and, at the same time, be the defendant in a civil lawsuit. Principally, the result of the latter has no influence on the criminal proceedings and vice versa.

51. A crucial purpose of criminal law is the prevention of criminal actions.[51] The threat of punishment in the forms of fines and confinement is intended to have a deterrent effect on potential offenders. In this area, criminal law partly intersects with the preventive function of tort law. However, the interests protected by criminal law go beyond those protected by tort law; as opposed to criminal law, tort law is not designed to prevent violations of legal assets of the general public. In addition to the prevention of criminal actions, German criminal law also aims at the rehabilitation of offenders. According to section 46(1) StGB, the effects which the punishment is expected to have on the perpetrator's future life in society are to be considered.

50. Wagner, *VersR* 1999, 1441, 1446; and J. Hager, in: Staudinger, BGB, Vor § 823 No. 7 (2017).
51. On the purpose of German criminal law, *see* Jescheck and Weigend, *Lehrbuch des Strafrechts*, Nos 60 et seq. (5th ed., 1996); and Kinzig, in: Schönke and Schröder, *Strafgesetzbuch*, Vorbem §§ 38 ff. Nos 2 et seq. (30th ed., 2019).

§5. Relationship Between Contractual and Tortious Responsibility

52. The German Civil Code basically provides a sharp distinction between tortious and contractual responsibility. Hence, tort law claims are principally independent of contractual liability in order to avoid disadvantages for the injured contracting party.[52] Breach of contract can also constitute a tort if it fulfils the definition of tortious conduct.[53] There is no rule of *non cumul.*[54] Moreover, the limitation of tort law actions has no influence on contractual claims.[55] However, an exception from the basic juxtaposition of tort law and contract law is acknowledged by the Federal Supreme Court for situations in which the tort law claim would exactly correspond to the contractual warranty for defects.[56] Furthermore, the limitation rules for tort law claims apply to contractual claims if the application is required by the specific purpose of the contract. This demonstrates that interactions between contractual and tortious responsibility are possible. For instance, statutory limitations of contractual liability frequently apply to tort law claims as well.[57] If the Civil Code requires a certain degree of culpability (e.g., gross negligence) in order to grant a contractual claim, the same degree of culpability is usually required for a respective tort law claim to prevent an evasion of the contractual party's privileged position.[58] However, contractual limitations of liability are only relevant for tort law claims if their applicability is explicitly or at least undoubtedly agreed upon.[59]

53. Despite these interactions, there are a number of differences in the foundation and scope of contractual and tortious liability, most evidently with respect to the recoverability of pure economic loss and the principles of vicarious liability. While pure economic loss is generally recoverable under the rules of contractual liability, tort law provides only limited protection to a victim sustaining such damages; pure economic loss is not recoverable unless it is caused by a person in privity of contract with the victim. According to section 826 BGB, an exception exists for wilful damage contrary to public policy. Furthermore, a person who infringes a statute intended for the protection of others is also liable for pure economic loss pursuant to section 823(2) BGB.

54. With regard to vicarious liability, the Civil Code provides a clear differentiation. According to section 278 BGB, the debtor of a contractual obligation is

52. *See* BGHZ 110, 323, 328; BGHZ 116, 297, 300; BGHZ 123, 394, 398; and BGH, *NJW* 1998, 2282, 2283.
53. *See* BGHZ 24, 188, 191 et seq.; BGH, *NJW* 1992, 1511, 1512; BGH, *NJW-RR* 1996, 1121, 1122; BGH, *ZIP* 1998, 1073, 1074; and BGH, *NJW-RR* 2005, 172.
54. Spickhoff, in: Soergel, BGB, Vor § 823 No. 73 (13th ed., 2005).
55. *See* BGHZ 66, 315, 319.
56. *See* BGH, *NJW-RR* 1993, 793, 794; and BGH, *ZIP* 1998, 1073, 1075.
57. *See* Spindler, in: BeckOGK, BGB, § 823 No. 0.24 (version 01.02.2023); and Sprau, in: Grüneberg, BGB, Einf. v. § 823 No. 10 (82nd ed., 2023).
58. For examples *see* Sprau, in: Grüneberg, BGB, Einf. v. § 823 Nos 9 et seq. (82nd ed., 2023); Wagner, in: Münchener Kommentar zum BGB, Vor § 823 Nos 88 et seq. (8th ed., 2020); and Teichmann, in: Jauernig, BGB, Vor. § 823 No. 4 (18th ed., 2021).
59. *See* BGH, *NJW* 1979, 2148.

responsible to the same extent as for his own fault for the fault of his legal representative and of persons whom he employs to perform his obligation. Under section 831 BGB, a person who employs another to do any work is bound to compensate for any damage which the other unlawfully causes to a third party in the performance of his work. However, the duty to compensate does not arise if the employer has exercised necessary care in the selection and supervision of the employee. Hence, unlike under contract law, the principal may proof his non-negligent behaviour and thus claim exemption from liability according to section 831 BGB. Other differences between contractual liability and tortious responsibility exist with respect to the burden of proof and, despite all efforts of harmonization, the rules of limitation.[60]

55. German courts have shown a tendency to overcome the differences in the foundation and scope of contractual and tortious liability by expanding the range of contractual instruments. An example of this tendency is the adoption of doctrines such as pre-contractual liability – *culpa in contrahendo* – or a contract with protective effects for a third party (*Vertrag mit Schutzwirkung zugunsten Dritter*) that allow the recovery of pure economic loss or the application of the stricter contractual vicarious liability rules to genuinely extra-contractual settings. This expansive application of contractual instruments is sometimes identified as a 'third track' between contractual and tortious liability. In later jurisdiction, the Federal Supreme Court shows a tendency of transferring contractual towards tortious liability as contractual duties might be regarded in the question of tortious liability.[61]

§6. Foundation of Claims

56. Unlike other legal systems, German tort law is not based on a general clause according to which a person is liable for an unlawful and culpable infliction of damage. To avoid uncertainty regarding tort law claims, the German system (codified in sections 823–853 BGB) distinguishes between different causes of action, each with specific prerequisites and legal consequences.

57. Alongside several special provisions, the Civil Code includes three causes of action, which can be described as 'minor' general clauses: sections 823(1), 823(2), and 826 BGB. While section 823(2) BGB requires the culpable violation of specific legally protected interests, such as life, body, health, freedom, property, or a so-called other right, section 823(2) BGB refers to the culpable violation of a protective law. Section 826 BGB, on the other hand, sanctions wilful damage contrary to public policy. The most significant difference regarding the legal consequences is that contrary to section 823(1) BGB, sections 823(2) and 826 BGB allow recovery of pure economic loss.

---

60. *See* Sprau, in: Grüneberg, BGB, Einf. v. § 823 Nos 9 et seq. (82nd ed., 2023).
61. BGHZ 166, 84, 86 et seq.; *see also* Spindler, *JZ* 2006, 741 et seq.

58. Certain special provisions of the Civil Code are relevant in connection with the violation of specific duties: According to section 824(1) BGB, a person who declares or publishes, contrary to the truth, a statement that is likely to endanger the credit of another, or to injure the other person's earnings or prosperity in any other manner, shall compensate the other for any damage arising from the statement, even if he does not know of its untruth, but should know of it.[62] Damage claims in connection with an inducement to cohabit can be based on section 825 BGB. Other provisions deal with liability for servants,[63] liability of persons exercising a duty of supervision,[64] liability of animal keepers and supervisors,[65] and liability for the collapse of a building.[66] Finally, section 839(1) BGB regulates responsibility for the violation of an official duty, and the recently introduced section 839a BGB deals with liability of court-appointed experts.

§7. Protected Interests

59. A necessary prerequisite for a tort law claim is the violation of an interest protected by sections 823–853 BGB. As discussed in the preceding section, German tort law is characterized by a subtle differentiation with respect to the requirements of a tort law claim, particularly regarding the degree of culpability (e.g., while ordinary negligence is sufficient for claims based on section 823(1) BGB, section 826 BGB allows recovery only for wilfully inflicted damage). The counterpart to the varying levels of culpability required by sections 823 et seq. BGB is a differentiation with respect to the legal consequences; the different causes of action deviate with respect to the protected interests.

60. Under section 823(1) BGB, the predominant rule of German tort law, the extra-contractual fault-based claim for compensation is limited to recovery for injury to life, body, health, freedom, property or 'other rights' (innominated rights) of another person. The term 'other right' (*sonstiges Recht*) refers to absolute rights (rights that can be asserted against everyone in contrast to relative rights, such as rights arising under a contract) comparable to property. It includes, *inter alia*, copyrights, patents, trademarks, possession, certain family relationships, and membership to an association.[67] Furthermore, it embodies the general right of a person to his personality (*allgemeines Persönlichkeitsrecht*) and the protection of an established and operating commercial business (*Recht am eingerichteten und ausgeübten Gewerbebetrieb*). Again, an important limitation of the legal consequences attached to section 823(1) BGB is the exclusion of pure economic loss, which sometimes causes substantial trouble concerning 'other rights' and their scope. A person's

---

62. However, a person who makes a communication, the untruth of which is unknown to him, does not thereby render himself liable to make compensation if he or the receiver of the communication has a lawful interest in it, *see* s. 824(2) BGB.
63. *See* s. 831 BGB.
64. *See* s. 832 BGB.
65. *See* s. 833 BGB and s. 834 BGB.
66. *See* ss 836–838 BGB.
67. *See* Spindler, in: BeckOGK, BGB, § 823 Nos 160 et seq. (version 01.02.2023).

wealth is protected as such, *inter alia*, by section 823(2) and, especially, by section 826 BGB. Thus, while the scope of section 826 BGB seems to be at first glance wider than section 823(1) BGB to the extent that its application is not limited to the violation of enumerated interests but provides for compensation even of pure economic loss, it is narrower insofar as it covers only wilfully inflicted damage.

In the following, the interests protected by section 823(1) BGB will be described in detail.

I. Life, Body, and Health

61. The violation of another person's right to life means the killing of another person. The statutory definition does not only cover born persons but also extends to the unborn child.[68] Section 823(1) BGB, in combination with section 844 BGB, forms the basis for wrongful death claims by relatives and other survivors whose support fell under the legal obligation of the deceased: If the deceased at the time of the injury stood in a relationship to a third party by virtue of which he was bound by law to furnish maintenance to such third party, and if in consequence of the death such third party is deprived of the right to claim maintenance, the person bound to make compensation shall compensate the third party by payment of a money annuity, cf. section 844(2) BGB. The assistance in the commission of suicide is not sufficient for a claim based on the injury of the deceased person's life.[69]

62. According to a common definition, injury to the body is a violation of a person's physical integrity, whereas injury to a person's health is the causation of an internal physical or intellectual dysfunction.[70] The infliction of pain is not a necessary requirement.[71] Damage to body and damage to health cannot be strictly separated and merged into one another.[72] The injury need not be of a purely physical nature.[73] A nervous shock amounts to an interference with the body/health of the affected person if it is a serious and immediate shock suffered by a close relative of the victim.[74] However, the shock must be accompanied by medically recognizable

68. BVerfG, *NJW* 1975, 573; 1993, 1751; J. Hager, in: Staudinger, BGB, § 823 No. B 3 (2017); and Spindler, in: BeckOGK, BGB, § 823 No. 104 (version 01.02.2023).
69. J. Hager, in: Staudinger, BGB, § 823 No. B 1 (2017).
70. *See* BGHZ 124, 52, 54; Larenz and Canaris, *Schuldrecht II/2*, § 77 II 1 a (13th ed., 1994); and Spickhoff, in: Soergel, BGB, § 823 Nos 33, 38 (13th ed., 2005).
71. *See* BGHZ 114, 284, 289; BGHZ 163, 209, 212 (HIV infection); BGH, *NJW* 1953, 1440; and AG Köln, *NJW-RR* 2001, 1675 et seq. (haircut).
72. J. Hager, in: Staudinger, BGB, § 823 No. B 5 (2017); and Wilhelmi, in: Erman, BGB, § 823 No. 17 (16th ed., 2020).
73. *See* BGHZ 137, 142, 145 et seq.; BGHZ 132, 341, 343 et seq.; BGH, *NJW* 1998, 813, 814; BGH, *NJW* 1997, 1640, 1641; BGH, *NJW* 2000, 862; and BGH, *NJW* 2007, 2764.
74. *See* BGHZ 93, 351, 355 et seq.; BGHZ 107, 359, 363; BGHZ 132, 341, 344; OLG Köln, *NJW-RR* 2000, 760; OLG Hamm, *NJW-RR* 2001, 1676; and Wilhelmi, in: Erman, BGB, § 823 No. 20 (16th ed., 2020).

infringements.[75] The Federal Supreme Court has also affirmed bodily injury pursuant to section 823(1) BGB in a factual situation in which sperm for an in vitro fertilization was destroyed.[76] Furthermore, the death of an unborn child is an injury to the mother's body.[77] Insomnia caused by noise or industrial emissions has been qualified as injury to health.[78]

II. Freedom

63. Injury to freedom is the deprivation of an individual's physical freedom,[79] such as private imprisonment, forcible abduction, and wilful illegal arrest.[80] The duration of the deprivation is generally irrelevant.[81] However, section 823(1) BGB does not apply if the deprivation of freedom is entirely insignificant.[82] In addition, the general freedom of action is not protected.[83]

III. Property

64. Section 823(1) BGB protects real property (immovables) as well as personal property (movables). An injury to property can be any interference with ownership, whether it amounts to deterioration, partial or total destruction, or deprivation of the affected object.[84] Interference with the substance is not necessary. Even a restriction of the designated use of an object is considered an injury to property.[85] For this reason, the Federal Supreme Court has affirmed an injury to property for a ship trapped by a collapsed embankment.[86] The intrusion of noxious substances or noise can be

75. *See* BGHZ 137, 142, 145 et seq.; BGHZ 132, 341, 343 et seq.; BGH, *NJW* 1998, 813, 814; BGH, *NJW* 1997, 1640, 1641; Wagner, in: Münchener Kommentar zum BGB, § 823 Nos 214 et seq. (8th ed., 2020).
76. BGHZ 124, 52, 54.
77. BGH, *NJW* 1972, 1126 et seq.; OLG Koblenz, *NJW* 1988, 2959, 2960; BGH, *NJW* 2009, 3025, 3026; and OLG Oldenburg, *NJW* 1991, 2355.
78. *See* BGHZ 122, 363, 370; BGH, *NJW* 1997, 2748; BGH, *NJW* 1995, 1160, 1161; and OLG Oldenburg, *NJW* 1990, 3215, 3216.
79. *See,* e.g., OLG München, OLGZ 1985, 466, 467; J. Hager, in: Staudinger, BGB, § 823 No. B 53 (2017); Wagner, in: Münchener Kommentar zum BGB, § 823 No. 239 (8th ed., 2020); and Wilhelmi, in: Erman, BGB, § 823 No. 23 (16th ed., 2020).
80. *See* Spindler, in: BeckOGK, BGB, § 823 No. 115 (version 01.02.2023); and Wilhelmi, in: Erman, BGB, § 823 No. 24 (16th ed., 2020).
81. *See* AG Regensburg, *NJW-RR* 1999, 1402.
82. Spindler, in: BeckOGK, BGB, § 823 No. 118 (version 01.02.2023); *see also* J. Hager, in: Staudinger, BGB, s. 823 No. B 54 (2017).
83. OLG München, *OLGZ* 1985, 466, 467; Wagner, in: Münchener Kommentar zum BGB, § 823 No. 239 (8th ed., 2020); and Lorenz, *Der Schutz vor dem unerwünschten Vertrag*, 380 et seq. (1997).
84. *See* BGHZ 41, 123, 125 et seq.; BGHZ 105, 346, 350; J. Hager, in: Staudinger, BGB, § 823 No. B 79 (2017); Spindler, in: BeckOGK, BGB, § 823 No. 120 (version 01.02.2023); and Sprau, in: Grüneberg, BGB, § 823 Nos 7 et seq. (82nd ed., 2023).
85. BGHZ 138, 230, 235; BGH, *NJW* 1994, 517, 518; BGH, *NJW-RR* 1995, 342 et seq.; Spindler, in: BeckOGK, BGB, § 823 No. 132 (version 01.02.2023); and Sprau, in: Grüneberg, BGB, § 823 No. 7 (82nd ed., 2023).
86. BGHZ 55, 153, 159.

an injury to real property.[87] Other possible injuries are the soiling of an object, provided the cleaning costs are significant,[88] interference with the systematic order of an archive or a library,[89] or a hindrance of the organic plant growth attributable to unsuitable potting compost.[90] Closely connected to this is the question of whether data or software are seen as property: although the prevailing opinion refers to the data embodiment in regard of the storage medium, data itself must also be protected by the norm directly and cannot be dependent on whether it is embodied or not.[91]

IV. Right of a Person to His Personality

65. The general right of a person to his personality is a basic right constitutionally guaranteed by Articles 1 and 2 of the Basic Law. It guarantees the protection of human dignity and the right to unhindered development of the personality.[92] Specific manifestations of the general right to personality are the right to one's name according to section 12 BGB and the right to one's own picture according to sections 22 et seq. of the Act on Artistic Creations (*Kunsturhebergesetz* (KUG)), which prohibit the publication of a person's picture without consent, unless the person is a so-called public figure. Other provisions that may be relevant with respect to the protection of a person's honour and reputation are section 826 BGB and section 824 BGB. If a defamatory or insulting statement is punishable under sections 185–187 StGB, claims may also be based on section 823(2) BGB.

66. However, the protection guaranteed by these provisions is still incomplete in the face of the manifold facets of the right to personality, in particular regarding mass media and the intrusions into private spheres. Therefore, since 1954, the Federal Supreme Court has recognized the right to personality as an 'other right' according to section 823(1) BGB,[93] although the right to personality has more similarities to protected interests, such as life, body, health, and freedom.[94] A specific feature of the right to personality is the possibility to award compensation for pain and suffering,[95] despite the explicit wording of section 253(2) BGB, which states that the injured party may demand fair compensation in money for non-pecuniary damage only in case of injuries to body, health, or freedom, or if the right of sexual self-determination is violated. The reasoning behind this exception to section 253 BGB

87. Spindler, in: BeckOGK, BGB, § 823 No. 121 (version 01.02.2023); *see also* BGHZ 120, 239, 249.
88. BGH, *DB* 1964, 65 (smoke on a wall); and AG Leipzig, *NJW-RR* 1998, 240 (graffiti).
89. BGHZ 76, 216, 220 = *NJW* 1980, 1518; and Sprau, in: Grüneberg, BGB, § 823 No. 7 (82nd ed., 2023).
90. BGH, *NJW-RR* 1993, 793 and 1113; and Sprau, in: Grüneberg, BGB, § 823 No. 9 (82nd ed., 2023).
91. Spindler, in: BeckOGK, BGB, § 823 Nos 137 and 185 et seq. (version 01.02.2023).
92. BGHZ 13, 334; *see also* with further references Förster, in: Beck'scher Online-Kommentar (BeckOK), BGB, § 12 No. 104 (65th ed., 2023).
93. Constant case law since BGHZ 13, 334, 338 (readers' letters).
94. *See* Götting, in: Götting and Schertz and Seitz, *Handbuch Persönlichkeitsrecht*, § 1 No. 2 (2nd ed., 2019).
95. *See* Sprau, in: Grüneberg, BGB, § 823 No. 111 (82nd ed., 2023); Teichmann, in: Jauernig, BGB, § 253 No. 10 (18th ed., 2021); and Ebert, in: Erman, BGB, § 253 No. 19 (16th ed., 2020).

refers to the constitutional protection of human dignity and personality.[96] The courts have developed certain categories of injuries to the right to personality, such as the invasion of somebody's privacy or defamatory statements.[97] To a certain degree, the Federal Supreme Court acknowledges the continuation of the right to personality even past death.[98] An invasion of the right of a person to his personality can only be established after weighing colliding interests with regard to the specific case.[99] To differentiate between qualities of invasion, the so-called theory of spheres (*Sphärentheorie*) has been developed with the inviolable private sphere, the surrounding privacy, and the social sphere.[100]

67. A specific feature of the right to one's personality is that infringements are not unlawful per se. In order to determine the unlawfulness, every individual case requires a balancing of the conflicting legally protected interests.[101]

V. Right to an Established and Operating Commercial Business

68. The judge-made right to an established and operating commercial business was developed by the Supreme Court of the German Reich (*Reichsgericht*) in the early twentieth century.[102] It was created as an omnibus clause to fill gaps in the codified law, especially in the area of industrial property protection, which resulted from the limited protection offered by the Civil Code in cases of pure economic loss.[103] The intention underlying the acknowledgement of the right to an established and operating commercial business was the protection of commercial enterprises against certain kinds of interference with their economic interests, although its specific content still remains vague. Today, the right is accepted as customary law.[104] However, commentators recently have shown some effort to limit its scope in order to make the application by the courts more predictable.[105]

---

96. BGHZ 128, 1, 14 et seq.; BGH, *NJW* 1996, 985, 986; and BVerfG, *NJW* 2000, 2195, 2198.
97. *See* BGH, *NJW* 2000, 2195, 2197 et seq.; BGHZ 169, 193 = *NJW* 2007, 684, 685; and BGH, *NJW* 2009, 751, 752.
98. *See* BGH, *NJW* 2000, 2195, 2197 et seq.; BGHZ 169, 193 = *NJW* 2007, 684, 685; and BGH, *NJW* 2009, 751, 752.
99. *See* Specht-Riemenschneider, in: BeckOGK, BGB, § 823 No. 1169 (version 01.02.2023); Wilhelmi, in: Erman, BGB, § 823 No. 48 (16th ed., 2020); and Götting, in: Götting and Schertz and Seitz, *Handbuch Persönlichkeitsrecht*, § 1 No. 2 (2nd ed., 2019).
100. *See* BVerfG, *NJW* 2000, 1021 et seq.; BVerfG *ZUM-RD* 2010, 657, 661; and Rixecker, in: Münchener Kommentar zum BGB, Anhang zu § 12 No. 29 (9th ed., 2021).
101. *See* BVerfG, *NJW* 1973, 1226; BGH, *NJW* 2005, 2766, 2770; Sprau, in: Grüneberg, BGB, § 823 Nos 95–106 (82nd ed., 2023); and Wilhelmi, in: Erman, BGB, § 823 No. 48 (16th ed., 2020).
102. *See* RGZ 58, 24, 30.
103. *See* Spindler, in: BeckOGK, BGB, § 823 No. 204 (version 01.02.2023); and Sprau, in: Grüneberg, BGB, § 823 No. 137 (82nd ed., 2023).
104. *See* Spindler, in: BeckOGK, BGB, § 823 No. 204 (version 01.02.2023); and Wilhelmi, in: Erman, BGB, § 823 No. 49 (16th ed., 2020).
105. *See* Spindler, in: BeckOGK, BGB, § 823 Nos 213 et seq. (version 01.02.2023).

69. The protection provided by the right to an established and operating commercial business includes the regular clientele,[106] business relations,[107] ways of communication (including unhindered e-mail communication),[108] know-how, good will,[109] and the organizational structure of an enterprise.[110] However, in order to limit the doctrine's field of application, the Federal Supreme Court requires a 'direct interference' with the commercial business.[111] The interference with the right needs to be 'business-related' (betriebsbezogener *Eingriff*), in contrast to a simple affection of rights and interests that are separable from the business as a functioning unit.[112] Hence, it must be in some way directed against the business as such, in a manner that is neither socially adequate nor a mere annoyance.[113] The field of application of the right to an established and operating commercial business is restricted not only by the requirement of business-related interference but also by its subsidiary nature.[114] Hence, it can only be invoked if no other, more specific provision is applicable to the case.[115] Moreover, as with the general right of a person to his personality, infringements of the right to an established and operating commercial business are not unlawful per se, and every case requires a careful balancing of the legally protected interests involved.[116]

---

106. BGHZ 23, 157, 162 et seq.; and BGH, *DB* 1971, 571 et seq.
107. BGH, *NJW* 2009, 2958; BGH, *NJW* 2005, 3141; BGH *NJW* 2006, 1432, 1433; Spindler, in: BeckOGK, BGB, § 823 No. 205 (version 01.02.2023).
108. Spindler, in: BeckOGK, BGB, § 823 No. 205 (version 01.02.2023).
109. Sprau, in: Grüneberg, BGB, § 823 No. 138 (82nd ed., 2023).
110. BGH, *VersR* 1990, 1283; Sprau, in: Grüneberg, BGB, § 823 No. 134 (82nd ed., 2023).
111. *See* BGHZ 86, 152, 156; BGHZ 90, 113, 123; BGHZ 138, 311, 318 et seq.; BGH, *NJW* 1997, 3304, 3308; and BGH, *GRUR* 2009, 980, 981.
112. BGH, *WM* 2014, 1532, 1533; Sprau, in: Grüneberg, BGB, § 823 No. 139 (82nd ed., 2023); and Spindler, in: BeckOGK, BGB, § 823 No. 208 (version 01.02.2023).
113. *See* BGHZ 138, 311, 317 et seq.; BGH, *NJW* 1985, 1620; BGH, *NJW* 2001, 3115, 3117; and BGH, *WM* 2014, 1532, 1533.
114. *See* BGHZ 69, 128, 138 et seq.; BGHZ 105, 346, 350; and BGH, *NJW* 1992, 41, 42.
115. *See* BGHZ 166, 84, 108; Spindler, in: BeckOGK, BGB, § 823 No. 214 (version 01.02.2023).
116. *See* BGHZ 90, 113, 123; BGHZ 138, 311, 318; BGHZ 166, 84, 108; Deutsch, *Allgemeines Haftungsrecht,* No. 69 (2nd ed., 1996); and Spindler, in: BeckOGK, BGB, § 823 No. 212 (version 01.02.2023).

Part I. Liability for One's Own Acts

Chapter 1. General Principles

§1. Unlawfulness and Fault

70. The mere violation of a legally protected interest is not sufficient to entail liability under the rules of German tort law; the injurious conduct must rather qualify as unlawful.[117] Unlawfulness can be described as a failure to conduct oneself within the boundaries set by the law.[118] Contrary to other legal systems, German tort law is characterized by a sharp distinction between unlawfulness (*Rechtswidrigkeit*) and fault (*Verschulden*).[119] Unlawfulness and fault are seen as separate concepts. Except for cases of strict liability, both are essential prerequisites in order to impose liability on a person causing damage. While the concept of unlawfulness describes the violation of a legal provision without justification, the concept of fault refers to a person's incapability to meet the expected standard of care.

71. Based on this distinction, the traditional and predominant doctrine considers a conduct unlawful if one of the interests enumerated in section 823(1) BGB is violated unless a ground of justification is substantiated by the tortfeasor (*Lehre vom Erfolgsunrecht*).[120] Hence, a specific assessment of unlawfulness is not necessary. In recent times, however, the traditional method to determine unlawfulness has been challenged by some commentators. According to this deviating view, the unlawfulness test must not apply to the result but rather to the injurious conduct itself (*Lehre vom Handlungsunrecht*).[121] Consequently, only those interferences with protected

117. Cf. v. Caemmerer, Festschrift zum Deutschen Juristentag II, 49, 126 et seq. (1960); Wiethölter, *Der Rechtfertigungsgrund des verkehrsrichtigen Verhaltens* 15 (1960); and Larenz and Canaris, *Schuldrecht II/2*, § 75 I 1 (13th ed., 1994).
118. *See* BGHZ 24, 21, 24; OLG Düsseldorf, *OLGR Düsseldorf* 1993, 294; Deutsch, *Allgemeines Haftungsrecht* No. 226 (2nd ed., 1996); and Stathopoulos, Festschrift für Larenz 631, 645 (1983).
119. Spindler, in: BeckOGK, BGB, § 823 No. 78 (version 01.02.2023).
120. Cf. BGHZ 39, 103, 108; BGHZ 74, 9, 14; BGHZ 118, 201, 207; BGH, *NJW* 1996, 3205, 3207; Pfeiffer, in: Soergel, BGB, § 276 No. 26 (13th ed., 2014); Steffen, in: Reichsgerichtsrätekommentar (RGRK), BGB, § 823 No. 114 (12th ed., 1989); Bindokat, *JZ* 1958, 553 et seq.; Böhmer, *MDR* 1958, 745 et seq.; Stoll, *JZ* 1958, 137 et seq.; Wussow, *NJW* 1958, 891 et seq.; Larenz, *Karlsruher Forum* 1959, 10, 13; and Weitnauer, *Karlsruher Forum* 1961, 28, 30 f.
121. *See* Nipperdey, *NJW* 1957, 1777, 1778; Brüggemeier, *Deliktsrecht* No. 95 (1986); Erwin Deutsch, *Fahrlässigkeit und erforderliche Sorgfalt* 213 et seq. (2nd ed., 1995); Deutsch, Festschrift für Medicus 77, 79 et seq. (1999); Esser and Weyers, *Schuldrecht II/2*, § 55 II 3 c (8th ed., 2000); Wiethölter,

interests that also violate a duty of care are treated as unlawful. If the examination of the wrongdoer's conduct proves no protective law to be infringed, the question of whether a duty of care has been breached can only be answered by a weighing of interests. The reasoning behind this view is the assumption that only actions can be lawful or unlawful and that unlawfulness is predominantly relevant with respect to the accountability of a violation. Furthermore, it is argued that the technique of inferring unlawful conduct from the result is not applicable in case of omissions.[122] According to this deviating view, unlawfulness and fault tend to be merged into the same stage of the enquiry.

72. Despite the theoretic differences, both ways to determine unlawfulness usually lead to the same results. In situations where the deviant view negates the unlawfulness of a conduct based on a comprehensive weighing of interests, the traditional view would infer the unlawfulness from the violation of a protected interest but subsequently assume a faultless violation with the consequence of no liability. However, the focus of the unlawfulness test on the injurious conduct as endorsed by the deviating view has some considerable disadvantages: e.g., neither self-defence nor a right to require the acting person to refrain from the respective conduct would be possible;[123] additionally, the clear distinction between unlawfulness and fault would be distorted.[124]

73. Nonetheless, the ever-increasing division of labour suggests that a concept of unlawfulness, which considers only a conduct's result, may lead to an escalation of tort liability. Therefore, most commentators and courts differentiate between direct and indirect violations of legally protected interests. In case of a direct violation, the interference usually indicates the unlawfulness.[125] In case of an indirect violation, the underlying conduct is not unlawful unless the wrongdoer's behaviour can be regarded as an infringement of his general duty to ensure public safety (*Verkehrspflicht*).[126] Such a duty to ensure public safety can result from previous activities. Whoever, by his property or by his actions, establishes a source of potential hazard that is likely to affect the legally protected interests of others has the obligation to ensure the protection of the endangered interests.[127] Thus, the unlawfulness of the wrongdoer's conduct arises from his failure to avoid danger caused by his previous actions. In any case, responsibility for a source of hazard is

---

Der Rechtfertigungsgrund des verkehrsrichtigen Verhaltens 34 (1960); Zippelius, 157 *AcP* 390, 395 (1957); and Stoll, 162 *AcP* 203, 209 et seq. (1962).

122. *See* BGHZ 24, 21, 26; Lorenz, *JZ* 1961, 433, 435; Nipperdey, *NJW* 1957, 1777, 1778; Zippelius, 157 *AcP*, 390, 395 (1957); and Esser and Weyers, *Schuldrecht II/2*, § 55 II 3 b (8th ed., 2000).

123. Cf. Spindler, in: BeckOGK, BGB, § 823 No. 78 (version 01.02.2023).

124. *See* Larenz, *Karlruher Forum* 1959, 10, 13.

125. Teichmann, in: Jauernig BGB, § 823 No. 48 (18th ed., 2021).

126. BGH, *NJW* 1986, 1865, 1866; *see* Larenz, Festschrift für Dölle 169, 192 et seq. (1963); Larenz and Canaris, *Schuldrecht II/2*, § 75 II 3 b (13th ed., 1994); v. Bar, *Verkehrspflichten* 155 et seq., 175 (1980); G. Hager, Festschrift für E. Wolf 133 et seq. (1985); J. Hager, in: Staudinger, BGB, § 823 No. H 16 (2021); U. Huber, Festschrift für E.R. Huber 253, 274 et seq. (1973); and Wagner, in: Münchener Kommentar, BGB, § 823 Nos 433 et seq. (8th ed., 2020).

127. BGH, *NJW* 1977, 1965 et seq.; BGH *NJW* 1978, 1629 et seq.; *see* Markesinis, Bell and Janssen, *Markesinis's German Law of Torts* 56 (5th ed., 2019).

an indispensable prerequisite for liability; there is no general duty to protect others from damage.[128] Additionally, neither the endangerment of others nor the inducement of others to self-endangerment is generally prohibited.[129]

§2. Concept of Fault

74. As a general rule, liability for tortious conduct is dependent on whether the tortfeasor acted with fault. Only a few provisions of the Civil Code do not necessitate fault as a prerequisite for the imposition of liability. With respect to the tort law rules codified in sections 823 to 853 BGB, strict liability only applies to keepers of luxury animals.[130] However, since the Civil Code went into force in 1900, a multitude of previously unknown hazardous activities arose in connection with technical evolution. The legislator reacted by introducing new forms of strict liability. Yet, the respective provisions were not integrated into the Civil Code but rather codified in special laws, such as the Road Traffic Act of 1952 (StVG), the Strict Liability Act (HPflG), or the Product Liability Act (*ProdHaftG*).

75. The German Civil Code distinguishes between negligent and wilful injuries.[131] An injury is considered wilful if it was caused knowingly and intentionally (*dolus directus*). A person persisting with his actions even though he realizes that he may cause injury also acts wilfully (*dolus eventualis*). In contrast, a person merely acts negligently if he does not exercise the ordinary care required in everyday life.[132] Therefore, negligence can be described as an unintentional failure to provide the necessary care in order to avoid an injury. German civil law basically distinguishes between ordinary negligence (einfache *Fahrlässigkeit*) and gross negligence (grobe *Fahrlässigkeit*).[133] Except for liability for wilful damage contrary to public policy, which requires intent,[134] the tort law rules generally require only simple negligence. Exceptionally, German courts apply a particular standard of liability based on equity to the benefit of employees if the tortious conduct is directly work-related.[135] According to the liability-restricting principles of in-company damage compensation (*innerbetrieblicher Schadensausgleich*), the concept of fault has to be adapted to the, not necessarily hazardous, nature of certain kinds of labour. The employee, nevertheless, remains fully liable for his or her

128. BGH, *NJW* 1953, 1180, 1182; BGH, *NJW* 1987, 2510; J. Hager, in: Staudinger, BGB, § 823 No. E 25 (2021); Larenz and Canaris, *Schuldrecht II/2*, § 76 III 4 a (13th ed., 1994); Spindler, in: Beck-OGK, BGB, § 823 No. 393 (version 01.02.2023); and Wagner, in: Münchener Kommentar, BGB, § 823 No. 476 (8th ed., 2020).
129. BGH, *NJW* 2011, 313, 314; BGH, *VersR* 2008, 1083 et seq.; and Sprau, in: Grüneberg, BGB, § 823 No. 46 (82nd ed., 2023).
130. *See* s. 833(1) sentence 1 BGB.
131. *See* s. 823(1) BGB in connection with § 276(1) BGB.
132. Negligence is defined in s. 276(2) BGB.
133. Provisions requiring gross negligence are, e.g., ss 521, 599, 680, 968 BGB.
134. *See* s. 826 BGB.
135. Constant case law of the Federal Labor Court: cf. BAG, *NZA* 2013, 622, 624; BAG, *NZA* 2007, 1230, 1233; and BAG GS, *NZA* 1994, 1083, 1084; *see also* Weidenkaff, in: Grüneberg, BGB, § 611 Nos 152 et seq. (82nd ed., 2023); and Deinert, *RdA* 2013, 146, 147 et seq.

actions or omissions committed with wilful intent. In cases of gross negligence, the employee is, as a rule, fully liable for the tortious conduct. A restriction of liability in cases of gross negligence is, however, possible under exceptional circumstances. In contrast, slight negligence of the employee amounts to full exemption from liability. Ordinary negligence results in a quota-based allocation of damages between employee and employer. In order to determine the co-liability of employee and employer, courts must take multiple factors into consideration, such as the hazardous nature of the respective work, the degree of fault, the tortious conduct and its consequences, as well as insured risks.[136]

76. Wrongful intent, as well as negligence, must cover not only the tortious conduct but also its unlawfulness.[137] The scope of necessary care is dependent on the extent of the potential danger and on generally accepted standards.[138] The general standard for evaluating negligence is an objective one; personal shortcomings of the wrongdoer are usually not taken into account.[139] As a practical result of this objective determination of negligence, the theoretical distinction between fault and risk-based liability, to some extent, becomes distorted,[140] particularly in cases where fault-based liability is modified by a statutory or judge-made reversal of the burden of proof.[141]

77. An exception applies if certain provisions, such as sections 690, 708, 1359, 1664(1) BGB, provide liability relief within the meaning of section 277 BGB. In this case, the standard for evaluating negligence is a subjective one, taking into account personal shortcomings (so-called *diligentia quam in suis*). However, these specific subjective standards, in general, apply only to contractual liability.

§3. Duty of Care

78. As already noted, according to the majority of German courts and commentators, the conduct underlying an indirect violation of a legally protected interest (or a violation 'caused' by an omission) is not automatically unlawful unless the wrongdoer violates his duty to ensure public safety (*Verkehrspflicht*).[142] According to the traditional idea, a preceding hazardous activity can give rise to a duty of care. Based on this thought, German courts have developed a differentiated system of specific duties of care to ensure the protection of the general public with respect to potential

136. Cf. BAG, *NZA* 2013, 622, 624; and Deinert, *RdA* 2013, 146, 147 et seq.
137. Cf. Deutsch, Festschrift für Medicus 77, 85 (1999).
138. BGHZ 113, 297, 303.
139. BGHZ 80, 193; BGH, *NJW* 1988, 909; BGH, *NJW 2000,* 2812, 2813; *see* Spickhoff, in: Soergel, BGB, § 823 No. 142 (13th ed., 2005); and Wagner, in: Münchener Kommentar, BGB, § 823 No. 38 (8th ed., 2020).
140. Cf. Markesinis, Bell and Janssen, *Markesinis's German Law of Torts* 54 (5th ed., 2019).
141. The burden of proof is reversed, e.g., in s. 831(1) BGB (liability for employees) and s. 836(1) BGB (liability for the collapse of a building); a judge-made reversal of the burden of proof is recognized with respect to the liability for defective products based on s. 823(1) BGB, *see* BGHZ 51, 91, 104 et seq.
142. *See* Part I, Ch. 1, §1.

hazards incurred by a person's activity or property.[143] The purpose of these duties is to delineate the range of relationships to be protected from careless interference and to limit the range of persons who could be held liable for particular injuries.[144] Among the relevant factors used to determine the specific content of such duties of care are the probability and predictability of an injury, the seriousness of the potential harm, and the necessary prevention costs.[145] In general, the respective measures necessary to prevent damages shall comprise those which are deemed necessary and sufficient for eliminating the danger by a circumspect person, taking into account the specific circumstances, the endangered legal positions, and the probability of harm.[146] Usually, the delictual duty to ensure public safety does not exceed the contractual obligation to protect other people's interests.[147] However, a generally applicable method of determination does not exist. As a result, the case law in this area is exceptionally diverse.[148]

§4. CAPACITY

79. Under German tort law, children who have not completed their seventh year of age are not responsible for any damage they cause to another person.[149] Likewise, a person who causes damage to another person while he is unconscious or suffering from a mental disturbance preventing the free exercise of his will is not responsible for the damage. However, if he has brought himself into a temporary condition of this kind by imbibing alcoholic beverages or similar means, he is responsible for any damage he unlawfully causes in this condition in the same manner as if negligence were imputable to him unless he has been brought into this condition without fault.[150] A minor who has completed his seventh but not his eighteenth year of age is not responsible for any damage if he did not have the necessary understanding in order to realize his responsibility at the time he committed the damaging act.[151] An exception was introduced in 2002 for road traffic accidents: pursuant to the new section 828(2) BGB, a person having completed the seventh, but not the tenth year of age, is not responsible for the damage caused by him in an accident involving a motor vehicle, a cable car, or a teleferic, unless he acts wilfully. This rule is based on the thought that minors are usually not capable of assessing the dynamics of motorized traffic and acting accordingly. In view of this

143. BGH, *NJW* 1988, 2667 et seq.; BGH, *NJW* 1990, 1236; BGH, *NJW-RR* 2003, 1459 et seq.; and BGH, *NJW-RR* 2011, 313; cf. Spindler, in: BeckOGK, BGB, § 823 Nos 394 et seq. (version 01.02.2023); *see also* Sprau, in: Grüneberg, BGB, § 823 Nos 45 et seq. (82nd ed., 2023).
144. Markesinis, Bell and Janssen, *Markesinis's German Law of Torts* 54 et seq. (5th ed., 2019).
145. Spindler, in: BeckOGK, BGB, § 823 No. 394 (version 01.02.2023); and Sprau, in: Grüneberg, BGB, § 823 No. 51 (82nd ed., 2023).
146. BGH, *NJW* 2013, 48; BGH, *NJW* 2011, 888 et seq.; BGH, *NJW* 2010, 1967; and BGH, *VersR* 2008, 1083.
147. BGH, *NJW* 2013, 48; BGH, *NJW-RR* 2013, 534.
148. For a comprehensive overview *see* Spindler, in: BeckOGK, BGB, § 823 Nos 394 et seq. (version 01.02.2023).
149. *See* s. 828(1) BGB.
150. *See* s. 827 BGB.
151. *See* s. 828(3) BGB.

intention, the exception is only applicable if the accident occurred in an excessive demand situation arising from a typical danger of motorized traffic.[152]

80. The victim of a tort committed by a person not responsible for his actions may nevertheless have a claim against the tortfeasor's parents or against other persons under a legal duty to supervise the tortfeasor. According to section 832(1) BGB, a person bound by law to exercise supervision over a person who needs supervision by reason of minority or by reason of his mental or physical condition is bound to make compensation for any damage the latter unlawfully causes to a third party. However, responsibility is not designed as a form of strict- liability. The duty to compensate does not arise if the supervisor can substantiate that he correctly fulfilled his duty or that the damage would have occurred notwithstanding the exercise of proper supervision. The scope of proper supervision is determined with respect to the age and character of the infant and with respect to the specific circumstances of each individual case.[153]

81. Even if liability is excluded due to a lack of capacity, section 829 BGB, under certain circumstances, postulates a duty to compensate for reasons of equity. Accordingly, a person who, in one of the cases specified in sections 823 to 826 BGB, is not responsible, by virtue of sections 827, 828 BGB, for any damage caused by him shall, nonetheless, make compensation as is reasonable under the circumstances as long as compensation cannot be obtained from a third party charged with a duty to supervise.[154] A duty to compensate particularly arises in cases where equity requires compensation according to the financial position of the parties, provided the tortfeasor is not deprived of the means he needs for his own reasonable maintenance and for the fulfilment of his obligations to furnish maintenance to others. Regarding the underlying equity test, multiple factors have to be taken into consideration. Among them are the natural capacity to understand the wrongfulness of an act, the financial circumstances, and the course of events leading to the injury.[155]

152. Sprau, in: Grüneberg BGB § 828 No. 3 (82nd ed., 2023).
153. BGH, *NJW* 1976, 1684, 1685; BGH, *NJW* 1980, 1044, 1045; BGH *NJW* 1993, 1003; and BGH, *NJW* 2013, 1441; *see also* Sprau, in: Grüneberg, BGB, § 832 No. 9 (82nd ed., 2023).
154. BGHZ 127, 186, 192 et seq.; and Sprau, in: Grüneberg, BGB, § 829 Nos 1 et seq. (82nd ed., 2023).
155. *See* Teichmann, in: Jauernig, BGB, § 829 No. 4 (18th ed., 2021).

Chapter 2. Specific Cases of Liability

§1. Liability of Professionals

I. In General

82. The term 'professional liability' refers to specific duties of care developed by the courts with respect to the exercise of a profession; the professional has to take all appropriate and necessary precautions a reasonable member of the respective profession would take to protect others from injury.[156] In some instances of severe violations, the courts have even reversed the burden of proof in favour of the tort victim, provided the violated duties were directed at the protection of life or health.[157] However, it remains doubtful if professional liability can actually be characterized as a specific category of German tort law since it is almost impossible to draw a clear line in order to define its field of application. In addition, the essence of professional liability does not go beyond defining the duty of care owed by the members of a particular profession.[158] In cases in which the tortfeasor and the victim are in privity of contract, contractual agreements may alter the delictual liability regime to be applied to the tortious conduct of the professional. Consequently, the delictual liability of professionals can be intrinsically influenced by deviant contractual agreements regarding, e.g., the restriction or increase of liability as well as the reduction or extension of limitation periods. Therefore, professional delictual liability and underlying contractual relationships are closely intertwined. The exercise of a profession cannot amount to liability without the violation of a duty of care. Moreover, it has to be kept in mind that compensation for pure economic loss is only available under the rigorous requirements of section 826 BGB (unless a protective law in terms of section 823(2) BGB is violated). Thus, even with respect to the exercise of a profession, pure economic loss is not compensable in case of negligent infringements.[159] In the following, the duty of care for selected professionals will be described.

II. Medical Practice

83. In recent years, along with medical progress, an ever-increasing number of cases involving medical practitioners' liability have been brought to the courts. The liability of medical practitioners can result from the violation of a contractual or a delictual duty. In the past, the main emphasis had clearly been on tort law. The underlying reasons were more favourable rules of limitation and the possibility of claiming compensation for pain and suffering. However, the predominance of tort

156. BGHZ 103, 298, 304; BGH, *NJW-RR* 1991, 1240, 1241; OLG Celle, *NJW-RR* 1996, 372, 373; and OLG München, *VersR* 1998, 326, 327.
157. *See* BGH, *NJW* 1962, 959, 960 (lifeguard); and OLG Köln, *VersR* 1970, 229, 230 (person running a kiosk).
158. Spindler, in: BeckOGK, BGB, § 823 No. 574 (version 01.02.2023); *see also* Kleindiek, *Deliktshaftung und juristische Person* 423 et seq. (1997).
159. Cf. Spindler, in: BeckOGK, BGB, § 823 No. 574 (version 01.02.2023).

law in the area of medical malpractice might vanish in the future, given that the legislator largely adjusted contractual and delictual liability in 2002.[160] This trend might be fuelled by the enactment of the law fostering patient's rights (*Gesetz zur Verbesserung der Rechte von Patientinnen und Patienten* or *Patientenrechtegesetz*) in 2013. Hereby, the German legislator sought to provide an encompassing framework for the contractual relationship of medical practitioners and patients (cf. sections 630a–630h BGB). Yet, the relationship between contractual duties stipulated in sections 630a–630h BGB and delictual liability of medical practitioners with regard to the burden of proof remains unclear.[161] Apart from that, contractual and delictual liability may differ in cases in which the contract with the medical practitioner unfolds protective effect to the benefit of third parties (*Vertrag mit Schutzwirkung zugunsten Dritter*).[162]

84. Delictual liability has its foundation in the medical practitioner's position as a guarantor for the patient's physical and mental integrity.[163] As a starting point, it is agreed upon that an improper medical treatment always amounts to an injury to body in terms of section 823(1) BGB.[164] Moreover, despite enduring criticism by commentators,[165] in order to protect the patient's free will, the Federal Supreme Court also considers a skilfully executed but unauthorized medical treatment to be an injury to body regardless of the treatment's success.[166] Hence, medical treatment without the patient's free and informed consent (*Einwilligung*), given the possibility of such consent, may result in the medical practitioner's liability based on the breach of a duty to inform (*Aufklärungspflichtverletzung*).[167] To exclude the unlawfulness of his conduct, the medical practitioner needs to inform the patient in advance about the nature, seriousness, and potential consequences of an envisaged medical treatment.[168] Only in extreme scenarios, the conduct of a medical

160. *See* Spindler and Rieckers, *JuS* 2004, 272 et seq.; and Mäsch, *NJW* 2013, 1354, 1356.
161. Mäsch, *NJW* 2013, 1354, 1356.
162. Spickhoff, *VersR* 2013, 276.
163. BGHZ 95, 63, 75.
164. *See*, e.g., BGHZ 76, 259; and Wagner, in: Münchener Kommentar, BGB, § 823 No. 1073 (8th ed., 2020).
165. Laufs, *NJW* 1997, 1609, 1610 et seq.; Kern/Rehborn, in: Laufs, Kern and Rehborn, Handbuch des Arztrechts § 102 Nos 4 et seq. (5th ed., 2019); Hart, Festschrift für Heinrichs 291, 308 (1998); Büttner, Festschrift für Geiß 353, 355 et seq. (2000); Mayer-Maly, Festschrift für Deutsch 667, 669 (1999); and Larenz and Canaris, *Schuldrecht II/2*, § 76 II 1 g (13th ed., 1994).
166. *See*, e.g., BGHZ 29, 46, 49; BGHZ 67, 48, 49; and BGHZ 106, 153, 156; *see also* OLG Bamberg, *VersR* 1998, 1025; BGH, *NJW* 2008, 2344, 2345; OLG Bamberg, *NJW-RR* 2012, 467, 468; and Wagner, in: Münchener Kommentar, BGB, § 823 Nos 1073 et seq. (8th ed., 2020).
167. Cf. BGHZ 29, 176, 179 et seq.; BGHZ 90, 103, 105 et seq.; BGHZ 106, 391, 394; Wagner, in: Münchener Kommentar zum BGB, § 823 No. 1074 (8th ed., 2020); and Michalski, *VersR* 1997, 137, 139; on consent in general *see* Neuner, *JuS* 2021, 617 et seq.
168. *See* BGHZ 29, 176, 180; BGHZ 90, 103, 106; BGHZ 106, 391, 398 et seq.; BGH, *NJW* 1985, 2192; BGH, *NJW* 1992, 2351, 2352; BGH, *NJW* 1995, 2410, 2411; BGH, *NJW* 1996, 777, 779; BGH, *NJW* 2000, 1784, 1786; OLG Oldenburg, *VersR* 1998, 769, 770; OLG Brandenburg, *NJW-RR* 2000, 24, 25; and OLG Bremen, *NJW-RR* 2001, 671.

practitioner not covered by the patient's consent may fall within the ambit of emergency assistance according to section 34 StGB (*Strafgesetzbuch* – code of criminal law).[169]

85. The scope of necessary information depends on the individual circumstances. Hence, German courts have developed a vast and diverse case law. As a rule, the medical practitioner has to consider intellectual capability as well as the patient's insight into his illness.[170] He must inform the patient not only about the possible risks but also about alternative methods of treatment. Yet, the selection of the treatment method is basically the physician's responsibility.[171] The information is intended to allow the patient to make an informed decision. With respect to potential risks resulting from a medical treatment, German courts in the past used to rely solely on the probability of complications. However, more recent decisions ask if the risks are of significance for a reasonable patient in a particular situation, provided the patient is duly informed about the situation.[172] This perspective allows consideration with regard to the urgency of an operation on the one hand and the seriousness of the potential consequences on the other.[173]

86. Despite the patient's informed consent, a medical practitioner can nevertheless become liable in case of medical malpractice (*Behandlungsfehler*). Diagnosis, therapy and aftercare have to comply with the rules of medical art and science (*Regeln der ärztlichen Kunst*).[174] The standard of care is dependent on the specific field of medicine.[175] The physician's conduct has to be in accordance with the hypothetic measures an attentive and reasonable medical practitioner with specific knowledge would have taken in the particular situation.[176] Operations executed by beginners have to be supervised by an experienced physician.[177] Guidelines to determine the duty of care are, on the one hand, protection of the patient, the patient's right of self-determination,[178] and, on the other hand, the insight that the complexity of bodily processes renders a guaranteed success of the medical

169. Cf. OLG Bamberg, *NJW-RR* 2012, 467, 469: fixation in case of self-endangerment; and Sprau, in: Grüneberg, BGB, § 823 No. 154 (82nd ed., 2023).
170. BGH, *NJW* 1988, 1514, 1515; OLG Köln, *VersR* 2011, 81, 82; and Spindler, in: BeckOGK, BGB, § 823 No. 867 (version 01.02.2023).
171. BGH, *NJW* 1981, 2121, 2122; BGH, *NJW* 1988, 763, 764; BGH, *NJW* 2000, 1788, 1789; BGH, *NJW-RR* 2003, 745; and Teichmann, in: Jauernig, BGB, § 823 Nos 127 et seq. (18th ed., 2021).
172. *See* BGHZ 144, 1, 5.
173. Cf. Teichmann, in: Jauernig, BGB, § 823 No. 128 (18th ed., 2021).
174. Cf. Spindler, in: BeckOGK, BGB, § 823 Nos 834, 941 et seq. (version 01.02.2023).
175. BGH, *NJW* 1995, 776 et seq.; and BGH, *NJW* 1999, 1778, 1779.
176. BGH, *NJW* 2011, 1672; BGH, *NJW* 1999, 1778, 1779; and BGH, *NJW* 1995, 776, 777.
177. BGH, *NJW* 1974, 1424, 1425; BGH, *NJW* 1983, 1374, 1375; BGH, *NJW* 1985, 2189, 2191; Wagner, in: Münchener Kommentar, BGB, § 823 No. 1076 (8th ed., 2020); and Teichmann, in: Jauernig, BGB, § 823 No. 116 (18th ed., 2021).
178. *See* BGHZ 29, 46, 54; BGHZ 113, 297, 301; and J. Hager, in: Staudinger, BGB, § 823 No. I 8 (2021).

treatment impossible.[179] The general risk of failure remains with the patient. Hence, an unsuccessful medical treatment does not by itself indicate a violation of the duty of care.[180]

87. As a particular feature of medical practitioners' liability, the burden of proof is reversed under certain circumstances. Principally, the patient has to prove not only the violation of a legally protected interest and the resulting damage but also the causation and the breach of a duty of care.[181] These rules have been modified by the courts for cases of grave medical malpractice (grobe *Behandlungsfehler*). According to the Federal Supreme Court, medical malpractice shall be considered grave if the medical practitioner clearly and obviously violated tried and tested rules of medical treatment or acted contrary to assured medical knowledge and, thereby, made a mistake that appears incomprehensible from a professional point of view.[182] If such malpractice is certain, the burden of proof regarding causation is reversed, provided the malpractice is generally apt to cause the respective injury.[183] By this, German courts take into account the patient's specific difficulties with respect to the production of clear evidence subsequent to severe malpractice.[184] Notwithstanding the burden of proof regarding causation between malpractice and the resulting injury, the medical practitioner also has to show that he correctly fulfilled his duty to inform the patient.[185]

III. Legal Practitioners

88. If legal practitioners provide erroneous information, they may, under certain circumstances, be liable under the rules of tort law. However, tort liability for negligent conduct is usually excluded since none of the interests protected by section 823(1) BGB will be infringed. Hence, legal practitioners are usually exposed to contractual liability only. Tort law claims can, however, be based on section 826 BGB. A prerequisite for such a claim would be the wilful infliction of damage contrary to

179. Spindler, in: BeckOGK, BGB, § 823 No. 835 (version 01.02.2023).
180. BGH, *NJW* 1978, 1681; BGH, *NJW* 1980, 1333; BGH, *NJW* 1995, 776 et seq.; Nüßgens, in: RGRK, BGB, § 823 Anh. II Nos 180 et seq. (12th ed., 1989); and Spindler, in: BeckOGK, BGB, § 823 No. 835 (version 01.02.2023).
181. BGH, *NJW* 2011, 1672, 1673; and Teichmann, in: Jauernig, BGB, § 823 No. 120 (18th ed., 2021).
182. Cf. BGH, *NJW* 2012, 227, 228; *see also* the criticism of Mäsch, *NJW* 2013, 1354, 1355.
183. *See* BGHZ 85, 212, 215; BGH, *NJW* 1994, 1594, 1595; BGH, *NJW* 1997, 796, 797; BGH, *NJW* 1998, 814, 815; BGH, *NJW* 1998, 1780, 1781; BGH, *NJW* 1998, 1782, 1784; OLG Brandenburg, *NJW-RR* 2000, 24, 26; BGH, *NJW-RR* 2010, 831, 832; cf. Sprau, in: Grüneberg, BGB, § 823 No. 162 (82nd ed., 2023); and Wagner, in: Münchener Kommentar, BGB, § 823 No. 1077 (8th ed., 2020).
184. Cf. BGH, *NJW-RR* 2010, 831, 832 et seq.; BGH, *NJW* 1988, 2303, 2304; BGH, *NJW* 1992, 754, 755; BGH, *NJW* 1995, 778, 779; BGH, *NJW* 1997, 794, 795; and OLG Zweibrücken, *VersR* 1998, 590, 591.
185. *See* BGH, *NJW* 1981, 2002, 2003; BGH, *NJW* 1984, 1807, 1808; BGH, *NJW* 1992, 741, 742; BGH, *VersR* 1992, 237; OLG Karlsruhe, *NJW-RR* 1998, 459, 460; H. Schmid, *NJW* 1994, 773; Larenz and Canaris, *Schuldrecht II/2*, § 76 II 1 g (13th ed., 1994); and J. Hager, in: Staudinger, BGB, § 823 No. I 127 (2021).

public policy. Principally, a claim based on section 826 BGB comes into consideration if the information is incorrect as a result of the information provider's recklessness, given that he knew of the information's importance for a third party.[186] Positive knowledge of the information's incorrectness is not necessary.[187] Nonetheless, recklessness usually requires a serious breach of the duty of care. In other words, it must have been obvious to the wrongdoer that the information was false.[188]

IV. Builders and Architects

89. Construction sites usually raise complex questions of liability. Principally, the builder is fully responsible for the protection of all persons who enter the construction site with permission.[189] He can, however, assign his duties to a construction manager.[190] In this case, the builder is merely exposed to a duty to supervise and coordinate.[191] Thus, the builder is still obliged to intervene if he recognizes (or should recognize) upcoming hazards. He also has to intervene if he has reasonable doubts regarding the construction manager's ability to meet the required safety standards or if the construction manager's activity is associated with particular risks the builder himself could have recognized or averted through specific prior arrangements.[192]

90. The scope of the architect's duties is dependent on the assigned tasks. Similar to other professionals, architects are not only liable under contracts with their clients. They are also subject to delictual liability towards their clients and towards third parties, who are not entitled to contractual claims.[193] An architect appointed as building site manager has to protect third parties who rightfully come into contact with the construction work.[194] The architect is liable for damages caused by insufficient planning or supervision of the construction.[195] Even after the completion of the construction, the architect remains liable for injuries to property or to the body and health of third parties. He is, e.g., responsible for water damage to a tenant's

186. Cf. BGH, *NJW* 1987, 1758, 1759; OLG Frankfurt, *WM* 1989, 1618, 1620; OLG Bremen, *VersR* 1999, 499, 501; *Landgericht* (LG) Frankenthal, *MedR* 1999, 184, 186; Zugehör, *NJW* 2000, 1601, 1608; and Sprau, in: Grüneberg, BGB, § 826 No. 27 (82nd ed., 2023).
187. Cf. BGH, *NJW* 1991, 3282, 3283; and BGH, *NJW* 1987, 1758 et seq.
188. *See* BGH, *NJW* 1991, 3282, 3283; BGH, *NJW* 1986, 180, 181; and BGH, *WM* 1962, 579, 581.
189. Cf. OLG Hamm, *NJW-RR* 2014, 715, 716.
190. BGH, *NJW* 1977, 898; and BGH, *NJW-RR* 1994, 1241; *see also* OLG Koblenz, *NZBau* 2008, 511; and Krause, in: Soergel, BGB, § 823 app. I No. 101 (13th ed., 2005).
191. BGH, *NJW* 1982, 2187; OLG Hamm, *NJW-RR* 1999, 319 et seq.; and OLG Zweibrücken, *NJW-RR* 2012, 94, 95; Sprau, in: Grüneberg, BGB, § 823 No. 221 (82nd ed., 2023).
192. BGH, *NJW* 1993, 1647, 1648; OLG Düsseldorf, *NJW-RR* 1999, 318; OLG Hamm, *NJW-RR* 2014, 715, 716; and Sprau, in: Grüneberg, BGB, § 823 No. 221 (82nd ed., 2023); *see also* Krause, in: Soergel, BGB, § 823 app. I No. 101 (13th ed., 2005).
193. Cf. BGH, *NJW-RR* 2007, 1027.
194. Cf. BGHZ 68, 169, 175 et seq.; BGH, *NJW* 1987, 1013; BGH, *NJW* 1991, 562, 563; and J. Hager, in: Staudinger, BGB, § 823 No. E 374 (2021).
195. OLG Hamm *NJW-RR* 1993, 594; and Spindler, in: BeckOGK, BGB, § 823 No. 528 (version 01.02.2023).

property caused by insufficiently supervised insulation works.[196] The duty of care is dependent on the function and the tasks exercised by the architect.[197] To a certain degree, the architect's contractual duties can be consulted in order to determine his (delictual) duty of care.[198]

91. The designation as site supervisor in charge typically justifies the assumption that the architect also assumed a respective duty of care, i.e., the obligation to secure and supervise the construction.[199] While known hazards have to be immediately eliminated by the architect, checks for hidden risks are required on a regular basis.[200] The architect carrying out the supervision of construction work and the builder are jointly and severally liable for damages caused by insufficient supervision.[201] The factual exercise of supervision is sufficient for accountability; a respective contractual obligation is not required.[202] The architect has to ensure compliance with official directives, technical rules, and safety regulations as long as they define the accepted engineering standards.[203] Among the architect's duties is the duty to secure the building site, including its scaffolding.[204] However, the architect is not liable for damages suffered by visitors who were brought to the construction site during the weekend by the architect's client.[205]

92. The demands on the architect regarding the supervision of the construction work are dependent on the specific factual situation of each individual case. A decisive factor is the reliability of the builder and his employees.[206] The architect can rely on the professional execution of simple construction work and the abidance of known safety rules.[207] However, the more complex the construction work, the more intensive the supervision in situ must be.[208] The same rule applies if the architect has indications of the builder's unreliability. Particularly diligent supervision is required with respect to work crucial for the construction's safety, especially if the determination of an insufficient execution is nearly impossible in retrospect.[209] If

196. *See* BGH, *NJW* 1987, 1013; and BGH, *NJW* 1991, 562, 563.
197. Spindler, in: BeckOGK, BGB, § 823 No. 528 (version 01.02.2023).
198. Cf. OLG Köln, *NJW-RR* 1997, 597, 598; *see also* Jagenburg and Kesselring, *NJW* 2001, 3302, 3313 et seq.; Part I, Ch. 2, §1, I.
199. *See* BGH, *NJW* 1970, 2290, 2291; 1985, 1078; OLG Frankfurt, *BauR* 1998, 152, 154; OLG Frankfurt aM, *NZBau* 2006, 185, 186; and BGH, *NJW-RR* 2007, 1027 et seq.
200. BGHZ 68, 169, 176; and OLG Frankfurt, *BauR* 1998, 152, 153.
201. BGHZ 68, 169, 175 et seq.; BGH, *NJW* 1987, 1013; BGH, *NJW* 1991, 562, 563; BGH, *NJW* 1997, 582, 583; and OLG Stuttgart, *NJW-RR* 2000, 752, 754.
202. BGH, *VersR* 1959, 904, 905.
203. Cf. BGHZ 68, 169, 176; and BGH, *NJW* 1980, 1101, 1102.
204. OLG Frankfurt, *BauR* 1998, 152, 154, OLG Stuttgart, *NJW-RR* 2000, 752, 754 (injury of a construction worker caused by an unsafe scaffolding); and OLG Frankfurt aM, *NZBau* 2006, 185, 186.
205. BGH, *NJW* 1985, 1078, 1079.
206. *See* BGHZ 68, 169, 174; OLG Hamm, *NJW-RR* 1993, 594, 596; and OLG Düsseldorf, *BauR* 1996, 731.
207. BGH, *NJW* 1984, 360, 362.
208. BGHZ 68, 169, 176; BGH, *NJW* 1994, 1276, 1277; and OLG Köln, *NJW-RR* 1995, 156 et seq.
209. *See* BGH, *NJW* 1991, 562, 563; OLG Hamm, *NJW-RR* 1993, 594, 596; OLG Hamm, *BauR* 1995, 269; and OLG Köln, *NJW-RR* 1995, 156, 157.

dangers become known, the architect has to take care of immediate risk elimination.[210] However, permanent presence at the building site is not required.[211]

V. Expert Opinions

93. Court-appointed experts used to be liable for pure economic loss only in case of wilful damage contrary to public policy in terms of section 826 BGB unless their conduct violated a rule of criminal law qualifying as a protective law under section 823(2) BGB. The expert's legal duty to take the oath before or subsequent to his expert testimony, as stipulated in section 410 ZPO, was not considered as protecting litigating parties.[212] However, the prerequisites for claims against court-appointed experts have been modified by the introduction of a new section 839a BGB, in force since 1 August 2002. Pursuant to section 839a(1) BGB, a court-appointed expert is liable for the damage caused by an erroneous expert opinion if he acted wilfully or with gross negligence. Yet, according to the Federal Supreme Court and the majority of German commentators, section 839a BGB is also analogously applicable to an erroneous expert opinion in preliminary investigations initiated by the public prosecutor.[213] Within its scope, section 839a BGB grants exhaustive damages for erroneous expert opinions and, therefore, excludes the applicability of other tort law provisions, such as section 823(1) BGB.[214]

94. An expert may also become liable for negligently violating one of the interests protected by section 823(1) BGB. However, court-appointed experts are regarded as assistants to the judge. Hence, they can refer to section 839(2) BGB, according to which an official who commits a breach of his official duty in giving judgment in an action is not responsible for any damage arising therefrom unless the breach of duty is punished with a penalty for a criminal offence. Consequently, experts are not liable for ordinary negligence in connection with an incorrect opinion.[215] An expert is, however, liable for an unlawful detention ordered by a criminal court on the basis of his testimony if the testimony is incorrect due to gross negligence.[216]

210. BGH, *VersR* 1974, 263, 264; OLG Celle, *VersR* 1977, 479, 480; and OLG Hamm, *BauR* 1980, 378, 379.
211. BGHZ 68, 169, 174.
212. BGHZ 42, 313, 317; and OLG Hamm, *BB* 1986, 1397.
213. BGH, NJW 2014, 1665, 1666; Wagner, in: Münchener Kommentar, BGB, § 839a No. 8 (8th ed., 2020); Mayen, in: Erman, BGB, § 839a No. 5 (16th ed., 2020); and Sprau, in: Grüneberg, BGB, § 839a No. 2 (82nd ed., 2023); opposing view: Spickhoff, in: Soergel, BGB, § 839a No. 16 (13th ed., 2005).
214. BGH, *NJW-RR* 2014, 90, 91; and OLG Nürnberg, *NJW-RR* 2011, 1216, 1217.
215. BGHZ 62, 54, 58.
216. *See* BVerfGE 49, 304, 319 et seq.; and OLG Schleswig, *NJW* 1995, 791, 792.

VI. Auditors

95. In addition to contractual claims and claims for damages based on section 323(1) of the Commercial Code (*Handelsgesetzbuch* (HGB)), an audited company (as well as third parties) may, under certain circumstances, claim damages against the auditor under the rules of tort law.[217] The relevant duty of care is described by section 323(1) sentences 1 and 2 HGB: the auditor has to conduct an impartial and conscientious audit. Further, he has an obligation of discretion and is not allowed to make use of trade secrets. With respect to negligent conduct, the main emphasis is on contractual claims and on claims in accordance with section 323(1) HGB since usually none of the interests protected by section 823(1) BGB will be infringed. Regarding tort law, the predominant rule for claims against auditors is section 826 BGB, which requires the infliction of wilful damage contrary to public policy. As with legal practitioners, auditors are exposed to section 826 BGB claims if they recklessly provide erroneous information they recognized to be important for a third party.[218] Even though auditors may be liable to their clients for reckless and unscrupulous conduct in connection with the execution of an audit,[219] they nevertheless are not liable for criminal acts of board members who violate the interests of a third party on the basis of trading relations that would not have been continued without the auditors' attestation,[220] or disclose incorrect capital market information to the detriment of the investing public.[221] Furthermore, recklessness is typically missing if auditors use erroneous information given to them by the audited company with fraudulent intentions.[222]

§2. Liability of Public Authorities

96. Public authorities, such as the federal states or the communities, may be held responsible for harm caused by an individual acting as their official representative in exercising public sovereign functions. Under German law, there is no rule of governmental and sovereign immunity. A specific rule regarding liability for breach of official duties (*Amtshaftung*) is codified in section 839 BGB. It overrides the Civil Code's more general provisions, such as section 823 BGB or section 824 BGB.[223]

---

217. Cf. Weber, *NZG* 1999, 1, 5; on the liability of auditors *see also* Arnold, *DStR* 2001, 488 et seq.; Ebke, *Wirtschaftsprüfer und Dritthaftung* (1983); Ebke, *JZ* 1998, 991; Ebke, Festschrift für Sandrock, 243 (2000); Ebke and Scheel, *WM* 1991, 389 et seq.; Ekkenga, *WM* 1996, Beil. 3; Feddersen, WM 1999, 105; Hopt, *WpG* 1986, 461, 498; Otto and Mittag, *WM* 1996, 333, 377; Schüppen, *DB* 1998, 1317; Weber, *NZG* 1999, 1; Zugehör, *NZG* 2000, 1601; Heukamp, *Abschlußprüfer und Haftung* (2000); and Wagner, in: Münchener Kommentar, BGB, § 826 Nos 138 et seq. (8th ed., 2020).
218. Cf. BGH, *NJW* 2001, 360, 365.
219. Cf. BGH, *NJW* 2014, 383, 384; BGH, *NJW* 2001, 360; BGH, *NJW* 1973, 321, 322; BGH, *VersR* 1979, 283, 284; BGH, *BB* 1961, 652; and Seibt and Wollenschäger, *DB* 2011, 1378, 1381.
220. Cf. OLG Karlsruhe, *ZIP* 1985, 409, 413 et seq.
221. Cf. BGH, *NJW-RR* 2008, 1004.
222. Cf. OLG Köln, *AG* 1992, 89, 90; *see also* Ebke, in: Münchener Kommentar zum HGB, § 323 No. 106 (4th ed., 2020); and Seibt and Wollenschäger, *DB* 2011, 1378, 1381.
223. Cf. OLG Frankfurt, *NJW-RR* 2007, 283; and Förster, *NJW* 2013, 1201, 1202.

97. According to section 839(1) BGB, an official wilfully or negligently committing a breach of official duty incumbent upon him as against a third party shall compensate the third party for any damage arising therefrom. Yet, if only negligence is imputable to the official, he may be held liable only if the injured party is unable to obtain compensation from other sources (e.g., social security and private insurance). Moreover, pursuant to section 839(2) BGB, an official committing a breach of official duty in giving judgment in an action is not responsible for any damage arising therefrom unless the breach of duty is punished with a public penalty to be enforced by criminal proceedings.[224] In addition, section 839(3) BGB states that the duty to make compensation does not arise if the injured party has wilfully or negligently omitted to avert the injury by making use of an available legal remedy. Although section 839 BGB, on the one hand, represents a partial reduction of liability, the rule, on the other hand, exceeds the general tort law provisions by allowing, e.g., recovery for pure economic loss outside the narrow boundaries of section 826 BGB. However, the tort victim can only claim pecuniary compensation; compensation in kind is generally not possible.[225]

98. Section 839 BGB only provides for an official's personal liability. However, the tort victim will usually prefer to seek liability from the state or other public body. To achieve this goal, section 839 BGB has to be read in connection with Article 34 of the Basic Law, which states that in case a person, in the exercise of a public office entrusted to him, violates his official duty to a third party, liability shall rest principally with the state or public body that employs him.[226] Hence, the Basic Law effectively shifts the official's liability under section 839 BGB onto the state or other employing public body; the latter is liable instead of the official. The claim against the public body can be pursued before the ordinary courts.[227] Liability under Article 34 of the Basic Law and section 839 BGB is not limited to officials in terms of administrative law; it also applies to the conduct of any other person, whether a private enterprise or an individual, performing acts that qualify as sovereign activities.[228] According to the Federal Supreme Court, a tortious conduct qualifies as a sovereign activity if the underlying objective pursued by the enterprise or individual can be attributed to the public sphere and, furthermore, if there is an internal and external connection between this pursued objective and the tortious conduct.[229] Nevertheless, Article 34 of the Basic Law applies to the execution of sovereign acts only. Consequently, a public official pursuing ordinary private law activities can be

224. This provision does not apply to a breach of duty consisting of refusal or delay in the exercise of the office, *see* s. 839(2) sentence 2 BGB; cf. BGH, *NJW* 2011, 1072 et seq.
225. *See* BGHZ 4, 77, 84; and BGHZ 34, 99, 101.
226. In the event of intentional wrongdoing or gross negligence, the right of recourse against the individual officer shall be preserved, *see* Art. 34 of the Basic Law; *see also* BGH, *VersR* 2006, 698, 699.
227. *See* Art. 34 of the Basic Law; according to s. 71(2) No. 2 GVG, the district courts have jurisdiction for respective claims.
228. *See* Papier/Shirvani, in: Münchener Kommentar zum BGB, § 839 Nos 181 et seq. (8th ed., 2020).
229. BGH, *NVwZ* 2012, 381, 382; BGH, *NVwZ-RR* 2011, 556; and BGH, *NJW* 2009, 993, 994.

held personally liable by the injured third party.[230] Yet, the state may become liable under the rules of vicarious liability or pursuant to section 31 BGB,[231] which regulates liability for acts of a statutorily appointed representative.

99. In order to obtain recovery, the tort victim not only has to substantiate the breach of an official duty and fault but must also establish that the duty was owed to him as an individual and that the damage falls within the protective ambit of the violated duty.[232] The question of whether an official duty is owed to an individual citizen (in contrast to the community at large) can only be answered by looking at the duty's purpose. The tort victim cannot claim damages unless he belongs to the group of people protected by the official duty.[233] For instance, claims of individuals have been denied by the courts with respect to legislative injustice.[234] Conversely, state supervision over banks originally had been considered (till the change of banking supervisory laws) to be not only in the interest of the general public but also in the interest of individual creditors.[235]

100. The limitations contained in section 839 BGB have been subject to growing criticism since their application nowadays seems old-fashioned and unsuitable for the modern state.[236] Section 839 BGB was first promulgated in a system of individual fault-based responsibility. The precondition set by section 839(1) BGB (that the tort victim cannot obtain compensation elsewhere), e.g., was meant to shield public officials from excessive liability, which otherwise might have led them into complete inactivity out of fear of being held liable for their activities.[237] With the transition of liability from the individual officer to the public body, this rule has become obsolete. The federal legislator has addressed these concerns with a special law promulgated in 1981, the Act on Governmental Liability (*Staatshaftungsgesetz*). However, the Federal Constitutional Court decided that the federal legislator did not have the competence to regulate the liability of public authorities and declared the law to be null and void.[238] Although the competence to regulate this area of law has explicitly shifted from the states to the federal legislator, a new law has not yet been enacted.

---

230. Cf. Markesinis, Bell and Janssen, *Markesinis's German Law of Torts* 179 (5th ed., 2019); Sprau, in: Grüneberg, BGB, § 839 No. 16 (82nd ed., 2023).
231. *See* Sprau, in: Grüneberg, BGB, § 839 No. 3 (82nd ed., 2023); and Teichmann, in: Jauernig, BGB, § 839 No. 7 (18th ed., 2021).
232. BGH, *NJW* 2013, 604, 605; and BGH, *VersR* 2010, 532 et seq.; *see also* Markesinis, Bell and Janssen, *Markesinis's German Law of Torts* 179 et seq. (5th ed., 2019); and Kümper, *DVBl* 2013, 1022, 1024.
233. BGHZ 110, 1, 8, 9; BGH, *NJW* 1991, 2696; BGH, *VersR* 2010, 532 et seq.; and BGH, *NJW* 2013, 604, 605.
234. Cf. BGHZ 87, 321, 335; and BGH, *NJW* 1989, 101.
235. Cf. BGHZ 74, 144; and BGHZ 75, 120.
236. Cf. BGHZ 42, 176, 181.
237. Vinke, in: Soergel, BGB, § 839 No. 189 (13th ed., 2005).
238. Cf. BVerfGE 61, 149.

§3. Abuse of Rights

101. Basically, everyone is free to exercise his rights within the limits set by the legal system. As long as the rights of third parties are not infringed, everyone may pursue his own personal goals. Nonetheless, nobody is allowed to abuse his rights.[239] Under certain circumstances, the abuse of a formal legal position may amount to wilful injury contrary to public policy under section 826 BGB, resulting in a duty to compensate the injured third party for damages.[240] An example of such an abuse of a formal legal position is a proxy abusing his representative authority. In such a case, the proxy may be liable under section 826 BGB.[241] Wilful damage contrary to public policy may also be caused in connection with the abuse of legal procedure (i.e., the abuse or acquisition by false pretences of a judgment or other title).[242]

102. Along this line, the Federal Supreme Court has pointed out the creditor's duty to refrain from executing an enforceable instrument, provided the title is incorrect, the creditor has knowledge, and the title's enforcement is accompanied by circumstances qualifying as reprehensible. In addition, the Federal Supreme Court grants the debtor a claim for damages and restitution of the title.[243] This practice, in effect, results in an exception from the principle of res judicata and the specific requirements for a reopening of proceedings codified in sections 578–591 ZPO.[244] German courts apply section 826 BGB even if a motion for a new trial would be successful.[245] This far-reaching application of section 826 BGB has been widely criticized by commentators due to the possible circumvention of the specific preconditions for a reopening codified in the Code of Civil Procedure.[246]

§4. Injury to Reputation and Privacy

103. A person's reputation and privacy are primarily protected by section 823(1) BGB, by recognizing the right of a person to his personality as an 'other right', and by section 824 BGB, which deals with credit endangering statements. Further, injuries to honour and reputation may also amount to the crimes of insult or defamation under sections 185–187 StGB, which are generally viewed as protective laws in terms of section 823(2) BGB. Hence, liability under section 823(1) or section 824 BGB may overlap with responsibility pursuant to section 823(2) BGB. If an injury to reputation and privacy is caused wilfully and contrary to public policy, claims

239. Cf. s. 226 BGB: The exercise of a right is inadmissible if its only purpose is to cause damage to another person.
240. Spindler, in: BeckOGK, BGB, § 826 No. 140 (version 01.02.2023).
241. *See* Spindler, in: BeckOGK, BGB, § 826 No. 45 (version 01.02.2023).
242. Cf. Spindler, in: BeckOGK, BGB, § 826 Nos 144 et seq. (version 01.02.2023).
243. *See* BGHZ 13, 71, 72; BGHZ 26, 391, 396 et seq.; BGHZ 42, 194, 204; *see also* Spindler, in: BeckOGK, BGB, § 826 No. 144 (version 01.02.2023).
244. *See* BGHZ 101, 380, 383.
245. BGHZ 50, 115, 120; and OLG Celle, OLGZ 1979, 64, 66.
246. *See* Prütting and Weth, *Rechtskraftdurchbrechung bei unrichtigen Titeln* Nos 176 et seq. (2nd ed., 1994); Münzberg, *NJW* 1986, 361; and Gaul, Festschrift für Flume 443 et seq. (1978).

may also be based on section 826 BGB. The different provisions do not exclude each other and can be applied next to each other.

104. Section 824 BGB imposes liability for oral or written statements that are likely to endanger another person's credit or otherwise damage his earnings or prosperity. Liability under section 824 BGB is dependent on an untrue allegation of facts. A mere expression of opinion or value judgment is not sufficient. Furthermore, culpable ignorance is required with regard to the falsity of the allegation.[247] To limit liability, the statement must refer to an identified or at least identifiable individual, as opposed to a larger group the individual is part of.[248] If the plaintiff proves a culpably inaccurate allegation of facts, the person making the allegation may avoid liability if he proves that he or the receiver of the communication had a lawful interest in it, provided the untruth of the statement was unknown to him.[249] This defence of 'justified interest' (*berechtigtes Interesse*) will be upheld only if an objective assessment of the communication's content, its form, and the accompanying circumstances suggest that it is the appropriate and necessary means for achieving a legitimate objective.[250] In case of a successful section 824 BGB claim, the plaintiff may recover his economic loss and demand withdrawal of the inaccurate statement.[251]

105. As described above, the constitutionally guaranteed right of a person to his personality protects human dignity and the unhindered development of the personality.[252] However, holders of the right are not only natural persons but also political parties, partnerships, and juristic persons as long as their function is affected.[253] Infringements to the right to one's personality are not unlawful per se. In order to limit the otherwise boundless applicability of the right to one's personality, each individual case requires a balancing of the conflicting legally protected interests.[254] The right to one's personality may especially conflict with another person's freedom of speech or the freedom of press, both guaranteed by Article 5(1) of the Basic Law.[255] The Federal Supreme Court has developed a rich and (in parts) confusing case law regarding the unlawfulness of infringements on the right to one's personality. Basically, the numerous cases dealing with the right to one's personality can be divided into certain categories. One category is the invasion of somebody's privacy, e.g., by secretly taking photographs in a private area.[256] Other categories include the publishing of intimate information, such as private letters or diaries,[257]

247. Cf. § 824(1) BGB.
248. BGH, *NJW* 1963, 1871; and BGH, *DB* 1989, 921.
249. *See* § 824(2) BGB.
250. BGHZ 3, 270, 281; *see also* Sprau, in: Grüneberg, BGB, § 824 No. 9 (82nd ed., 2023).
251. BGHZ 70, 39 et seq.; BGH, *NJW* 1984, 1607; OLG Frankfurt, *NJW-RR* 1988, 562, 565; *see* Sprau, in: Grüneberg, BGB, § 824 Nos 11 et seq. (82nd ed., 2023); and Teichmann, in: Jauernig, BGB, § 824 No. 14 in combination with § 823 Nos 85 et seq. (18th ed., 2021).
252. *See* General Introduction, § 6 IV.
253. Cf. OLG München, *NJW* 1996, 2515; KG, *NJW* 2000, 2210; and Sprau, in: Grüneberg, BGB, § 823 Nos 91 et seq. (82nd ed., 2023).
254. *See* BGHZ 24, 72, 80; BGHZ 36, 77, 82, 83; and BGHZ 45, 296, 307.
255. Cf. BGH, *NJW* 2014, 768, 769.
256. *See* BGHZ 24, 200.
257. *See* BGHZ 13, 334; and BGHZ 15, 249.

defamatory statements,[258] disclosure of family relationships[259] or sexual preferences,[260] and violations of the right of self-determination, e.g., by transplanting the organs of a deceased without permission.[261] If the plaintiff is successful, he may not only demand the withdrawal of the inaccurate statement but also recover his economic loss. Furthermore, under certain circumstances, the plaintiff may also claim compensation in money for non-pecuniary damage.[262]

§5. Interference by a Third Person with Contractual Relations

106. Contractual obligations are only of a relative nature and, therefore, not protected under section 823(1) BGB.[263] However, the contracting party may have a claim based on section 826 BGB if a third party interferes with the contractual relation. The systematic and reckless inducement of the contracting party to breach the contract usually amounts to wilful damage contrary to public policy in terms of section 826 BGB.[264] However, in a market economy, not all interferences with contractual relations by taking advantage of a contracting party's willingness to breach the contract may result in delictual responsibility.[265] The specific circumstances of each individual case need to be thoroughly scrutinized, especially the aim of the interference, its means, and the underlying motivation.[266] The more a contract is determined by a fiduciary relation, the more likely is a qualification of the interference as a violation of public morals.[267] A mere outbidding does not by itself amount to liability under section 826 BGB.[268] However, liability is not excluded if the outbidding is accompanied by additional circumstances qualifying as reprehensible.[269] Interference with unilateral contractual duties may also qualify as wilful infliction of damage contrary to public policy in terms of section 826 BGB.[270]

107. An objective interest of the interfering party usually excludes a violation of moral principles.[271] A claim based on section 826 BGB typically requires a collusive acting of the interfering and the contracting party, aiming at the thwarting of the

258. *See* BGHZ 31, 308; and BGHZ 39, 124.
259. *See* BGH, *NJW* 2014, 768.
260. *See* BGH, *NJW* 2013, 1681; and BGH, *NJW* 2012, 767.
261. *See* LG Bonn, *JZ* 1971, 56.
262. Cf. Sprau, in: Grüneberg, BGB, § 823 No. 111 (82nd ed., 2023); and Teichmann, in: Jauernig, BGB, § 823 Nos 85 et seq. (18th ed., 2021).
263. Cf. BGHZ 12, 308, 317 et seq.
264. Cf. BGH, *NJW* 1994, 128, 129; BGH, *VersR* 1995, 1451, 1454; *see also* BGH, *NJW* 1992, 2152, 2153.
265. *See* BGHZ 12, 308, 317 et seq.; BGH, *NJW* 1994, 128, 129; BGH, *VersR* 1995, 1451, 1454; and BGH, *NJW-RR* 1999, 1186.
266. BGH, *NJW* 1981, 2184, 2185; and OLG Hamm, *VersR* 1987, 509.
267. *See* BGHZ 12, 308, 319 et seq.; and Spindler, in: BeckOGK, BGB, § 826 No. 41 (version 01.02.2023).
268. Dubischar, *JuS* 1970, 6, 8; Spindler, in: BeckOGK, BGB, § 826 No. 41.1 (version 01.02.2023); but *see also* Hönn, in: Soergel, BGB, § 826 No. 126 (13th ed., 2005).
269. Cf. BGH, *NJW* 1981, 624, 625; BGH, *NJW* 1995, 404, 405; and BGH, *NJW-RR* 1999, 1186, 1187.
270. BGH, *NJW* 1992, 2152, 2153 (legacy).
271. *See* OLG Stuttgart, *NJW-RR* 1997, 362, 363.

other contracting party's contractual claim. If this precondition is fulfilled, the interfering and the contracting party are jointly and severally liable.[272] However, even in the case of an objective interest, the use of immoral means, as well as a disproportion of the means regarding the specific aim, can amount to a violation of public morals.[273]

108. The courts are more willing to affirm a wilful violation of moral principles if the interfering party acts in order to achieve a competitive advantage.[274] In such a case, the instigation as well as the aiding and abetting of a breach of contract are usually considered a violation of public morals (even without additional circumstances). Otherwise, the interfering party would be able to gain an unjustified advantage vis-à-vis his competitors.[275] According to the Federal Supreme Court, it is sufficient if a competitor, without further knowledge, incorrectly advises a contracting party that the conclusion of a contract with him would be possible, notwithstanding the latter's existing contractual obligation.[276] Even the mere utilization of a breach of contract (without influencing the contracting party) may, under certain circumstances, amount to a violation of public morals.[277]

109. The party injured by a breach of contract can claim compensation with respect to any pecuniary damage he suffers from the interference. In the case of interference with a contract of sale, the injured party may also claim specific restitution.[278]

§6. Others

110. Especially in connection with liability for wilfully inflicted damage contrary to public policy in terms of section 826 BGB, the Federal Supreme Court has developed a vast case law addressing numerous factual situations. The court has awarded compensation based on section 826 BGB, e.g., in the case of an asset manager executing financial transactions not covered by the client's interest (so-called churning).[279] Further, damage caused to investors by an intentional manipulation of the stock exchange price by publishing erroneous ad-hoc announcements was also considered a wilful infliction of damage contrary to public policy.[280] The same applies, *inter alia*,[281] to the dishonest utilization of company secrets;[282] the

272. Cf. Friedrich, 178 AcP 468, 486 et seq. (1978); Sprau, in: Grüneberg, BGB, § 826 No. 23 (82nd ed., 2023); *see also* OLG Stuttgart, *BauR* 2007, 420.
273. BGH, *NJW* 1981, 2184, 2185; and BGH, *VersR* 1995, 1451, 1454.
274. *See* Spindler, in: BeckOGK, BGB, § 826 No. 43 (version 01.02.2023).
275. Cf. BGH, *WM* 1981, 624, 625; BGH, *NJW* 1975, 1361, 1362; and BGH, *NJW-RR* 1989, 234.
276. *See* BGH, *NJW* 1975, 1361, 1362.
277. Cf. BGH, *BB* 1973, 1229; and Spindler, in: BeckOGK, BGB, § 826 No. 43 (version 01.02.2023).
278. *See* RGZ 108, 58, 59.
279. BGH, *NJW* 2004, 3423.
280. BGH, *NJW* 2004, 2664; BGH, *NJW* 2004, 2971; BGH, *NJW* 2005, 2450, 2451; and OLG Frankfurt, *AG* 2006, 584 et seq.
281. For further examples *see* Spindler, in: BeckOGK, BGB, § 826 Nos 31 et seq. (version 01.02.2023).
282. BGH, *NJW* 1977, 1062.

cooperation of the debtor and a third person in order to hide seizable assets from creditors;[283] or the exploitation of a person's passion for gambling.[284]

111. More recently, in particular, the so-called Diesel-Gate has fuelled the discussion about liability under section 826 BGB: In September 2015, it became known that Volkswagen AG (*Aktiengesellschaft*, German corporation) used software in the engine design of its diesel vehicles that detects the test situation for determining exhaust gas values and, in this case, optimizes the exhaust gas treatment in such a way that less nitrogen oxides are emitted (so-called defeat device).[285] Since then, the German courts have been seized not only with requests for subsequent performance,[286] claims for reduction in price,[287] and return claims[288] against the sellers but also with claims for damages against the vehicle manufacturer itself.[289] Since contractual claims predominantly fail due to the statute of limitations[290] or the priority of subsequent performance, tort claims against the vehicle manufacturer are shifting more and more into the focus of the current discussion.[291]

112. In this regard, it was first of all discussed which action should be considered as an immoral act of damage. The generally accepted starting point of the accusation of immorality in the so-called emissions scandal is the wilful deception of the car buyer by the manufacturer.[292] This can be seen in the fact that the manufacturer has violated a duty to provide information and has thus been misled by omission.[293] Or the action in question is the placing on the market of the manipulated vehicles or the issuance of the so-called certificate of conformity (cf. section 6 EG-FGV, Article 18 in conjunction with Annex IX Directive 2007/46/EC) combined with a declaration that the vehicle is fully eligible for registration, i.e., an active misleading act.[294]

113. In addition, the loss experienced is questionable since the strict use of the difference hypothesis means that there may not be any pecuniary loss at all.

283. BGH, *NJW* 2005, 1121, 1124.
284. BGH, *LM* § 761 No. 1.
285. LG Bielefeld, *BeckRS* 2017, 131627 No. 24; LG Düsseldorf, *BeckRS* 2018, 1444 No. 20; Riehm, *DAR* 2016, 12; zur zeitlichen Abfolge in der Angelegenheit: https://www.epa.gov/vw/learn-about-volkswagen-violations#timeline (accessed 20 Apr. 2023); Witt, *NJW* 2017, 3681; Heintz, *jM* 2017, 354.
286. OLG Hamm, *BeckRS* 2016, 13954; LG Bamberg, *BeckRS* 2016, 124467.
287. LG Braunschweig, *BeckRS* 2017, 117245; LG Kempten, *BeckRS* 2017, 106279.
288. OLG München, *NJW* 2017, 1238; OLG Köln, *NZV* 2018, 72.
289. Cf. Sievers, *DAR* 2016, 543.
290. OLG Düsseldorf, *BeckRS* 2017, 119626 No. 4; Riehm, *DAR* 2016, 12.
291. Riehm, *DAR* 2016, 12; Legner, *VuR* 2018, 251.
292. BGHZ 225, 316 No. 16; KG Berlin, *BeckRS* 2019, 22714 Nos 52 ff.; OLG Koblenz, *BeckRS* 2019, 11148 No. 16; OLG Karlsruhe, *ZIP* 2019, 864; OLG Köln, *NZV* 2019, 249 No. 23; LG Hildesheim, *VuR* 2017, 111 No. 25; LG Bielefeld, *BeckRS* 2017, 131627 No. 25; Heese, *NJW* 2019, 257 (259).
293. LG Braunschweig, *BeckRS* 2017, 111214 No. 41; Legner, *VuR* 2018, 251 et seq.; Oechsler, *NJW* 2017, 2865 et seq.
294. OLG Koblenz, *BeckRS* 2019, 11148 No. 16; OLG Karlsruhe, *ZIP* 2019, 864; OLG Köln, *NZV* 2019, 249 No. 23; LG Hildesheim, *VuR* 2017, 111 No. 25; LG Bielefeld, *BeckRS* 2017, 131627 No. 25; Heese, *NJW* 2019, 257 (259).

Although an affected vehicle was originally subject to the risk of an operating prohibition, at least after installation of offered software updates – one could argue – the vehicle was fully usable in road traffic so that the purchaser did not suffer any damage.[295] Within the framework of economic consideration, the lowered resale value of the vehicle equipped with harmful software was also taken into account when determining damage[296] – although this is a question of evidence. Relying on its previously established case law, the Federal Court of Justice also stated that an assessment of damage according to the difference hypothesis is always subject to normative review.[297] Such an 'evaluative review' encompasses the protection purpose of liability, as well as the compensatory function of damages.[298] With regard to the conclusion of a contract, even if the performance and the consideration are objectively valuable, someone can obtain damage by the fact that the performance is not fully usable for its purposes; however, this assumes that 'the performance obtained by the undesirable contract is not only regarded as damage from a purely subjectively arbitrary point of view but also that the view of the market, taking into account the prevailing circumstances, regards the conclusion of the contract as unreasonable, not appropriate to the concrete pecuniary interests and thus as disadvantageous'.[299] The Federal Court of Justice justifies the lack of usability of the purchased vehicle by pointing out that the defeat device could have led to an operating restriction or prohibition.[300] Since the conclusion of the contract for a vehicle with a defeat device is thus to be regarded as unreasonable not only subjectively but also according to the view of the market, the purchaser has suffered damage as a result of the unintentional conclusion of the contract.[301] In addition, the argument that the installation of software updates eliminates the damage is predominantly rejected on the basis that the damage – be it the disadvantageous conclusion of the contract[302] or the disappointed expectation of use[303] – arose with the acquisition of the vehicle and thus continues to exist regardless of any subsequent measure.[304]

295. Lorenz, *NJW* 2020, 1924 et seq.
296. OLG Frankfurt a. M., *BeckRS* 2019, 22222 No. 18; OLG Koblenz, *BeckRS* 2019, 11148 No. 70; LG Hildesheim, *VuR* 2017, 111 No. 26; LG Bielefeld, *BeckRS* 2017, 131627 No. 22; LG Dortmund, *BeckRS* 2017, 123451 No. 24; LG Duisburg, *BeckRS* 2018, 1903 No. 28; LG Düsseldorf, *BeckRS* 2018, 1444 No. 18; Harke, *VuR* 2017, 83 (89 f.); Oechsler *NJW* 2017, 2865 (2867 et seq.).
297. BGHZ 225, 316 No. 45.
298. BGHZ 225, 316 No. 45.
299. BGHZ 225, 316 No. 46.
300. BGHZ 225, 316 No. 53.
301. BGHZ 225, 316 No. 48; BGH, *BeckRS* 2021, 12218 No. 23.
302. OLG Köln, *BeckRS* 2019, 22774 No. 16.
303. KG Berlin, *BeckRS* 2019, 22714 No. 33.
304. BGHZ 225, 316 No. 58; OLG Frankfurt a. M., *BeckRS* 2019, 22222 No. 19; OLG Köln, *BeckRS* 2019, 22774 No. 16; OLG Koblenz, *WM* 2019, 1229 No. 85; KG Berlin, *BeckRS* 2019, 22714 No. 33.

Part II. Liability for Acts of Others

Chapter 1. Vicarious Liability

§1. Employee/Employer

114. The German Civil Code does not specifically provide for the liability of an employer for damages caused by his employees during the course of their employment. Section 831(1) BGB rather provides a more general rule by stating that a person who appoints another to do any work is bound to compensate for any damage the other unlawfully causes to a third party in the performance of his work unless the master has exercised the necessary care in the selection and supervision of the servant (*Verrichtungsgehilfe*). Contrary to other legal systems,[305] the master is not strictly liable for injuries caused by his servants under German tort law.[306] Liability under section 831 BGB is based on the master's own fault with respect to an inadequate selection or supervision of his servants.

115. A precondition for the master's liability is the causation of damage by a person appointed to do any work for him. The test, most commonly applied to determine a master-servant relationship, refers to the degree of direction and control exercised by the master.[307] According to the Federal Supreme Court, a person is a servant in terms of section 831 BGB if he is – generally or for a specific occasion – entrusted with the performance of a function in the master's sphere of influence, provided the relation between master and servant is determined by social and economic dependency.[308] In principle, liability, according to section 831 BGB, only relates to the employment of persons who act in the master's interest and are bound by the master's directives.[309] Without this prerequisite, the master's liability for incidents occurring in his organizational sphere could not be justified.[310] However,

305. Cf. Kadel, *ZfRV* 1997, 56; and Baums, Festschrift für Lukes 623 (1989).
306. *See* Bernau, in: Staudinger, BGB, § 831 No. 5 (2022); on the history of § 831 BGB *see* Seiler, *JZ* 1967, 525, 527 et seq.; and Martinek, *Repräsentantenhaftung* 197 et seq. (1979).
307. Cf. Markesinis, Bell and Janssen, *Markesinis's German Law of Torts* 119 (5th ed., 2019).
308. BGH, *VersR* 1998, 862 et seq.; BGHZ 45, 311, 313; BGHZ 103, 298, 303; and BGH, *NJW* 2009, 1740, 1741.
309. *See* BGH, *NJW* 2013, 1002, 1003; BGHZ 80, 1, 3; BGHZ 45, 311, 313; BGH, *VersR* 1998, 862 et seq.; BGH, *VersR* 1979, 844 et seq.; BGH, *NJW* 1994, 2756, 2757; OLG Karlsruhe, *VersR* 1990, 860 et seq.; OLG Köln, *TranspR* 1995, 440, 441; Steffen, in: RGRK, BGB, § 831 Nos 16 et seq. (12th ed., 1989); and Bernau, in: Staudinger, BGB, § 831 Nos 101 et seq. (2022).
310. Cf. Spindler, in: BeckOGK, BGB, § 831 No. 15 (version 01.02.2023).

it is neither relevant whether the servant acts with or without payment nor if the appointment is based on a contract or is of a mere factual nature.[311] Furthermore, it is unimportant whether the servant was appointed by tacit or by explicit agreement.[312]

116. Dependency in the context of section 831 BGB is often described as a personal relation of subordination.[313] However, the line between activities bound by directions and the independent fulfilment of an assigned task is not easy to draw. The classic dependency test fails, e.g., with respect to highly specialized employees, such as employees in the areas of health care or finance, who de facto exercise discretion and can hardly be considered dependent in the sense of a personal relation of subordination.[314] Moreover, modern tendencies to outsource numerous activities to independent enterprises in combination with the resulting contractual relations cast doubts on the appropriateness of the traditional dependency test. Independent contractors are usually not seen as servants in terms of section 831 BGB by German courts, regardless of whether their relationship with the principal is determined by economic dependency.[315] The same rules apply to subcontractors unless they are integrated into the master's organizational sphere and bound by his directives.[316]

117. To bridge these liability gaps, German courts increasingly show a tendency to transfer organizational duties (regarding an enterprise's external sphere) from section 831 BGB to contractual relations with independent contractors by requiring a diligent selection and supervision even outside the scope of section 831 BGB.[317] However, the Federal Supreme Court considers a freelancer, who also works for other enterprises, a servant only if he is strictly bound by the master's directives in

311. Cf. RGZ 91, 363 et seq.; BGH *FamRZ* 1964, 84; Spindler, in: BeckOGK, BGB, § 831 No. 15 (version 01.02.2023); and Wagner, in: Münchener Kommentar, BGB, § 831 No. 14 (8th ed., 2020).
312. *See* Spindler, in: BeckOGK, BGB, § 831 No. 15 (version 01.02.2023); and Wagner, in: Münchener Kommentar, BGB, § 831 No. 14 (8th ed., 2020).
313. *See* Krause, in: Soergel, BGB, § 831 No. 19 (13th ed., 2005).
314. BGH, *NJW* 1980, 1901, 1902; cf. Spindler, in: BeckOGK, BGB, § 831 No. 16 (version 01.02.2023).
315. *See* BGHZ 24, 247 et seq.; BGHZ 26, 152, 159; BGH, *NJW* 1976, 46, 47; BGH, *NJW-RR* 2003, 1457, 1458; BGH, *NJW* 2013, 1002, 1003; OLG Düsseldorf, *VersR* 1995, 1363, 1364; Schlechtriem, Festschrift für Heiermann 281, 282 et seq. (1995); Krause, in: Soergel, BGB, § 831 No. 21 (13th ed., 2005); and Wagner, in: Münchener Kommentar, BGB, § 831 No. 16 (8th ed., 2020).
316. Cf. BGH, *VersR* 1998, 862 et seq.; BGHZ 45, 311, 313; BGH, *NJW* 1980, 941; BGH, *WM* 1989, 1047, 1050; OLG Düsseldorf, *VersR* 1996, 511; Wilhelmi, in: Erman, BGB, § 831 Nos 6 et seq. (16th ed., 2020); Bernau, in: Staudinger, BGB, § 831 No. 108 (2022); Larenz and Canaris, *Schuldrecht II/2*, § 79 III 2 a (13th ed., 1994); and Wagner, in: Münchener Kommentar, BGB, § 831 No. 17 (8th ed., 2020).
317. Cf. BGH, *NJW* 1976, 46, 47 et seq.; OLG Dresden, *VersR* 1995, 836; and OLG Düsseldorf, *VersR* 1995, 1363, 1364; for further references *see* Spindler, in: BeckOGK, BGB, § 831 No. 21 (version 01.02.2023).

the individual case and the master can limit or withdraw the activity from the servant at any time.[318] The predominant criterion is the quality and scope of the master's authority to give directives.[319] Hence, to some degree, not only socially and economically dependent persons may qualify as servants in terms of section 831 BGB but also independent contractors as long as they are bound by detailed directives and by the master's will.[320]

118. Liability under section 831 BGB requires that the damage has been inflicted by the servant in the exercise of the assigned functions (*in Ausübung der Verrichtung*).[321] Whether the servant acts in the course of his employment is a question of fact. The Federal Supreme Court refers to an internal connection, i.e., an inseparable link, between the functions assigned to the servant (with respect to their quality and aim) and the servant's injurious conduct.[322] This criterion is only met if the servant's activities do not exceed the general scope of the assigned tasks.[323] Alongside the exact determination of the assigned function, the question of whether the appointment of the servant results in an increase in risk and whether the master can be viewed as a guarantor with respect to the servant's misconduct is a decisive factor.[324] What is crucial is not the servant's general field of activity, e.g., as a company's driver, but rather the specifically assigned task. Hence, the master is not liable for the servant's activities en route to his place of work.[325]

119. A wilful crime, executed only incidentally to the assigned work (*gelegentlich der Verrichtung*), is not covered by section 831 BGB as long as it has no connection with the assigned function as such.[326] For example, fraudulent investments by an employee of a credit institution are not executed in the course of employment.[327] However, the situation may be different if the crime overlaps with the assigned duties (e.g., the theft of luggage by a baggage handler[328] or a knowingly false report by an employed restaurant critic).[329] Nevertheless, the courts' tendency to attribute criminal activities to the servant's assigned functions often appears too

318. Cf. BGH, *VersR* 2014, 466, 467; BGH, *NJW* 2013, 1002, 1003; BGH, *NJW* 2009, 1740, 1741; BGH, *VersR* 1998, 862 et seq.; and BGHZ 45, 311, 313.
319. *See* BGHZ 45, 311, 313; BGH, *VersR* 2014, 466, 467; BGH, *NJW* 2013, 1002, 1003; BGH, *NJW* 2009, 1740, 1741; and Bernau, in: Staudinger, BGB, § 831 No. 99 (2022).
320. *See* BGH, *NJW* 1956, 1715.
321. *See* s. 831(1) sentence 1 BGB.
322. Cf. BGHZ 11, 151, 153; BGH, *LM* BGB § 831 (D) No. 2; BGH, *NJW* 1958, 1774 et seq.; BGH, *NJW* 1971, 31 et seq.; BGH, *NJW-RR* 1989, 723, 725; OLG Naumburg, *NJW-RR* 2009, 1032, 1033; and OLG Hamm, *NJW-RR* 2010, 454.
323. Spindler, in: BeckOGK, BGB, § 831 No. 31 (version 01.02.2023).
324. Cf. OLG Saarbrücken, *NJW-RR* 1986, 672; Spindler, in: BeckOGK, BGB, § 831 No. 31 (version 01.02.2023).
325. BGH, *NJW* 1958, 1774 et seq.
326. OLG Hamm, *NJW-RR* 2010, 454; BGH, *NJW-RR* 1989, 723, 725; BGH, *WM* 1999, 791, 796; Spindler, in: BeckOGK, BGB, § 831 No. 32 (version 01.02.2023); and Wagner, in: Münchener Kommentar, BGB, § 831 No. 30 (8th ed., 2020).
327. *See* BGH, *WM* 1999, 791, 796; BGHZ 11, 153 et seq.; and Spindler, in: BeckOGK, BGB, § 831 No. 33.1 (version 01.02.2023).
328. *See* BGHZ 24, 188, 196 et seq.
329. *See* BGH, *VersR* 1998, 862 et seq.; BGHZ 49, 19, 23.

generous, especially in cases where a crime has simply been enabled by the assignment of a specific task in combination with a lack of supervision. According to the Federal Supreme Court, thefts by employees on a third party's premises are attributed to the master if the latter employed the servants on the premises and the occurrence of thefts was foreseeable.[330] Even the high-handed acting of the servant and the wilful disregard of the master's directives do not necessarily qualify the conduct as being outside the boundaries of the assigned functions.[331] Hence, a servant assigned the task of securing barracks intended for the company's drivers and employees still acts in the course of his employment if he allows a tourist to spend the night in the barracks.[332] Likewise, a driver assisting with the unloading of a truck acts in the course of his employment, even if the unloading is not covered by the contract.[333] Servants who unintentionally exceed their assigned functions are also covered by section 831 BGB (e.g., employees of a demolition firm who tear down the wrong part of a building).[334] Similarly, a driver still acts in the course of his employment if he deviates from an assigned route.[335] However, the unauthorized use of a motor vehicle by an employed driver exceeds the assigned function and is not attributable to the master.[336]

120. Section 831 BGB further requires an unlawful infliction of damage. Responsibility on the part of the servant is not a prerequisite for liability under section 831 BGB.[337] Hence, even if the servant acts faultlessly, the master may remain liable for damages caused by the servant.[338] This may lead to a situation where the master is liable for the servant's conduct, although if he had acted himself, he would have acted without fault. As a consequence, the Federal Supreme Court denies liability under section 831 BGB if the master's own conduct would not have resulted in liability had he acted instead of the servant[339] or if the servant acted in accordance with the highest possible standard of care.[340] A further exception is made in cases in which the liability for an unlawful infliction of damages depends on certain subjective elements, such as wilful intent within the meaning of section 826 BGB. In these cases, the subjective requirements of section 826 BGB must be personally met by the servant.[341] This restrictive application of section 831 BGB is

---

330. Cf. BGHZ 11, 151, 153; *see also* Larenz and Canaris, *Schuldrecht II/2*, § 79 III 2 d (13th ed., 1994); and Bernau, in: Staudinger, BGB, § 831 Nos 127 et seq. (2022).
331. Cf. BGHZ 49, 19, 23; BGH, *NJW* 1971, 31 et seq.
332. *See* BGH, *VersR* 1967, 353 et seq.
333. Spindler, in: BeckOGK, BGB, § 831 No. 33.1 (version 01.02.2023); *different* OLG Hamburg, *VersR* 1974, 52 et seq.; and OLG Köln, *VersR* 1996, 523 et seq.; Bernau, in: Staudinger, BGB, § 831 No. 126 (2022).
334. Cf. BGHZ 11, 151, 153.
335. *See* BGH, *VersR* 1955, 345 et seq.
336. Cf. BGHZ 1, 388, 390 et seq.; BGH, *NJW* 1971, 31 et seq.; BGH, *NJW-RR* 1989, 723, 725; and RGZ 136, 15, 16.
337. *See* BGH, *NJW* 2014, 1380, 1381; BGH, *NJW* 1996, 3205, 3207; and Wagner, in: Münchener Kommentar, BGB, § 831 No. 34 (8th ed., 2020).
338. BGH, *NJW* 2014, 1380, 1381; and BGH, *WM* 2010, 928, 932.
339. Cf. BGH, *VersR* 1975, 447, 449; and BGH, *NJW* 1996, 3205, 3207.
340. Cf. BGHZ 12, 94, 96; BGH, *NJW* 1996, 3205, 3207; *see also* OLG Hamm, *NJW-RR* 1998, 1402; and OLG Oldenburg, *NJW-RR* 1988, 38.
341. BGH, *NJW* 2014, 1380, 1381; and BGH, *WM* 2010, 928, 932.

in conformity with the rule's purpose, which is to prevent evasion of liability through the appointment of a servant lacking capacity.[342]

121. For the evaluation of the servant's conduct, the two theories on the definition of unlawfulness, i.e., the traditional theory looking at the result and the more modern theory looking at the conduct,[343] are of specific relevance. Section 831 BGB is one of the few situations where the two theories could lead to deviating results. Under the more modern theory, the violation of a protected interest would not be unlawful per se; the victim would have to prove that the servant did not attain the necessary standard of care.[344] However, a straightforward application of the traditional unlawfulness doctrine would require the victim merely to prove that he had been injured by the servant's (non-culpable) conduct; with respect to the presumption of the master's fault under section 831 BGB, it would be for the master to submit evidence in order to adduce the exculpatory proof.[345] However, even the supporters of the traditional view require a connection between the master's fault and the risk of infringement, which must have been increased by the insufficient selection or supervision of the servant.[346] In the end, it is generally agreed that the liability of the master is appropriate only in cases where the servant's non-culpable conduct results from an insufficient selection or supervision or from an inadequate provision of equipment or devices.[347] As a result, since unlawfulness is not indicated simply by an infringement of a protected interest, the victim has to prove that the servant breached a duty of care.[348]

122. Although section 831 BGB is not a rule of strict liability, the master's fault is presumed if the above-mentioned criteria are met. Therefore, the master will be held liable unless he proves that he has diligently selected, instructed, and trained the servant, that he has properly supplied the servant with the appropriate equipment and devices, or that the damage would have occurred even if he had fulfilled these duties.[349] The duty of care owed by the master has to be determined for each individual case by recourse to both generally accepted standards and the specific circumstances.[350] Particularly, decisive factors include the kind of activity exercised by

342. Cf. Stoll, *JZ* 1958, 137, 138; v. Caemmerer, Festschrift 100 Jahre DJT II, 49, 120 (1960); and Kupisch, *JuS* 1984, 250, 253.
343. *See* Part I, Ch. 1, §1.
344. Cf. Nipperdey, *NJW* 1957, 1777, 1779; and v. Caemmerer, Festschrift 100 Jahre DJT II, 49, 119 et seq. (1960).
345. *See* Markesinis, Bell and Janssen, *Markesinis's German Law of Torts* 123 (5th ed., 2019).
346. Cf. Wilhelmi, in: Erman, BGB, § 831 No. 13 (16th ed., 2020).
347. *See* v. Caemmerer, Festschrift 100 Jahre DJT II, 49, 123 (1960); Stoll, *JZ* 1958, 137 et seq.; Larenz and Canaris, *Schuldrecht II/2*, § 79 III 2 c (13th ed., 1994); and Spindler, in: BeckOGK, BGB, § 831 No. 3 (version 01.02.2023).
348. *See* v. Caemmerer, Festschrift 100 Jahre DJT II, 49, 125 (1960); Stoll, *JZ* 1958, 137 et seq.; Larenz and Canaris, *Schuldrecht II/2*, § 79 III 2 c. (13th ed., 1994); Spindler, in: BeckOGK, BGB, § 831 No. 35 (version 01.02.2023); and Krause, in: Soergel, BGB, § 831 No. 37 (13th ed., 2005).
349. *See* s. 831(1) sentence 2 BGB.
350. Sprau, in: Grüneberg, BGB, § 831 No. 10 (82nd ed., 2023).

the servant and the respective risk potential.[351] The more likely the infringement of protected interests becomes, the more intense and complex are the necessary precautionary measures to be taken by the master in order to exonerate himself.[352] Therefore, German courts usually place high demands on the necessary supervision and require, e.g., regular unannounced checks, which may vary with regard to their intensity depending on the extent of the risk and the personal suitability of the respective servant.[353] The checks have to be suitable to avoid hazards for third parties.[354] The instruction of servants in terms of section 831 BGB typically requires the compilation and realization of service regulations and guidelines,[355] especially in cases where safety regulations require special precautions.[356]

123. Proof that every employee has been carefully selected and supervised is almost impossible with respect to large organizations. Therefore, German courts developed the doctrine of decentralized exoneration, the so-called decentralized exculpatory proof (*dezentralisierter Entlastungsbeweis*). According to this theory, the master only has to prove proper care and diligence in the selection and supervision of the leading employees, who stand in an intermediate position in the organization's hierarchy.[357] Large enterprises are particularly favoured by the system of decentralized exoneration because it enables them to shift the delictual risk to others.[358] Although it has been extensively criticized by commentators,[359] and even the Federal Supreme Court has occasionally expressed doubts,[360] German courts principally adhere to the decentralized exculpatory proof doctrine.[361] Meanwhile, however, they have more or less balanced the privilege for large businesses by setting significantly higher standards for exoneration and by introducing far-reaching corporate organizational duties.[362] According to these duties, the exculpatory proof has

351. *See* BGH, *NJW-RR* 1996, 867 et seq.; BGH, *NJW-RR* 1987, 1469 et seq.; and Wagner, in: Münchener Kommentar, BGB, § 831 No. 42 (8th ed., 2020).
352. Cf. BGH, *VersR* 2003, 75, 76; OLG Hamm, *VersR* 2010, 917, 918; and Wagner, in: Münchener Kommentar, BGB, § 831 No. 44 (8th ed., 2020).
353. BGH *LM* BGB § 823 (Dc) No. 23; OLG Hamm, *NJW-RR* 1998, 1403 et seq.; BGH, *NJW-RR* 1996, 867 et seq.
354. Cf. LG Hanau, *WM* 1996, 1540, 1545; and Wagner, in: Münchener Kommentar, BGB, § 831 No. 44 (8th ed., 2020).
355. *See* BGH, *VersR* 1969, 518 et seq.; OLG Stuttgart, *VersR* 1984, 1078 et seq.; and Spindler, in: BeckOGK, BGB, § 831 No. 41 (version 01.02.2023).
356. Cf. BGH, *VersR* 1964, 241, 243; and Steffen, in: RGRK, BGB, § 831 No. 51. (12th ed., 1989).
357. Constant case law since RGZ 78, 107, 108 et seq.; *see also* BGHZ 4, 1, 2; BGH, *VersR* 1964, 297; on the history of decentralized exoneration *see* Helm, 166 AcP 389, 394 et seq. (1966); Brüggemeier, *Deliktsrecht* Nos 122 et seq. (1986); Heiss, *Der dezentralisierte Entlastungsbeweis und die Versuche zu seiner Überwindung* 22 et seq. (1969); Krause, in: Soergel, BGB, § 831 No. 46. (13th ed., 2005); and Schmitz, *Die deliktische Haftung für Arbeitnehmer* 28 et seq., 97 et seq. (1994).
358. Cf. Helm, 166 *AcP* 389, 395 et seq. (1966); and Spindler, in: BeckOGK, BGB, § 831 No. 46 (version 01.02.2023).
359. Cf. Wilhelmi, in: Erman, BGB, § 831 No. 21. (16th ed., 2020); *see also* Helm, 166 *AcP* 389, 395 (1966); v. Caemmerer, Festschrift 100 Jahre DJT II, 49, 115 et seq. (1960).
360. *See* BGH, *NJW* 1968, 247, 248.
361. Cf. BGH, *NJW* 1973, 1602, 1603 et seq.
362. Cf. Spindler, in: BeckOGK, BGB, § 831 No. 46 (version 01.02.2023).

to cover not only the careful selection and supervision of the intermediary employees but also the instalment of a safety system; the organizational structure must guarantee that the intermediary employees are informed on a regular basis about the subordinated servants' conduct.[363]

124. In the past, German courts have shown a tendency to evade the possibility of exoneration envisaged by section 831 BGB by increasingly assuming liability for structural defects through an extension of the duties of care under section 823(1) BGB. The organizational duties in terms of section 823(1) BGB sometimes seem inseparable from the master's duty to provide for proper supervision and instruction in order to prevent damage to third parties caused by insufficient work routines.[364]

125. A second way to bypass section 831 BGB is a far-reaching application of section 31 BGB,[365] which orders an absolute liability of a legal entity for acts of its organs or other duly appointed representatives without the possibility of exoneration. The Federal Supreme Court has extensively interpreted the term 'duly appointed representative' as including not only representatives empowered by law to represent the entity but also representatives simply having the right to make autonomous decisions in their own sphere of work.[366]

126. Another way to circumvent section 831 BGB is an expansive recourse to contract law, especially to section 278 BGB, which states that a debtor is responsible for the fault of his statutory agent and of persons whom he employs in fulfilling his obligation, to the same extent as he is for his own fault. Section 278 BGB can be characterized as strict liability for faults of the persons the debtor uses in the course of fulfilling his contractual obligations.[367] Although German courts have repeatedly denied an analogous application of section 278 BGB in the area of tort law,[368] they have, however, extended the scope of contractual protection by including the pre-contractual phase via the rules of *culpa in contrahendo*, which allows compensation for a breach of duty prior to contract,[369] and by conceding compensation to persons other than the immediate contracting parties.[370]

363. Constant case law since RGZ 87, 1, 4; *see also* BGHZ 4, 1, 2 et seq.; BGHZ 11, 151, 154 et seq.; Steffen, in: RGRK, BGB, § 831 No. 54 (12th ed., 1989); and Brandes, *Die Haftung für Organisationspflichtverletzung* 196 et seq. (1994).
364. Cf. BGH *NJW* 1968, 247, 249; BGH *VersR* 1964, 297; RGZ 87, 1, 4; *see also* Spindler, in: BeckOGK, BGB, § 831 No. 46 (version 01.02.2023).
365. Cf. Spindler, in: BeckOGK, BGB, § 831 No. 9 (version 01.02.2023); *see also* Part II, Ch. 1, §§ 2, 3.
366. *See* BGHZ 49, 19, 21.
367. *See* Markesinis, Bell and Janssen, *Markesinis's German Law of Torts* 128 et seq. (5th ed., 2019).
368. Cf., e.g., RGZ 113, 293, 296; BGHZ 1, 3, 4.
369. On the rules of *culpa in contrahendo see* Grüneberg, in: Grüneberg, BGB, § 311 Nos 11 et seq. (82nd ed., 2023); and Emmerich, in: Münchener Kommentar, BGB, § 311 Nos 37 et seq. (9th ed., 2022).
370. *See* General Introduction, Part V.

§2. INDEPENDENT CONTRACTORS

127. As discussed in the preceding section, independent contractors usually do not fall under the definition of 'servant' in terms of section 831 BGB unless they are entirely bound by the master's directives. Nonetheless, in an individual case, it may be extremely difficult to draw a clear line between a dependent condition as demanded by section 831 BGB on the one hand and the independent exercise of certain functions for the principal on the other hand. To avoid unreasonable differentiations with regard to vicarious liability, German courts have found various ways to establish the principal's liability for damages caused by independent contractors.

128. While section 831 BGB does not usually apply to independent contractors, a person whom the debtor, in terms of section 278 BGB, employs in fulfilling his contractual obligations does not need to be bound by the debtor's directives.[371] Neither does section 278 BGB require a relation characterized by social and economic dependency.[372] Hence, besides the effort to facilitate recovery of pure economic loss via the rules of contract law and the tendency to bypass the exculpatory proof as envisaged by section 831 BGB, the possibility to extend the master's responsibility to acts of 'independent servants' is another reason for the courts' expansive recourse to contract law, especially to the rules of *culpa in contrahendo*.[373]

129. Similar to independent contractors, certain employees operating in largely independent positions also do not meet the criteria to qualify as servants under section 831 BGB, e.g., the head doctor of a hospital, who acts in a discretionary manner and is not bound by directives.[374] However, in such a case, the doctor is usually regarded as a duly appointed representative in terms of section 31 BGB with the consequence of an absolute liability of the employing legal entity.[375]

§3. LIABILITY OF LEGAL ENTITIES FOR ACTS OF THEIR ORGANS

130. The organs of a legal entity do not fall within the scope of vicarious liability under section 831 BGB. However, with section 31 BGB, the Civil Code offers an explicit provision ordering an absolute liability of legal entities for acts of their organs and other duly appointed representatives (i.e., persons entrusted with the power to act without being an organ). Legal entities are not capable of acting on their own and, therefore, depend on their organs to act on their behalf in accordance with their articles of incorporation. A necessary consequence is the accountability

---

371. *See* BGHZ 62, 119, 124; and BGH, *NJW* 1996, 452; *see also* BGH, *NJW* 2013, 1002, 1003.
372. Cf. BGH, *NJW* 2013, 1002, 1003 with regard to the differences between s. 831 and s. 278.
373. *See* Part II, Ch. 1, §1.
374. *See* Spindler, in: BeckOGK, BGB, § 831 No. 26.3 (version 01.02.2023).
375. Cf. BGHZ 77, 74, 79; *see also* Part II, Ch. 1, §§ 1, 3.

of legal entities for acts of their organs. A precondition for the application of section 31 BGB is a claim according to another civil law provision; the rule only regulates accountability and is not, in and of itself, a foundation of claims.[376] Hence, claims cannot be based solely on section 31 BGB. Yet, it does not necessarily preclude the joint and several liability of the natural person acting as an organ.[377] The provision applies to all kinds of juristic persons,[378] such as stock corporations (*Aktiengesellschaft* (AG)) and limited companies (*Gesellschaft mit beschränkter Haftung* or *GmbH*). Furthermore, the rule also applies to the partnerships of the Civil Code and the Commercial Code, i.e., the *Gesellschaft bürgerlichen Rechts* (*GbR*), the *offene Handelsgesellschaft* (OHG), and the *Kommanditgesellschaft* (abbreviated as KG in Germany, whereby this abbreviation can also be used for the Berlin Court of Appeal (*Kammergericht*); for the sake of consistency, the *Kommanditgesellschaft* will not be referred to as 'KG' below).[379]

131. Section 31 BGB requires an act of an organ or other duly appointed representatives. While the organs of a legal entity are determined by law, the term 'duly appointed representative' needs further clarification. In accordance with the wording of section 31 BGB, the term certainly covers representatives whose appointment is envisaged by the articles of association. However, the Federal Supreme Court has given the phrase a far broader interpretation by including all persons who, in accordance with general internal company regulations and with sole responsibility, independently execute important functions of the legal entity and thereby represent the latter.[380] Legal authority to represent the entity is not required.[381]

132. The Federal Supreme Court has even imposed liability for organizational deficiencies on legal entities failing to appoint a special representative for certain important tasks the entity's organs do not perform themselves. The servant carrying out the respective tasks is treated as if he were a duly appointed representative in terms of section 31 BGB in order to prevent a circumvention of the rule's strict liability by disallowing exoneration according to section 831(1) sentence 2 BGB.[382]

133. As with section 831 BGB, the legal entity's accountability under section 31 BGB requires that the organ or other duly appointed representative acted in the exercise of the assigned functions. This precondition is only fulfilled if a material link – in contrast to a mere incidental connection with respect to time and location – between the conduct causing the damage and the functions executed by the organ

376. *See* BGHZ 99, 298, 302.
377. Cf. BGH, *NJW* 2006, 830, 842; BGH, *NJW* 1996, 1535, 1536; and Ellenberger, in: Grüneberg, BGB, § 31 No. 13 (82nd ed., 2023).
378. Section 31 BGB also applies to legal entities of public law, *see* s. 89 BGB.
379. BGH, NJW 2003, 1445; BAG, *NZA* 2008, 348, 353; Ellenberger, in: Grüneberg, BGB, § 31 No. 3 (82nd ed., 2023); and Wagner, in: Münchener Kommentar, BGB, § 831 No. 20 (8th ed., 2020).
380. *See*, e.g., BGHZ 49, 19, 21.
381. Cf. BGHZ 49, 19, 21.
382. *See* RGZ 157, 228, 235; BGHZ 24, 200, 213; and BGH, *NJW* 1980, 2810, 2811; *see also* Part II, Ch. 1, §§ 1, 2.

or representative exists.[383] However, it is not required that the conduct be covered by the organ's or representative's legal authority as long as this authority is not clearly exceeded.[384]

383. Cf. BGHZ 49, 19, 23; and BGHZ 98, 148, 151.
384. Cf. BGHZ 98, 148, 152; and BGHZ 99, 298, 300.

Chapter 2. Liability of Parents, Teachers, and Instructors

134. Section 832 BGB imposes liability upon persons who are under a legal or contractual duty to supervise others, such as minors and mentally or physically incapacitated persons, for damages caused by the latter. Supervisory duties deriving directly from the codified law are, e.g., the duties of parents with respect to their children (sections 1626 et seq., 1631 BGB)[385] and the obligations of legal guardians (sections 1793, 1797, 1800, 1909, 1915 BGB). Contractual duties to supervise may be taken upon by explicit as well as by tacit agreement.[386] It is not important whether the duty is taken upon permanently or only temporarily.[387] Neither is the charging of a fee relevant.[388] Typical examples of persons or institutions accepting contractual obligations to supervise other persons are, *inter alia*, private nursery schools or children's homes,[389] Boy Scout camps,[390] nursing homes,[391] or doctors and nurses in an open psychiatric clinic.[392] The supervisor might also be held liable for violating his duty to ensure public safety according to section 823 BGB if he or she wilfully or negligently induced the injurious conduct of the incapacitated person.[393]

135. Comparable to vicarious liability under section 831 BGB, the supervisor's liability is dependent on an unlawful infliction of damage by the supervised person. If this criterion is met, the supervisor is presumed to have culpably failed to properly discharge his duty to supervise. Moreover, it is presumed that the damage was caused by neglect of the supervisory duty.[394] The supervisor may nevertheless exonerate himself by proving that he fulfilled his duty or that the damage would have been caused notwithstanding the exercise of proper care. The necessary standard of care in supervision has to be determined in accordance with the circumstances of each individual case. With respect to the supervision of children, it primarily depends on the age, disposition, character, education, and development of the child.[395] German courts regularly ask which practical measures reasonable parents

385. For illegitimate children *see* s. 1626a BGB.
386. *See* OLG Celle, *NJW-RR* 1987, 1384; and LG Bremen, *NJW-RR* 1999, 969.
387. *Reichsgericht*, *HRR* 1934, No. 1449; Bernau, in: Staudinger, BGB, § 832 No. 38 (2022); and Spindler, in: BeckOK, BGB, § 832 No. 12 (65th ed., 2023).
388. OLG Düsseldorf, *VersR* 1992, 310, 311; Bernau, in: Staudinger, BGB, § 832 No. 35 (2022); and Wagner, in: Münchener Kommentar, BGB, § 832 Nos 19 et seq. (8th ed., 2020).
389. BGH, *VersR* 1965, 48.
390. LG Landau, *NJW* 2000, 2904.
391. OLG Koblenz, *NJW-RR* 1997, 345.
392. BGH, *NJW* 1985, 677, 678.
393. OLG Naumburg, *NJW-RR* 2013, 1109; *see also* Part I, Ch. 1, §3.
394. *See* s. 831(1) sentence 2 BGB.
395. Cf. BGHZ 111, 282, 286; BGH, *NJW* 1984, 2574, 2575; BGH, *NJW* 1985, 677, 678; OLG Hamm, *VersR* 1990, 743; OLG Hamm, *MDR* 2013, 655; BGH, *NJW* 2009, 1952; BGH, *NJW* 2013, 1441; for further references *see* Schoof, *Die Aufsichtspflicht* 43 et seq. (1999); and Wagner, in: Münchener Kommentar, BGB, § 832 No. 27 (8th ed., 2020).

would have taken in the specific situation in order to prevent injury to third parties.[396] As a rule, the requirements regarding the exculpatory proof are rather strict. With respect to mentally or physically incapacitated persons, the content of the supervisory duty is dependent on the specific incapacity.[397] Heightened demands may result from a known disposition of the incapacitated person to show aggressive behaviour or from an acknowledged indication of danger to third parties.[398] Yet, the Federal Supreme Court also acknowledges that absolute security cannot be reasonably required. Therefore, the exculpatory proof does not require continuous monitoring 'around the clock' and 'at every turn'.[399]

136. If the supervisor successfully exonerates himself, the tort victim may run the risk of being left without any compensation (provided the tortfeasor is incapable of fault according to sections 827, 828 BGB).[400] In such a situation, the tort victim's only option to claim recovery for his damages is a reference to section 829 BGB, which, under certain circumstances, allows compensation for reasons of equity. The rule allows the judge to pass a judgment according to which the tortfeasor, although not responsible for any damage caused by him, has to compensate the tort victim as equity demands. In such a case, the financial position of the parties is specifically taken into account.[401]

---

396. *See* BGH, *NJW* 1980, 1044, 1045; BGH, *NJW* 1993, 1003; BGH, *NJW* 2013, 1441; and OLG Hamm, *MDR* 2013, 655.
397. BGH, *NJW* 1985, 677, 678.
398. OLG Koblenz, *NJW-RR* 1997, 345, 346; cf. Sprau, in: Grüneberg, BGB, § 832 No. 10 (82nd ed., 2023).
399. Cf. BGH, *NJW* 2009, 1945, 1955: scratching the paint of parked cars by a seven year old; BGH, *VersR* 2012, 865, 866: setting a barn on fire by a ten year old; *see also* Wagner, in: Münchener Kommentar, BGB, § 832 No. 29 (8th ed., 2020).
400. Cf. Markesinis, Bell and Janssen, *Markesinis's German Law of Torts* 134 et seq. (5th ed., 2019).
401. *See* Part I, Ch. 1, §4.

Chapter 3. Liability for Things and Animals

137. The Civil Code includes specific provisions on the liability of possessors of real property built-up with buildings and other constructions and of animal keepers (*Tierhalter*) and supervisors (*Tieraufseher*). The relevant provisions with respect to damage caused by a collapsing building or other man-made structure are sections 836–838 BGB. Liability for damage inflicted by an animal is codified in section 833 BGB (animal keeper) and section 834 BGB (animal supervisor).

138. According to section 836(1) BGB, the possessor of real property is bound to compensate for any damage caused by the collapse of a building or other structure attached to a piece of land or by the detachment of parts, provided a person is killed, the body or health of a person is injured, or a thing is damaged. Further, the collapse or detachment must have been caused by defective construction or inadequate maintenance unless the possessor exercised proper care in order to protect third parties. With respect to the liability of the possessor of real property, section 836 BGB states a specific expression of the general duty to ensure public safety, combined with a reversal of the burden of proof.[402] In this context, it is not only presumed that the possessor acted culpably with respect to the proper construction and maintenance of the structure but also that the structure's collapse is causally connected with a breach of the duty of care.[403] However, the tort victim still has to prove his damage.[404] The reasons underlying section 836 BGB are the specific risk potentials of buildings and other structures erected or maintained in violation of the general rules of art and science of engineering[405] and the consideration that it is usually easier for the possessor to produce evidence regarding the specific hazards of a structure built on his property.[406]

139. According to section 836(3) BGB, 'possessor' in the context of section 836(1) BGB is the proprietary possessor. A former possessor may be liable under section 836(2) BGB. Furthermore, if a person possesses a building or other structure on another's real property in the exercise of a right, the responsibility specified in section 836 BGB attaches to him instead of the possessor of the land. Sections 836 and 837 BGB are supplemented by section 838 BGB, according to which a person who undertakes for the possessor the maintenance of a building or other structure attached to land or who has to maintain the building or the structure by virtue of a right of use belonging to him, is responsible for any damage caused by the structure's collapse or the detachment of parts in the same manner as the possessor.

402. Cf. BGHZ 58, 149, 156; BGH, *NJW* 1985, 1076; BGH, *NJW-RR* 1988, 853, 854; BGH, *NJW-RR* 1990, 1500, 1501; and OLG München, *NJW-RR* 1995, 540, 541.
403. *See* BGH, *LM* BGB § 836 No. 4; and BGH, *NJW-RR* 1988, 853, 854.
404. BGH, *LM* BGB § 836 No. 4.
405. Cf. Bernau, in: Staudinger, BGB, § 836 Nos 10 et seq. (2022); and Spindler, in: BeckOK, BGB, § 836 No. 1 (65th ed., 2023).
406. *See* Bernau, in: Staudinger, BGB, § 836 No. 2 (2022); and Larenz and Canaris, *Schuldrecht II/2*, § 79 VI 1 a (13th ed., 1994).

140. As a prerequisite for claims based on sections 836–838 BGB, the damage must have been caused by the (complete) collapse of a building or other structure or by a detachment of its parts, i.e., the disconnection or loosening of single parts of the whole structure, leaving the structure otherwise intact. Examples of the detachment of building parts include falling roofing tiles,[407] the breaking of a sewer pipe,[408] or the collapse of a loggia railing.[409] The range of the rule is, however, limited by the requirement that the detachment must have been non-systematic. Thus, compensation for damage caused by building parts falling down in the course of demolition work cannot be claimed under section 836 BGB.[410]

141. With regard to the liability of animal keepers under section 833 BGB, an important distinction has to be made. While section 833 sentence 1 BGB imposes strict liability on the keeper for damage caused by so-called luxury animals,[411] keepers of so-called domestic animals are liable under section 833 sentence 2 BGB only if they fail to rebut the presumption of fault. The term 'domestic animal' refers to animals which, according to their intended purpose, aid the business, the earnings, or the prosperity of the animal keeper,[412] such as police dogs,[413] hunting dogs of a forest ranger,[414] watchdogs in commercial buildings,[415] cats used on a farm to protect the supplies,[416] racing horses,[417] or slaughter cattle of a meat wholesaler.[418]

142. Animal keeper, in terms of section 833 BGB, is the person who has the power to decide over the animal's fate, pays for the animal's maintenance, bears the risk of loss, and has an ownership interest in the animal.[419] Section 834 BGB extends liability to persons who undertake to supervise an animal under a contract with the keeper. However, even with regard to damages caused by luxury animals, the animal supervisor is not strictly liable; according to section 834 BGB, responsibility does not arise if the supervisor has exercised proper care in the supervision or if the damage would have occurred notwithstanding the exercise of such care.

407. OLG Frankfurt, *NJW-RR* 1992, 164.
408. BGH, *VersR* 1983, 588.
409. BGH, *NJW* 1985, 1076; *see also* OLG Hamm, *VersR* 1972, 1173.
410. *See* BGH, *VersR* 1978, 1160.
411. Section 833 sentence 1 BGB is the only tort law provision of the German Civil Code ordering strict liability.
412. Cf. BGH, *NJW* 2011, 1961, 1962; BGH, *NJW-RR* 2005, 1183.
413. BGH, *VersR* 1972, 1047, 1048; OLG Düsseldorf, *NJW-RR* 1995, 661; and OLG Hamm, *VersR* 1998, 495, 496.
414. OLG Bamberg, *NJW-RR* 1990, 735.
415. BGH, *LM* BGB § 833 No. 3a; OLG München, *VersR* 1984, 1095, 1096; and OLG Hamm, *NJW-RR* 1995, 599.
416. LG Kiel, *NJW* 1984, 2297; and LG Ravensburg, *VersR* 1986, 823.
417. OLG Düsseldorf, *VersR* 1993, 115.
418. OLG Düsseldorf, *VersR* 1983, 543.
419. Cf. BGH, *NJW-RR* 1988, 655, 656; BGH, *VersR* 1976, 1175, 1176; RGZ 168, 331, 332 et seq.; OLG Hamm, *VersR* 1993, 238, 239; Eberl-Borges, in: Staudinger, BGB, § 833 Nos 67 et seq. (2022); Spindler, in: BeckOK, BGB, § 833 No. 13 (65th ed., 2023); and Krause, in: Soergel, BGB, § 833 No. 12 (13th ed., 2005).

143. Liability under section 833 BGB presupposes that an animal kills a person, causes injury to the body or health of a person, or damages an object. The damage must be a consequence of the specific hazards associated with the animal's savageness.[420] Section 833 BGB is applied by the Federal Supreme Court even if the victim has voluntarily exposed himself to the risks emanating from the animal, e.g., horse riding,[421] running a dog pension,[422] or providing veterinary treatment.[423] However, the keeper of an animal is not liable under section 833 BGB if the victim, acting predominantly in his own interest, willingly accepts an increased danger that exceeds the usual risk resulting from the animal's behaviour.[424] Hence, the Federal Supreme Court has denied liability in a case in which a rider took over an obviously wicked horse in order to demonstrate his superior riding skills.[425]

420. *See* BGHZ 67, 129, 132; BGH, *NJW* 1982, 763, 764; BGH, *NJW* 1992, 2474; BGH, *NJW* 1999, 3119; OLG Karlsruhe, *VersR* 1995, 927 et seq.; and OLG Hamm, *NJW-RR* 2013, 1038.
421. Cf. BGH, *NJW* 1992, 2474 et seq.; BGH, *NJW* 1977, 2158; and BGH, *NJW* 1982, 763.
422. Cf. BGH, *NJW* 2014, 2434.
423. Cf. OLG Celle, *MDR* 2012, 1162.
424. *See* BGH, *NJW* 1992, 2474.
425. BGH, *NJW* 1974, 234, 235 f.

Part III. Strict Liability and Specific Torts

Chapter 1. Road and Traffic Accidents

144. Except for strict liability of the keeper of a luxury animal under section 833 sentence 1 BGB, the tort law rules of the Civil Code do not order any form of strict liability. However, numerous special laws provide rules for risk-based liability. One of them is the Road Traffic Act (StVG). The practical significance of liability for road and traffic accidents can be illustrated by a brief look at the social cost invoked by such accidents: In 2022, approximately 2.40 million car accidents, with 2,776 people killed and more than 358,665 people injured, were registered by the German police.[426]

145. The predominant provision of the Road Traffic Act is section 7(1) StVG, which imposes upon the keeper of a motor vehicle (*Fahrzeughalter*) strict liability for personal injury, death and damage to property resulting from the vehicle's operation. According to section 1(2) StVG, the term 'motor vehicle' includes all land vehicles driven by mechanical force, such as forklift trucks,[427] tractors,[428] or any other kind of self-propelled machine,[429] as long as they are not attached to railway tracks. Nevertheless, section 8 No. 1 StVG excludes all slow-moving vehicles, which cannot exceed a maximum speed at the ground level of 20 kilometres per hour, from the Road Traffic Act's range of application.

146. The keeper of a motor vehicle will frequently be identical to the vehicle's owner, although such identity is not a necessity. In accordance with a common definition, the keeper is described as the person who uses a car at his own expense and who has the power of disposal associated with such use.[430] Even a person using a car under a long-term hiring agreement may become the car's keeper, provided he completely bears the running costs.[431] However, a person renting a car only on the

426. *See* https://www.destatis.de/DE/Themen/Gesellschaft-Umwelt/Verkehrsunfaelle/Tabellen/liste-strassenverkehrsunfaelle.html#251628 (accessed 20 Apr. 2023).
427. OLG Köln, *VersR* 1988, 194.
428. OLG Frankfurt, *VersR* 2000, 197.
429. OLG Rostock, *DAR* 1998, 474.
430. *See*, e.g., BGHZ 13, 351; Fuchs, Pauker and Baumgärtner, *Deliktsrecht,* 248 (9th ed., 2016); and G. Wagner, *Deliktsrecht* Ch. 8 No. 49 (14th ed., 2021).
431. Cf. BGHZ 87, 133.

basis of a typical short-term agreement does not yet become its keeper.[432] Principally, the keeper is liable regardless of who was driving the vehicle at the time of the accident. Special rules apply, however, for so-called joyrides (*Schwarzfahrten*), i.e., the use of a motor vehicle without the keeper's knowledge and consent (e.g., by a thief). According to section 7(3) StVG, the keeper is liable for damages caused by the joyrider only if he has granted the latter the vehicle's use or if the joyrider was employed for the operation of the vehicle. The relevant factor for determining whether or not a motor vehicle is used without the keeper's knowledge and consent is the overall character of the respective ride.[433] The keeper also remains strictly liable under the Road Traffic Act if his negligence has facilitated unauthorized use.

147. Liability under section 7(1) StVG presupposes that the damage was caused in the course of the vehicle's operation. The question of whether a motor vehicle is in operation is one of the most controversial problems in connection with the keeper's liability and has given rise to a considerably rich case law. The cases decided by German courts show a tendency towards an extensive protection of the victims of traffic accidents because even the proper operation of a vehicle constitutes a source of danger.[434] No problem occurs, however, if a moving motor vehicle collides with another moving or immovable object or with a person (e.g., a pedestrian). These accidents are clearly within the scope of section 7(1) StVG. More difficulties arise in situations where a motor vehicle has already come to a halt. The Federal Supreme Court and most commentators usually require the vehicle's typical 'operational hazard' (*Betriebsgefahr*) having resulted in the accident. In other words, the accident must have had a close connection in location and time with an operational process.[435] According to this perspective, it is irrelevant whether or not the vehicle's motor was still running at the time of the accident.[436] The Federal Supreme Court decided, e.g., that an accident happening while the engine of a specialized truck was merely running in order to operate the vehicle's unloading device still occurred in the course of operation in terms of section 7(1) StVG.[437] Even evasive manoeuvres with no contact whatsoever between the parties concerned can be considered a result of the operational hazard leading to an accident.[438]

148. Until 2002, liability under section 7(1) StVG was excluded if the holder was able to prove that the accident was caused by an 'unavoidable event' (*unabwendbares Ereignis*), which was attributable neither to a defect in the vehicle's construction nor to a failure of any of its functional parts. According to the definition

432. *See* BGHZ 32, 331.
433. Cf. OLG Nürnberg, *NVZ* 2011, 538, 539: joyride with suicidal intent.
434. BGH *NJW* 1962, 2676, 2677; BGH, *NJW* 1991, 2568; BGH, *NJW-RR* 2008, 764; BGH, *NJW* 2005, 2081; BGH, *NJW* 2010, 3713; BGH, *NJW* 2012, 1951, 1953; BGH, *NJW* 2013, 1679, 1680; cf. Fuchs, Pauker and Baumgärtner, *Deliktsrecht*, 242 (9th ed., 2016); and G. Wagner, *Deliktsrecht* Ch. 8 No. 50 (14th ed., 2021).
435. *See* BGHZ 29, 163, 169; BGH, *NJW* 1975, 1886, 1887; BGH, *NJW-RR* 2008, 764; 765; and BGH, *NJW* 2013, 1679, 1680.
436. Cf. BGH, *NJW* 1975, 1886, 1887.
437. BGH, *NJW* 1975, 1886, 1887.
438. Cf. BGH, *NJW* 2010, 3713; and BGH, *NJW* 2005, 2081.

included in the former section 7(2) sentence 2 StVG, an unavoidable event was, *inter alia*, an event that was due to the conduct of the victim or a third party not involved in the vehicle's operation or of an animal, provided the keeper and the driver have applied proper care with respect to the specific circumstances. This concept has endured much criticism since it introduces elements of fault into the Road Traffic Act's regime of strict liability. The legislator drew conclusions and modified the respective provision of the Road Traffic Act. The new section 7(2) BGB, in force since 1 August 2002, no longer requires an unavoidable event but rather an Act of God (*höhere Gewalt*). Despite the narrow scope of this defence, according to section 9 StVG in connection with section 254 BGB, contributory fault may nevertheless result in a reduction of the compensation awarded to the victim. Therefore, in practice, the amendment to section 7(2) StVG will have consequences predominantly in cases where children incapable of fault are involved.

149. Two further exceptions from the keeper's strict liability are stated in section 8 StVG. Section 7 StVG does not apply if the victim participated in the operation of the vehicle.[439] Neither does the provision apply if damage is caused to an object transported by the vehicle unless the object is carried by a passenger.[440] Another historic exception with respect to the injury or death of a person was stated in the former section 8a StVG, which limited the scope of section 7 StVG to passengers transported for a consideration. However, this exception was abolished with the tort law reform of 2002.

150. If two or more motor vehicles are involved in an accident, liability is distributed between the keepers according to section 17 StVG. In principle, every keeper is liable for the risk inherent to the specific vehicle (*Betriebsgefahr*). If none of the involved drivers acted negligently, liability is distributed in equal shares. However, if an involved party can prove that one of the drivers failed to apply the necessary degree of care, the culpable causation usually outweighs the other vehicle's inherent risk. Hence, despite the design of section 7 StVG as a provision of strict liability, the outcome of a case often depends on questions of fault. In practice, accidents usually have to be reconstructed by court-appointed experts in order to determine the degree of fault involved on either side.

151. In contrast to the keeper, the driver of a motor vehicle is not strictly liable under the Road Traffic Act. Section 18 StVG merely establishes prima facie liability of a motor vehicle's driver. According to section 18 StVG, the driver's fault is regularly presumed and has to be rebutted by proving that he did not act culpably with respect to the causation of an accident. However, in practice, the courts place rather high demands on exculpatory proof to ensure a comprehensive protection of the victims of car accidents. Therefore, the driver's liability under section 18 StVG comes close to strict liability.

---

439. *See* s. 8 No. 2 Straßenverkehrsgesetz (StVG).
440. *See* s. 8 No. 3 StVG.

152. Strict liability of motor vehicle keepers is accompanied by a mandatory system of liability insurance under the Obligatory Insurance Act (*Pflichtversicherungsgesetz* (PflVG)).[441] Hence, to register a motor vehicle and to receive a licence plate, the vehicle's keeper has to show that he concluded an insurance contract providing sufficient coverage as required by the appendix to the Obligatory Insurance Act.[442] The victim of a road traffic accident may bring his action against the keeper and the driver of a vehicle and, at the same time, against the insurance company that has insured the keeper's risk of being held responsible in connection with the operation of a motor vehicle. According to section 115 of the Insurance Act (*Versicherungsvertragsgesetz* (VVG)), the victim has a direct claim against the insurer. Hence, there is no need for the victim of an accident to primarily sue the person causing the accident in order to bring a claim for insurance coverage into existence. The regime of mandatory liability insurance assures that the victim is not burdened with the keeper's or driver's risk of insolvency.

153. The rules of the Road Traffic Act do not supersede the general rules of tort law. In most cases, a person injured in a road traffic accident will – with the help of a court-appointed expert – already be able to bring a claim under section 823(1) BGB. Since, in the past, it was not possible to obtain compensation for pain and suffering under the rules of the Road Traffic Act, the strict liability regime was of only minor importance. However, following the recent tort law reform, this notion might change in the future: Since 1 August 2002, the new section 253(2) BGB allows recovery for pain and suffering regardless of the claim's foundation. The combination of such compensation with strict liability has the advantage that it is no longer necessary to call in a court-appointed expert in order to determine the driver's fault. In theory, this could lead to a considerable reduction in litigation costs.

441. *See* s. 1 *Pflichtversicherungsgesetz.*

442. The minimum amount of insurance is EUR 7.5 million for personal injury, EUR 1.22 million for damage to property, and EUR 50,000 for economic loss directly or indirectly resulting from personal injury or damage to property.

Chapter 2. Product Liability

154. Based on the European Community's Directive on Product Liability of 25 July 1985,[443] the German legislator promulgated the Product Liability Act (ProdHaftG), which has been in force since 1 January 1990. Section 1 ProdHaftG establishes the manufacturer's strict liability for personal injury and damage to property caused by a defective product. Property damage, however, is limited to consumers' private property.[444] Furthermore, there is no compensation for damage caused to the defective product itself.[445] Hence, the so-called insidious spreading loss (*Weiterfresserschäden*), i.e., damage to an object caused by a defective integral part, is not covered by the Product Liability Act. Neither can claims for the recovery of pure economic loss be based on section 1 ProdHaftG. Further limitations with respect to the claimable damage are included in sections 10 and 11 ProdHaftG. According to section 10(1) ProdHaftG, the manufacturer can only be liable up to a maximum of EUR 85 million for personal injury caused by a defect of a particular product or a group of similar products. Regarding property damage, section 11 ProdHaftG states that the victim himself has to bear the first EUR 500 of his damage.

155. The term 'product' is defined by section 2 ProdHaftG: Product within the meaning of the Product Liability Act is every chattel, even if it forms the part of another chattel or immovable object, as well as electricity.[446] A controversial debate among German commentators has evolved on the question of whether this definition also includes software. The better arguments speak for an extension of section 2 ProdHaftG to software as long as it is stored in a medium.[447] In accordance with the definition given by section 3(1) ProdHaftG, a product is defective if it lacks the safety one is entitled to expect from it. This so-called consumer expectation test refers to the objectively defined safety expectations of the public at large; the subjective expectations of the individual product user are irrelevant.[448] In more recent decisions, the Federal Supreme Court ruled that people, in general, cannot reasonably expect absolute safety.[449] Therefore, the manufacturer, within the meaning of section 4 ProdHaftG, is not required to take preventive measures against all kinds of conceivable dangers.[450] Section 3(1) No. 1 ProdHaftG explicitly names the presentation of the product, the use to which it could reasonably be put, and the time the product was put into circulation as relevant factors for the determination of the

443. Directive 85/374/EEC, O.J.EC 1985 L 210/29.
444. OLG Saarbrücken, *NJW-RR* 2013, 271.
445. *See* s. 1(1) sentence 2 Produkthaftungsgesetz (ProdHaftG).
446. BGH, *NJW* 2014, 2106, 2107; *see also* Sprau, in: Grüneberg, BGB, § 2 ProdHaftG No. 1 (82nd ed., 2023).
447. Cf. Spindler, *NJW* 1999, 3737, 3742; Spindler and Klöhn, *VersR* 2003, 410, 412 et seq.; Sprau, in: Grüneberg, BGB, § 2 ProdHaftG No. 1 (82nd ed., 2023); and Wagner, in: Münchener Kommentar zum BGB, § 2 ProdHaftG Nos 16 et seq. (8th ed., 2020).
448. Cf. BGH, *NJW* 2014, 2106, 2107; BGH, *NJW* 2013, 1302 et seq.; BGH, *NJW* 2009, 2952, 2953; BGH, *NJW* 2009, 1669, 1670; OLG Hamm, *NJW-RR* 2001, 1248, 1249; and Oechsler, *NJW* 2014, 2080.
449. BGH, *NJW* 2013, 1302, 1303; and BGH, *NJW* 2009, 1669, 1670.
450. BGH, *NJW* 2013, 1302, 1303.

safety standard the general public is entitled to expect from a product. In this context, the use to which a product could reasonably be put is not only the designated use of a product but also its foreseeable misuse.[451]

156. The strict liability envisaged by the Product Liability Act falls on the defective product's manufacturer (*Hersteller*). According to section 4 ProdHaftG, 'manufacturer' in terms of the Product Liability Act is not only the person who actually produced and not merely repacked or portioned a finished product,[452] one of its component parts or a basic substance for the product's manufacture in his organizational sphere,[453] but also anyone presenting himself as the manufacturer by affixing to the product his name, trademark, or other distinguishing mark.[454] Additionally, the importer of a defective product manufactured outside the European Economic Area is also regarded as its manufacturer for the purpose of the Product Liability Act. If the producer of a product is unidentifiable, any person supplying a product may also be liable.[455] Where, as a result of the provisions of the Product Liability Act, two or more persons are responsible for the same damage, they are jointly and severally liable.[456]

157. To claim damages, the injured person must prove the actual damage, the defect in the product, and the causal relationship between damage and defect. As the Product Liability Act provides for strict liability, it is not necessary to prove negligence or fault of the manufacturer.[457] The concept of fault is, however, not completely irrelevant with respect to liability under the Product Liability Act since contributory negligence of the victim is an available defence for the manufacturer according to section 6(1) ProdHaftG in connection with section 254 BGB. This might be the case, e.g., if the consumer ignores instruction manuals and warnings or uses the product incorrectly and not in accordance with its purpose.[458] Other defences for the manufacturer are codified in section 1(2)–(3) ProdHaftG. The manufacturer is exempt from all liability if he proves that he did not put the product into circulation, that the defect causing the damage came into being after the product was put into circulation by him, that the product was not manufactured for profit-making sale, that the defect is due to compliance of the product with mandatory regulations issued by the public authorities, or that the state of scientific and technical knowledge at the time the product was put into circulation was not such as to enable the defect's discovery (so-called *development risk defence*).[459] In case of a manufacturer of a component part of the final product, liability is excluded if

451. Cf. BGHZ 116, 60, 65.
452. Cf. OLG Saarbrücken, *NJW-RR* 2001, 458.
453. BGH, *NJW* 2014, 2106, 2108; and Sprau, in: Grüneberg, BGB, § 4 ProdHaftG No. 2 (82nd ed., 2023).
454. *See* s. 4(1) ProdHaftG.
455. *See* s. 4(3) ProdHaftG; cf. OLG Saarbrücken, *MDR* 2007, 768, 769.
456. *See* s. 5 ProdHaftG.
457. *See* s. 1(4) ProdHaftG.
458. Cf. OLG Bamberg, *NJW-RR* 2010, 902, 903 et seq.: contributory negligence resulting from the improper handling of fresh concrete and causing chemical burns.
459. *See* s. 1(2) ProdHaftG.

the component part manufacturer proves that the defect is attributable to the design of the product or the instructions given by the manufacturer of the final product.[460] Other than these exceptions, all kinds of exemption clauses are null and void.[461]

158. According to section 15(2) ProdHaftG, the application of other contractual or tortious liability rules is not affected by the Product Liability Act. Therefore, the victim may still refer to other provisions if they are more favourable than those of the Product Liability Act. The general tort law rules of the Civil Code particularly remain important with respect to damage to commercially used products. Recourse to sections 823 et seq. BGB can also be more favourable if the inflicted property damage is less than the deductible of EUR 500 or if the maximum of EUR 85 million for personal injury is exceeded. Furthermore, until the recent amendments in the course of the 2002 tort law reform, it was not possible to claim damages for pain and suffering under the rules of the Product Liability Act.[462]

159. The Federal Supreme Court established specific rules for the application of the general tort law provisions in product liability cases in a 1968 landmark decision, the so-called Fowl Pest case (*Hühnerpest-Fall*): Rejecting all contractual and quasi-contractual theories developed by German scholars, the Federal Supreme Court solved the problem that tort law actions in connection with defective products regularly failed due to the plaintiff's inability to prove the manufacturer's fault by a reversal of the burden of proof for claims based on section 823(1) BGB.[463] In the specific case, the plaintiff ran a chicken farm and had the chickens vaccinated by a veterinarian. However, the vaccine contained insufficiently immunized active virus and bacterial impurities. As a result, a fowl pest broke out a few days later, killing more than 4,000 chickens. After being sued by the plaintiff, the company manufacturing the vaccine denied a causal connection between the use of its vaccine and the outbreak of fowl pests and produced evidence in order to exonerate itself from vicarious liability under section 831 BGB. The Federal Supreme Court, however, decided that a plaintiff who suffered damage from a defective product, which was used according to its purpose, only has to prove that the damage was caused by an objective defect of the product that made it unsuitable to be put into circulation.[464] Once the plaintiff has produced such evidence, the defendant manufacturer has to prove that he and every individual involved in the production process acted without fault.[465]

160. A distinctive feature of product liability cases is the absence of direct interference with one of the interests protected by section 823(1) BGB. Therefore, the victim principally has to prove that the manufacturer violated a duty of care in order to successfully claim damages. Although the case law in this area is extremely rich, the different duties of care are commonly subdivided into four categories of duties

460. *See* s. 1(3) ProdHaftG.
461. *See* s. 14 ProdHaftG.
462. *See now* s. 8 sentence 2 ProdHaftG.
463. BGHZ 51, 91, 104 et seq.
464. Cf. BGHZ 51, 91, 104 et seq.
465. *See* BGH, *NJW* 1973, 1602.

being relevant for both the fault-based liability within the meaning of section 823(1) BGB and the strict liability within the meaning of section 1 ProdHaftG:[466] (1) those concerning the manufacture, (2) those concerning the design, (3) those concerning instructions regarding the use, and (4) those concerning the monitoring of a product.[467]

161. The already mentioned 'Fowl Pest' case is an illustration of defects in the manufacture of a product (*Herstellungsfehler*). Such defects are characterized by the faulty manufacture of an individual product.[468] The manufacturer has the duty to avoid any defects during the production process, which might make the particular product less safe than usual. The relevant standard of care is determined with respect to the objective expectancies of the general public, the state of scientific and technical knowledge, the danger inherent to the product, and the relation between the hazard and the cost to avoid it.[469] The duty relates to the whole production process, including the examination of incoming goods;[470] the selection of raw materials and component parts;[471] the proper maintenance of the machinery and other production equipment, including quality checks;[472] and the proper packaging and labelling of the product.[473] In contrast to the responsibility under the rules of the Product Liability Act, the manufacturer's liability according to section 823(1) BGB is – at least theoretically – excluded with respect to isolated defective products, so-called outliers (*Ausreißer*), provided the defect was unavoidable notwithstanding all safety measures.[474] The mere theoretic nature of this exception can be illustrated by a look at the so-called Soft Drink Bottle case (*Limondenflaschen-Fall*):[475] The plaintiff was injured by an exploding soft drink bottle and sued the bottle's manufacturer for damages. In accordance with the state of scientific and technical knowledge, explosions of such bottles could not be entirely avoided. Nevertheless, the Federal Supreme Court ruled in favour of the plaintiff, stating that the manufacturer had violated his duty to properly examine the safe condition of the reusable glass bottles before they left the factory and to document the results of this examination. Thus, the manufacturer had to prove that the damage was attributable to an unforeseeable mishandling after the bottle left his sphere of influence.[476]

---

466. BGH, *NJW* 2009, 2952, 2953; and BGH, *NJW* 2009, 1669, 1670.
467. *See* Spindler, in: BeckOGK, BGB, § 823 Nos 638 et seq. (version 01.02.2023); and Wagner, *VersR* 2014, 905, 906.
468. Cf. BGH, *VersR* 1956, 410, 411; and Michalski, *BB* 1998, 961, 962.
469. Cf. BGHZ 105, 346, 352; Kullmann, in: Kullmann, Pfister, Stöhr and Spindler, Produzentenhaftung, No. 1520, pp. 10 et seq. (version 02/09); and Spindler, in: BeckOGK, BGB, § 823 No. 629 (version 01.02.2023).
470. OLG Düsseldorf, *NJW* 1978, 1693.
471. BGH, *NJW* 1968, 247, 248; and BGH, *VersR* 1972, 559, 560.
472. *See* Spindler, in: BeckOGK, BGB, § 823 No. 645 (version 01.02.2023).
473. BGHZ 66, 208; and OLG Hamm, *VersR* 1993, 765, 766.
474. BGHZ 51, 91, 105; BGHZ 129, 353, 358; BGH, *NJW* 1975, 1827, 1828; BGH, *VersR* 1956, 410, 411; BGH, *VersR* 1960, 855; and Sprau, in: Grüneberg, BGB, § 823 No. 176 (82nd ed., 2023).
475. BGHZ 104, 323.
476. Cf. BGHZ 104, 323, 332 et seq.; *see also* BGH, *NJW* 1993, 528, 529; BGHZ 129, 353, 361 et seq., 365 et seq.; BGH, *NJW* 2013, 1302, 1303; and Kunz, *BB* 1994, 450, 453 et seq.

162. The rules established by the Federal Supreme Court in the 'Fowl Pest' case were later extended to cases in which damage was caused by a product that had a defect in design (*Konstruktionsfehler*).[477] Other than manufacturing defects, which concern only a single product, defects in design are attached to a whole line of products.[478] Design defects may not only result from faulty construction[479] but also from the use of unsuitable component parts.[480] The manufacturer generally has the duty to design products in a way that makes them safe for ordinary use[481] and comparable to the liability under the Product Liability Act, even for foreseeable misuse.[482] However, the best possible safety standard is not required; the 'necessary' safety standard with respect to the specific circumstances is sufficient.[483] The manufacturer has to take organizational measures in order to ensure that all relevant technical rules are obeyed and that production does not start until the product and the materials used to produce it have been properly tested.[484] Furthermore, he has to investigate consumer expectations,[485] which then have to be passed on to the development department.[486]

163. To avoid instruction defects (*Instruktionsfehler*), the manufacturer has to provide proper instructions regarding the use of the product. If he fails to provide sufficient instructions, he is liable for damages resulting from dangers inherent to the product, notwithstanding a proper manufacture.[487] The duty to supply proper instructions not only relates to hazards arising from the product's designated use but

477. *See*, e.g., BGH, *NJW* 2009, 2952, 2953; BGHZ 67, 359, 362; OLG Saarbrücken, *NJW-RR* 2013, 271 et seq.; and Wagner, in: Münchener Kommentar zum BGB, § 3 ProdHaftG Nos 44 et seq. (8th ed., 2020).
478. Cf. Michalski, *BB* 1998, 961, 962.
479. BGH, *VersR* 1960, 855, BGH, *VersR* 1960, 1095 et seq.; and OLG Frankfurt, *VersR* 1990, 981, 982.
480. BGHZ 67, 359, 362; BGHZ 104, 323, 327; and Foerste, in: Foerste and Graf von Westphalen, Produkthaftungs-Handbuch, § 24 No. 131 (3rd ed., 2012).
481. BGH, *NJW* 2009, 2952, 2953; and BGH, *NJW-RR* 1999, 25, 26.
482. *See* BGHZ 104, 323, 328; BGHZ 105, 346, 351; OLG Düsseldorf, *NJW* 1997, 2333, 2333; and OLG Celle, *VersR* 1978, 258 et seq.; for further references *see* Foerste, in: Foerste and Graf von Westphalen, Produkthaftungs-Handbuch, § 24 Nos 72 et seq., 88 et seq. (3rd ed., 2012); Schmidt-Salzer, *Produkthaftung*, Vol. III/1, Nos 4.866 et seq., 4.873 et seq. (2nd ed., 1990); and Kullmann, in: Kullmann, Pfister, Stöhr and Spindler, Produzentenhaftung, No. 1520, pp. 11 et seq. (version 02/09).
483. Cf. BGH, *VersR* 1972, 559, 560; OLG Saarbrücken, *NJW-RR* 1993, 990, 991; OLG Saarbrücken, *NJW-RR* 2013, 271, 272; and J. Hager, in: Staudinger, BGB, § 823 No. F 12 (2021).
484. On the requirements *see* BGHZ 104, 323, 327; BGH, *VersR* 1971, 80 et seq.; and BGH, *NJW* 1990, 906 907 et seq.
485. *See* Kullmann, *NJW* 2002, 30, 32; and Spindler, in: BeckOGK, BGB, § 823 No. 642 (version 01.02.2023).
486. Steffen, in: RGRK, § 823 No. 283 (12th ed., 1989); Kullmann, in: Kullmann, Pfister, Stöhr and Spindler, Produzentenhaftung, No. 1520, pp. 14 et seq., 56 et seq. (version 01/11); and Dietrich, *Produktbeobachtungspflicht* 76 et seq. (1994).
487. *See* BGH, *NJW* 2009, 2952, 2954; BGHZ 139, 79, 83; BGHZ 116, 60, 65 et seq.; BGHZ 64, 46, 49; BGH, *NJW* 1999, 2815; BGH, *NJW* 1987, 372, OLG Bamberg, *NJW-RR* 2010, 902; and Wagner, in: Münchener Kommentar zum BGB, § 3 ProdHaftG Nos 46, 50 (8th ed., 2020).

also relates to hazards resulting from foreseeable misuse.[488] No instructions or warnings have to be supplied if the manufacturer reasonably assumes that the product is only used by persons who are familiar with its risks[489] or if the danger inherent to the product is obvious.[490] The content and scope of the manufacturer's duty to provide instructions have to be determined in view of the least informed group of product users.[491] Relevant factors for the determination are the degree of danger resulting from the product's use and the interests likely to be affected.[492] Discreetly placed instructions may not be sufficient.[493] Particularly where products are manufactured and consumed on a massive scale, a warning notice placed on an instruction leaflet, which is usually read only superficially, is not sufficient if the notice is not clearly set apart from other information.[494] Hence, in the so-called *Milupa* case, the Federal Supreme Court ruled that a manufacturer of sweetened children's tea, which has to be drunk out of plastic bottles, is accountable for cavities developed from constant sucking of the tea if he fails to place a clear warning on the product.[495]

164. After a product has been put into circulation, the manufacturer still has a monitoring duty (*Produktbeobachtungspflicht*). He has to check whether the product continues to be safe in light of new developments regarding scientific and technical knowledge and, if necessary, update the instructions that originally accompanied the product.[496] The manufacturer has the duty to consult specialist literature, recent technical regulations, and the results of scientific congresses on a regular basis.[497] Furthermore, he has to take note of the experiences of his competitors as well as their product developments with respect to improved safety standards.[498] Manufacturers acting on a worldwide scale have the duty to look globally

---

488. Cf. BGH, *NJW* 2009, 2952, 2954; BGHZ 116, 60, 65; BGHZ 106, 273, 283; BGHZ 105, 346, 351; BGH, *NJW* 1999, 2815, 2816; BGH, *NJW* 1994, 3349, 3350; OLG Nürnberg, *NJW-RR* 2014, 1304; and OLG Bamberg, *NJW-RR* 2010, 902.
489. BGHZ 116, 60, 65 et seq.; BGH, *NJW* 1999, 2815, 2816; BGH, *NJW* 1992, 2016; BGH, *NJW* 1986, 1863; OLG Bamberg, *NJW-RR* 2010, 902; Foerste, in: Foerste and Graf von Westphalen, Produkthaftungs-Handbuch, § 24 Nos 246 et seq. (3rd ed., 2012); and Kullmann, *NJW* 2000, 1912, 1913.
490. BGH, *NJW* 1995, 2631, 2632; *see also* OLG Bamberg, *NJW-RR* 2010, 902; and OLG Hamm, *NJW-RR* 2001, 1248, 1249.
491. *See* BGH, *NJW* 2009, 2952, 2954; and BGH, *NJW* 1994, 932.
492. Cf. BGH, *NJW* 2009, 2952, 2594 et seq.; BGHZ 106, 273, 281; BGHZ 59, 172; *see also* OLG Frankfurt, *VersR* 1995, 660, 661; BVerfG, *NJW* 1997, 249, 149 et seq.; BGHZ 116, 60, 67 et seq.; BGHZ 80, 186, 192; OLG Frankfurt, *NJW-RR* 1995, 406, 408; OLG Karlsruhe, *VersR* 1998, 63; and Kullmann, *NJW* 1997, 1746, 1748.
493. Cf. BGHZ 116, 60, 68; BGHZ 99, 167, 181; and BGH, *NJW* 1995, 1286, 1288.
494. *See* BGHZ 116, 60, 68; OLG Düsseldorf, *NJW-RR* 1995, 25, 26; and J. Hager, in: Staudinger, BGB, § 823 No. F 15 (2021).
495. *See* BGHZ 116, 60.
496. Cf. BGHZ 99, 167, 171 et seq.; BGHZ 80, 199, 202 et seq.; BGH, *NJW* 1994, 3349, 3350; Michalski, *BB* 1998, 961, 963; Pfeifer, *Produktfehler oder Fehlverhalten des Produzenten* 93 (1987); and Wagner, *VersR* 2014, 905, 906.
497. *See* BGHZ 116, 60, 70 et seq.; BGHZ 80, 186, 191; BGHZ 80, 199, 203; BGH, *NJW* 1995, 1286, 1287 et seq.; BGH, *VersR* 1971, 80, 81 et seq.; Foerste, in: Foerste and Graf von Westphalen, Produkthaftungs-Handbuch, § 24 Nos 377 et seq. (3rd ed., 2012); Kullmann, in: Kullmann, Pfister,

for new information regarding the safety of their products.[499] The efforts owed by the manufacturer are dependent on the degree of danger posed by the product; if no personal injury is to be expected, a passive observation of the product can be sufficient.[500] According to the Federal Supreme Court, the manufacturer can even be obligated to monitor the product's use for dangers resulting from the installation of accessories manufactured by third parties.[501] Under certain circumstances, especially in a situation where the hazards inherent to a product pose a serious danger to life or body of the product users, the manufacturer may be under a duty to recall the product.[502] The duty depends on the likelihood of injury and on the chance that a mere warning will reach the product users in time, provided such a warning is sufficient to prevent the injury.[503]

165. Claims in connection with damage caused by defective products can be based not only on section 823(1) BGB or section 1 ProdHaftG but also on section 823(2) BGB if the manufacturer has violated a protective law. In the context of product liability, section 3 of the Act on Providing Products in the Market in 2011 (*Produktsicherheitsgesetz* (ProdSG)), which is the result of the implementation of several EU directives concerning product safety by the German Federal Legislator, is widely recognized as such a protective law.[504] Prior to the enactment of the ProdSG, the Federal Supreme Court held that the preceding section 3 of the former Act on the Safety of Technical Equipment (*Gerätesicherheitsgesetz* (GSG)) could be qualified as protecting individuals, thus indirectly attributing their tort claims.[505] The same applied to section 4 of the Act on Technical Work Equipment and Consumer Products (*Gesetz über* technische *Arbeitsmittel und Verbraucherprodukte* or (GPSG)), which replaced section 3 GSG. Insofar, section 3 ProdSG functionally correlates with the preceding standard of section 4 GPSG.[506] Although the Act on Providing Products in the Market does not deviate substantially from the preceding

---

Stöhr and Spindler, Produzentenhaftung, No. 1520, pp. 14 et seq., 54 et seq. (version 01/11); Deutsch, Festschrift für Larenz 111, 120 et seq. (1983); and Wagner, *VersR* 2014, 905, 906; Brüggemeier, *WM* 1982, 1294, 1301 et seq.

498. Cf. BGH, *NJW* 1990, 906, 907; v. Westphalen, *ZIP* 1992, 18, 22 et seq.; Kunz, *BB* 1994, 450, 450; and Michalski, *BB* 1998, 961, 963; *see also* Dietrich, *Produktbeobachtungspflicht* 111 et seq. (1994).

499. *See* BGHZ 80, 199, 203; Foerste, in: Foerste and Graf von Westphalen, Produkthaftungs-Handbuch, § 24 No. 384. (3rd ed., 2012); and Wagner, *VersR* 2014, 905, 906.

500. Kullmann and Stöhr, in: Kullmann, Pfister, Stöhr and Spindler, Produzentenhaftung, No. 1520, pp. 14 et seq., 57 (version 02/16).

501. BGHZ 99, 167, 172 et seq.; and BGH, *NJW* 1995, 1286, 1287 et seq.; *see also* Klinger, *Die Produktbeobachtungspflicht bezüglich Zubehörteilen* 56 et seq. (1998); Kunz, *BB* 1994, 450, 451; Dietrich, *Produktbeobachtungspflicht* 76 et seq. (1994); and Ulmer, 152 ZHR 564, 575 et seq. (1988).

502. Cf. BGHSt 37, 106; OLG Karlsruhe, *NJW-RR* 1995, 594, 597; and OLG Düsseldorf, *NJW-RR* 1997, 1344, 1345.

503. *See* Bodewig, *Der Rückruf fehlerhafter Produkte* 216 et seq. (1999); Foerste, in: Foerste and Graf von Westphalen, Produkthaftungs-Handbuch, 24 Nos 314 et seq., 323 (3rd ed., 2012); Schwenzer, *JZ* 1987, 1059, 1062; and Spindler, in: BeckOGK, BGB, § 823 Nos 670 et seq. (version 01.02.2023).

504. Sprau, in: Grüneberg, BGB, § 823 No. 68 (82nd ed., 2023); Klindt, in: Klindt, ProdSG, § 3 No. 55 (3rd ed., 2021); and Wagner, *VersR* 2014, 905, 913.

505. BGH, *NJW* 1980, 1219, 1220; *see also* Wagner, *VersR* 2014, 905, 913.

506. Klindt, in: Klindt, ProdSG, § 3 No. 1 (3rd ed., 2021).

framework of product safety legislation, it must be seen in the broader context of the harmonization procedure on the EU level. By issuing several detailed directives requiring national implementation, the EU legislator aimed to provide a specific EU-wide safety standard for certain types of products, such as electrical equipment, toys, pressure containers, personal protective gear, or motor boots. However, section 8(1) ProdSG grants the German legislator the power to set safety standards by ordinance and to regulate the requirements for compliance with the ProdSG more specifically.

Chapter 3. Liability for Services

166. German tort law does not provide rules stipulating strict liability for services. In particular, services cannot be regarded as 'products' in terms of the Product Liability Act. According to section 2 ProdHaftG, except for electricity, only chattels fall within the range of the Product Liability Act. However, in some cases, a service may be rendered in direct connection with a product (e.g., blood transfusion/blood serum).[507] Taking into account the definition of 'manufacturer' provided by section 1(1) sentence 1 ProdHaftG in connection with section 4 ProdHaftG, it has to be decided for each individual case if an overall view in the context of generally accepted principles justifies the conclusion that the respective incident can primarily be described not as rendering a service, but as manufacturing a product.[508]

507. *See* Graf von Westphalen, in: Foerste and Graf von Westphalen, Produkthaftungs-Handbuch, § 47 No. 14 (3rd ed., 2012).
508. Graf von Westphalen, in: Foerste and Graf von Westphalen, Produkthaftungs-Handbuch, § 47 No. 14 (3rd ed., 2012).

Chapter 4. Environmental Liability

167. Prior to the enactment of the Environmental Liability Act (UmweltHG), German environmental law consisted of a patchwork of numerous provisions prohibiting specific polluting activities or requiring polluters to compensate for damages caused by pollution. Each provision had a relatively narrow field of application.[509]

168. Section 823(1) BGB is the basis for environmental liability. The polluter is liable if the pollution amounts to an unlawful and culpable violation of an interest or right protected by section 823(1) BGB.[510] According to the general concept regarding duties of care, anyone creating a hazardous situation has an obligation to apply reasonable care in order to prevent the injury of third parties. The operator of a facility has to comply with the limits for emissions imposed by administrative law, although these limits are generally not strictly binding with respect to civil law.[511] Nonetheless, to define the proper standard of care, a reference to the rules of administrative law is permissible.[512] They are, however, not final in a way that would prohibit the placing of more extensive demands regarding the duties of care under civil law.[513] Yet, the facility operator usually may presuppose that he applies proper care if he acts in accordance with the emission limits set by the rules of administrative law.[514] Only if he has indications that observing these limits is insufficient in order to prevent the injury of third parties is he obligated to apply further safety measures.[515]

169. Under the general rules of tort law, the plaintiff has to prove not only the damaging act and the damage but also causation, unlawfulness, and fault. In practice, usually, it is extremely difficult for plaintiffs in environmental liability to produce the necessary evidence. In the famous *Cupola Oven* case (*Kupolofen-Fall*), the Federal Supreme Court eased the plaintiff's burden of proof by adopting its product liability jurisprudence and the rules developed under section 906 BGB.[516] In the specific case, the defendant ran a cupola oven. The plaintiffs' cars, which stood in

509. *See* Ruffert, *NVwZ* 2010, 1177, 1178.
510. Cf. Medicus, *JZ* 1986, 778, 780, 783; Gerlach, *Privatrecht und Umweltschutz im System des Umweltrechts* 285 (1989); Kohler, in: Staudinger, BGB, Einl. UmweltHR No. 64 (2017); Wagner, in: Münchener Kommentar zum BGB, § 823 No. 1046 (8th ed., 2020); cf. Ruffert, *NVwZ* 2010, 1177, 1178: 'polluter-pays-principle'.
511. Spindler, in: BeckOGK, BGB, § 823 No. 802 (version 01.02.2023).
512. Wagner, *VersR* 2014, 905, 911 et seq.
513. Kohler, in: Staudinger, BGB, Einl. UmweltHR No. 299 (2017); Gerlach, *JZ* 1988, 161, 164; and Taupitz, 53 *UTR* 203 215 et seq. (2000).
514. *See* BGHZ 92, 143, 151 et seq.; and Hager, *NJW* 1986, 1961, 1966.
515. Cf. BGHZ 92, 143, 152; BGH, *NJW* 1997, 2748, 2749 et seq.; *see also* Salje, *VersR* 1998, 797, 798; v. Bar, 62. DJT 1998, A 1, 35; v. Bar, *Karlsruher Forum* 1987, 4, 12; Marburger, 56. DJT 1986, C 9, 121; Marburger, in: Waldschäden als Rechtsproblem 109, 135 et seq. (1987); Gerlach, *Privatrecht und Umweltschutz im System des Umweltrechts* 103 et seq. (1989); and G. Wagner, *EWiR* § 6 Umwelthaftungsgesetz (UmweltHG) 1/98, 83, 84; Petersen, *NJW* 1998, 2099.
516. *See* BGHZ 92, 143, 146 et seq.

a parking lot alongside the defendant's premises, were damaged by the oven's emissions. The Federal Supreme Court decided that the plaintiffs could bring an action neither under section 14 sentence 2 of the Federal Emissions Control Act (*Bundesimmissionsschutzgesetz* (BImSchG))[517] nor under section 906(2) sentence 2 BGB, which only affords protection to private use interest in land.[518] However, the Federal Supreme Court ruled that the plaintiff only has to prove that the damage was caused by the emissions of the defendant's facility. It is then up to the defendant to prove that the emissions were immaterial or in accordance with local customs and that he undertook all reasonable and economically feasible measures in order to avoid the damage. In the same decision, the Federal Supreme Court even considered a modification of the burden of proof with respect to the causal connection between emissions and the damage suffered by the plaintiff whenever the facility operator exceeds the limits set by the rules of administrative law.[519]

170. Before the Environmental Liability Act came into force, strict liability for environmental damage had been limited to certain particularly dangerous activities and specific types of facilities, such as nuclear reactors or mining facilities. The most important strict liability provision used to be section 89 of the Water Resources Act (WHG), which imposes strict liability for bodily injury, property damage and even pure economic loss caused by any change in the physical, chemical or biological composition of a water source.

171. The Environmental Liability Act now provides for strict liability of the operators of numerous environmentally relevant facilities with respect to damages caused by an environmental impact on soil, air, or water. It complements the preexisting laws, which are still applicable alongside the Environmental Liability Act.[520] Section 1 UmweltHG states that the operator of a facility listed in Appendix

---

517. Cf. s. 14 BImSchG:

> To the extent that licensing of a facility has become final, nobody shall have the right to request cessation of the facility's operation on the basis of civil law claims to prevent detrimental impact any piece of land may have upon neighboring premises, unless the claims are based on specific titles; only such precautionary measures as are necessary to prevent the detrimental impact may be demanded. Compensation may be claimed for the actual damage suffered if such measures are economically unviable or technically unfeasible according to the state of technical knowledge.

518. Cf. s. 906 BGB:

> (1) A landowner is not entitled to prohibit the intrusion of gases, vapors, smells, smoke, soot, heat, noises, shocks and similar interferences emanating from another piece of land to the extent the interference no or only negligible impact on the use of his land.
> (2) The same applies in so far as a substantial prejudice is caused by the use of another piece of land in conformity with local custom, provided it cannot be reasonably prevented. The landowner is entitled to compensation for the economic consequences of the interference.

519. Cf. BGHZ 92, 143, 146 et seq.
520. *See* s. 18(1) UmweltHG.

1 to the Environmental Liability Act is strictly liable if anyone suffers death, personal injury, or property damage due to an environmental impact emitted from the facility.[521] Hence, liability under the Environmental Liability Act requires the violation of a particular individual's protected interests; section 1 UmweltHG does not impose liability for abstract ecological damage. The term 'environmental impact' is defined in section 3(1) UmweltHG and includes harmful effects caused by substances, vibrations, noise, pressure, radiation, gas, steam, heat, or other comparable influences spreading within soil, air, or water. Section 4 UmweltHG excludes liability if the damage was caused by an Act of God. Furthermore, according to section 5 UmweltHG, recovery for property damage is excluded if the facility was properly operated, provided the damage is not substantial. The operator's liability is limited to a maximum amount of EUR 85 million for bodily injury and EUR 85 million for property damage caused by the same environmental impact.[522]

172. Since the proof of causation can present an almost insurmountable barrier to the plaintiff in an environmental liability case, section 6 UmweltHG includes a special provision easing the plaintiff's burden of proof.[523] According to section 6(1) UmweltHG, causation will be presumed upon a prima facie showing that the particular facility is generally likely to cause the respective damage.[524] However, section 6(1) UmweltHG does not apply if the facility was operated without interruption and in conformity with all applicable regulations.[525] The operator may also rebut the presumption of causation by reference to section 7 UmweltHG, according to which the presumption is rebutted if other circumstances equally appear to be inherently likely to have caused the damage.

521. Since the tort law reform of 2002, it is also possible to claim damages for pain and suffering under the rules of the Environmental Liability Act, *see* s. 13 sentence 2 UmweltHG.
522. *See* s. 15 UmweltHG.
523. Cf. OLG Düsseldorf, *NJW-RR* 2002, 26.
524. OLG Düsseldorf, *NJW-RR* 2002, 26; a similar presumption was developed by the courts with respect to liability under the Water Resources Act, *see* BGHZ 57, 257, 264.
525. *See* s. 6(1) UmweltHG.

Chapter 5. Others

§1. Strict Liability under the Civil Code

173. As described above, the liability of the keeper of a luxury animal under section 833 sentence 1 BGB is the only form of strict liability codified in the tort law section of the Civil Code. There are, however, other provisions of the Civil Code which order strict liability for damages resulting from certain activities.

174. A strict liability provision included in the general part of the Civil Code is section 231 BGB, which orders a duty to compensate for damages caused by erroneous self-redress, i.e., activities which were executed in the erroneous assumption of a situation that would grant the self-help defence of section 229 BGB. Moreover, section 701(1) BGB also imposes liability without fault on innkeepers for damage to their customers' property.[526] Another example of liability without fault is the duty to compensate the owner for property damage resulting from interference in an emergency situation under section 904 sentence 2 BGB. The rule is the necessary counterpart to the owner's obligation under section 904 sentence 1 BGB, which states that the owner of an object is not entitled to prohibit another's interference with the object if the interference is necessary in order to avoid a present danger, provided the impending damage is disproportionately large compared to the damage caused by the interference.

§2. Other Provisions of Strict Liability

175. Outside the Civil Code, numerous special laws impose strict liability for damages caused by particularly dangerous activities. The most important provisions, next to the already mentioned section 7 StVG, section 1 ProdHaftG, section 89 WHG and section 1 UmweltHG,[527] are section 1 of the Strict Liability Act (HPflG), sections 33–43 of the Air Traffic Act (LuftVG), sections 25 and 26 of the Atomic Energy Act (*AtG*), section 84 of the Pharmaceutical Products Act (*Arzneimittelgesetz* (AMG)), and section 32 of the Genetic Engineering Act (GenTG).

176. The Strict Liability Act has its roots in the Imperial Compulsory Liability Act of 1871 (*Reichshaftpflichtgesetz*), which was modelled after the Prussian Railways Act of 1838 (*Preußisches Eisenbahngesetz*). Section 1 HPflG imposes strict liability on the operator of a railway or a teleferic for bodily injury or damage to property caused in the course of operation (with an exception for Acts of God and damage to stored objects as well as objects transported by the railway, unless carried by a passenger). The Strict Liability Act also includes a provision regarding the liability for bodily injury and property damage caused by electricity, gas, steam or fluids escaping from cables, pipelines, or other facilities for the provision of such

526. The innkeeper's strict liability is limited to certain ceiling amounts, *see* s. 702(1) BGB.
527. *See* Part III, Ch. 3.

energy or substances.[528] Moreover, section 3 HPflG provides for vicarious liability on the operators of mines, quarries, pits, and factories for damage caused by the culpable conduct of their authorized agents or representatives. In contrast to the general provision of section 831 BGB, the provision of the Strict Liability Act allows no exoneration. Comparable to other strict liability statutes, the Strict Liability Act also limits the compensation to certain ceiling amounts.[529] Likewise, it also contains a contributory fault defence.[530]

177. While sections 33–43 LuftVG impose strict liability on aircraft operators, sections 25–26 AtG order risk-based liability for the operators of facilities designated for the production and fission of nuclear materials. Unlike other strict liability laws, the Air Traffic Act and the Atomic Energy Act invoke liability even for damage caused by an Act of God; a force majeure defence is not available. Section 84 AMG establishes strict liability for pharmaceutical products. Producers of pharmaceutical products are strictly liable for considerable bodily injury caused by the prescribed use of the product, provided the product's harmful effects exceed those to be tolerated with respect to the current state of medical science or the injury results from a labelling, specialized information, or directions that were not in accordance with the current state of medical science. Section 84(2) AMG eases the plaintiff's burden of proof regarding the causal connection between the damage and the use of the pharmaceutical product. According to section 32 GenTG, the operator of a genetic engineering facility is strictly liable if a person is killed or injured or if damage to property is caused by the characteristics of a genetically modified organism.

178. The provisions of strict liability codified in the Civil Code and in the described special laws may not be utilized by way of an analogous application with respect to comparable factual situations, even if they involve similarly dangerous activities. German courts have repeatedly held that the imposition of strict- liability is a matter for the legislator and not for the judiciary.[531]

528. *See* s. 2 *Haftpflichtgesetz* (HPflG).
529. *See* ss 9, 10 HPflG.
530. *See* s. 4 HPflG.
531. *See*, e.g., RGZ 78, 171, 172; BGHZ 51, 91, 98; BGHZ 54, 332, 337; and BGHZ 55, 229, 234.

Part IV. Defences and Exception Clauses

Chapter 1. Limitation of Action

179. According to section 195(1) BGB, claims are subject to statutory limitation. With respect to actions brought under the general rules of tort law, the Civil Code provides a relative and an absolute limitation period; section 199(1) BGB states a limitation period of three years, running from the end of the year in which the claim arose and in which the tort victim became aware (or without gross negligence should have become aware) of the tortfeasor and the circumstances underlying the claim. This general principle, however, is modified by a maximum limitation period of thirty years as far as injury to life, health, or freedom is concerned.[532] In this case, the limitation period starts running from the day the damage was caused. With respect to property damage, the absolute limitation period is ten years.[533] The limitation period for all claims arising from a particular damaging event usually ends uniformly. This rule applies even to consequential damage, provided it was foreseeable at the time the first damage was caused.[534] Only if further damage was unforeseeable would the limitation period start running with the occurrence of the damage.[535]

180. A special provision regarding the limitation of tort law claims is codified in section 852 BGB. If the person bound to make compensation under the rules of tort law has, at the expense of the injured party, acquired anything by the tortious act, he is, notwithstanding the expiration of the limitation period, bound to return it under the law of unjust enrichment. Specific provisions on statutory limitation are also included in the numerous special laws providing strict liability for particular hazardous activities. Comparable to the general limitation rules, they usually combine a relative with an absolute limitation period.[536] Most special laws, however, simply refer to the general rules of the Civil Code.[537]

181. The limitation periods are subject to suspension and interruption (i.e., a new beginning of the limitation period). The respective provisions are included in

532. *See* s. 199(2) BGB.
533. *See* s. 199(3) BGB.
534. BGH, *NJW* 2010, 596, 600; BGH, *NJW* 1998, 1488, 1489; and Ellenberger, in: Grüneberg, BGB, § 199 No. 14 (82nd ed., 2023).
535. Spindler, in: BeckOK, BGB, § 199 No. 6 (65th ed., 2023).
536. *See,* e.g., s. 12(1) ProdHaftG.
537. *See,* e.g., s. 10 HaftPflG, s. 14 StVG, s. 17 UmweltHG.

sections 203–213 BGB. In case of a suspension, the respective period of time is not taken into account for the calculation of the limitation period.[538] The running of the limitation period is suspended by, *inter alia*, pending negotiations between the parties,[539] the prosecution of an action,[540] the hindrance of such prosecution due to an Act of God,[541] the granting of a right to withhold performance,[542] and certain family reasons.[543] In contrast, the limitation period begins anew if the debtor acknowledges the creditor's claim by means of an interim payment, an interest payment, the provision of security, or in any other comparable manner.[544] Furthermore, the issuance of a writ of execution and the carrying out of execution measures also let the limitation period begin anew.[545]

182. Since the limitation defence is not considered by the court ex officio, the defendant has to raise it explicitly. If the limitation period expires, the claim becomes unenforceable.[546] Nevertheless, the debtor still acts in the performance of a – now unenforceable – debt. Hence, if he fulfils his obligation, a claim for restitution is unavailable to him, regardless of whether he knew about the expiration of the limitation period.[547]

538. *See* s. 209 BGB.
539. *See* s. 203 BGB.
540. *See* s. 204 BGB.
541. *See* s. 206 BGB.
542. *See* s. 205 BGB.
543. *See* s. 207 BGB.
544. *See* s. 212 No. 1 BGB.
545. *See* s. 212 No. 1 BGB.
546. *See* s. 214(1) BGB; *see also* BGH, *NJW* 2010, 2422, 2424.
547. *See* s. 214(2) BGB.

Chapter 2. Grounds of Justification

§1. CONSENT

183. The unlawfulness of an injurious conduct may be eliminated by the victim's consent (*Einwilligung*).[548] The victim's consent is of particular importance with respect to the liability of medical practitioners since German courts consider even a skilfully executed medical treatment to be an injury to body unless the patient has expressed his consent.[549] Moreover, it also has significance regarding injuries resulting from hazardous sports activities.

184. Consent must particularly refer to the infringement of a specific interest or right; it is not sufficient if the victim merely agrees with the tortfeasor's actions without being aware of the infringement of a legally protected interest.[550] As a precondition for the exclusion of unlawfulness, the victim's consent must be in accordance with public morals. This restriction regularly becomes relevant with respect to bodily injury: A person may not consent to his own killing or mutilation.[551] However, the demands are considerably lower with respect to a patient's disposal of his body or health in the course of medical treatment, provided the patient has been properly informed.[552] No such limitations apply to property damage. Hence, the injured party's consent may eliminate unlawfulness, even in case of an arranged traffic accident.[553] Consent may also exclude any claim regarding the infringement of a person's honour or personal freedom.

185. The victim must have consented voluntarily, i.e., without being forced, threatened, or intentionally deceived; a mere mistake as to motivation, however, does not exclude the consent's voluntary nature.[554] Special rules apply for medical treatment.[555] The expression of consent is treated in accordance with the general rules applicable to the expression of one's will. Thus, consent may be articulated either explicitly or tacitly.[556] However, a person does not need to be competent in contracting.[557] Consent expressed by a person of restricted capacity to contract may be fully effective if the person is, according to his maturity and personal development, able to understand the infringement's scope and consequences.[558]

548. On consent in general *see* Neuner, *JuS* 2021, 617 et seq.
549. *See* Part I, Ch. 2, §1, II.
550. BGH, *NJW-RR* 1995, 857, 858.
551. RGZ 66, 306, 308.
552. *See* BGHZ 67, 48, 54; and Sprau, in: Grüneberg, BGB, § 823 Nos 38 et seq. (82nd ed., 2023).
553. Cf. BGHZ 71, 339, 340 et seq.; and OLG Frankfurt, *VersR* 1983, 642.
554. BGH, *NJW* 1994, 2755, 2756; BGH, *NJW* 1964, 1177, 1178; OLG Frankfurt, *VersR* 1997, 572, 573; and Sprau, in: Grüneberg, BGB, § 823 No. 39 (82nd ed., 2023).
555. *See* Part I, Ch. 2, §1, II.
556. BGH, *NJW* 1961, 261, 262.
557. Cf. Spindler, in: BeckOGK, BGB, § 823 No. 84 (version 01.02.2023).
558. *See* BGHZ 29, 33, 36; BGH, *NJW* 1972, 335, 337; and Hauck, *NJW* 2012, 2398, 2399 et seq.

Nevertheless, in case of minors, usually the parents' consent is required for more serious infringements unless the violation of the legally protected interest is urgent (e.g., in case of medical treatment).[559]

§2. NECESSITY

186. The tortfeasor's conduct may be justified if he caused damage to another person in a state of emergency (*Notstand*). According to section 228 BGB, a person causing harm to another person's property in an attempt to overcome an imminent danger which cannot otherwise be averted does not act unlawfully if, upon weighing the conflicting interests, the protected interest is not substantially outweighed by the one interfered with. However, he has to compensate the other person for losses if he culpably invoked the danger. Moreover, the necessity defence of section 228 BGB only allows the destruction of the object from which the danger emanates.[560] The damaging of an object that is not the source of the danger can nevertheless be justified under section 904 BGB: The owner of an object is not entitled to prohibit another's interference with the object if the interference is necessary in order to avoid a present danger, provided the impending damage is disproportionately large compared to the damage caused by the interference. However, the interferer has to compensate the owner for the property damage.

§3. SELF-HELP AND SELF-DEFENCE

187. The Civil Code also includes provisions on self-defence (*Notwehr*) and self-help (*Nothilfe*). According to section 227 BGB, action taken in order to repel an immediate unlawful attack upon oneself or another person is not unlawful. The underlying reason is the thought that law does not need to give way to injustice. Besides the protection of individual interests, the rules on self-defence also serve the protection of the legal system as a whole.[561] Section 227 BGB presupposes an attack. The term 'attack' only refers to pending violations of legally protected interests caused by human actions, although human conduct does not need to be culpable.[562] Hence, even a child can be an attacker in terms of section 227 BGB.[563] Animal attacks, on the other hand, fall exclusively under section 228 BGB unless the animal was used as a tool (or weapon) by a human.[564]

188. Section 227 BGB is applicable with respect to all kinds of legally protected interests, especially life, health, and freedom, but also property, the right to

559. *See* BGH, *NJW* 1972, 335, 337.
560. Cf. OLG Hamm, *NJW* 1995, 279: killing a shepherd dog in order to protect a flock of sheep.
561. Cf. Ellenberger, in: Grüneberg, BGB, § 227 No. 1 (82nd ed., 2023).
562. Ellenberger, in: Grüneberg, BGB, § 227 No. 2 (82nd ed., 2023); and Grothe, in: Münchener Kommentar zum BGB, § 227 Nos 4 et seq. (9th ed., 2021).
563. *See* Bayerisches Oberstes Landesgericht, *NJW* 1991, 2031.
564. Ellenberger, in: Grüneberg, BGB, § 227 No. 2 (82nd ed., 2023); and Mansel, in: Jauernig, BGB, § 227 No. 2 (18th ed., 2021).

one's personality, the right to one's own picture,[565] or even the freedom of movement in traffic.[566] The defence does apply not only with respect to the acting person's legally protected interests but also with respect to the protection of someone else's interests unless the self-help is against the will of that person.[567] Self-defence is limited by the principle of proportionality; the measures of self-defence shall be sufficient to avert the injury that may result from the attack, but the means also must be reasonable in light of the specific circumstances. Which defence would have been reasonable is determined by an objective test; the individual assessment of the person defending against an attack is irrelevant.[568] Anyone acting in self-defence usually has to choose the least harmful means in order to prevent an injury. However, he is not burdened with the risk of an insufficient defence.[569]

189. Rules on self-help are provided by sections 229–231 BGB. The term 'self-help' refers to the temporary enforcement or securing of a claim by means of private force.[570] According to section 229 BGB, the self-help defence requires an enforceable claim, i.e., a claim that can be enforced in judicial proceedings. A further requirement is that timely assistance from the competent legal authorities must not be available. Additionally, the realization of the claim must be endangered or significantly aggravated without an immediate intervention. The means of self-help are explicitly determined by section 229 BGB: the removal, destruction or damaging of an object; the arrest of a suspect (provided a risk of flight exists); and the overcoming of resistance against an action the other person is entitled to tolerate. Self-help is, however, not limitless. According to section 230(1) BGB, it may only be applied as long as it is necessary to avoid the danger. Furthermore, certain cases of self-help require subsequent confirmation by the court.[571] If a person acts in the erroneous assumption of a self-help situation, section 231 BGB entitles him to compensate the victim for damages regardless of whether his assumption was culpable or not. Specific self-help provisions are codified in section 562b BGB for landlords, in section 859 BGB for possessors of a chattel or real property, and in section 1029 BGB for possessors of real property who are disturbed in the execution of a real servitude.

§4. Others

190. Grounds of justification relevant for civil law claims may be found not only in the Civil Code but also in the Criminal Code (e.g., the necessity provision of

565. *See* OLG Hamburg, *NJW* 1972, 1290.
566. *See* OLG Schleswig, *NJW* 1984, 1470.
567. Ellenberger, in: Grüneberg, BGB, § 227 No. 3 (82nd ed., 2023); and Mansel, in: Jauernig, BGB, § 227 No. 3 (18th ed., 2021).
568. Cf. BGH, *NJW* 1974, 154; and Ellenberger, in: Grüneberg, BGB, § 227 No. 7 (82nd ed., 2023).
569. BGH, *NJW* 1976, 41, 42; and BGH, *NJW* 1991, 503, 504.
570. Ellenberger, in: Grüneberg, BGB, § 229 No. 1 (82nd ed., 2023); and Grothe, in: Münchener Kommentar zum BGB, § 229 No. 1 (9th ed., 2021).
571. For details *see* s. 230(2)–(4) BGB.

section 34 StGB). Likewise, a statutory authorization or a formal decree of a public authority authorizing certain activities which are suitable to cause damage to third parties may exclude unlawfulness.[572]

191. Another ground of justification, which is of specific importance regarding the right to one's personality, is the safeguarding of legitimate interests that can be derived as a general defence from the more specific section 824(2) BGB and section 193 StGB.[573] An infringement of protected interests is further not unlawful if the victim has an obligation to tolerate under section 906 BGB or section 14 BImSchG. Otherwise, the duty to compensate codified in section 906(2) sentence 2 BGB could be circumvented.[574]

192. The initiation of judicial proceedings generally is not unlawful with respect to the participating parties, provided the party initiating the proceedings acts in good faith (regardless of whether the claim later turns out to be unfounded).[575] The other party is obligated to rely on the judicial remedies provided by the legal system in order to look after his rights and interests.[576] However, unlawfulness is not excluded in cases of intentional abuse of legal proceedings or if a third party who is not involved in the proceedings is injured.[577]

572. Cf. Spindler, in: BeckOGK, BGB, § 823 Nos 90 et seq. (version 01.02.2023).
573. Spindler, in: BeckOGK, BGB, § 823 No. 81 (version 01.02.2023).
574. Cf. BGHZ 90, 255, 258; BGHZ 92, 143, 148; BGHZ 117, 110, 111; BGHZ 120, 239, 249; BGH, *NJW-RR* 2000, 537; and OLG Stuttgart, *NJW-RR* 2001, 1313, 1314.
575. Spindler, in: BeckOGK, BGB, § 823 No. 88 (version 01.02.2023).
576. *See* BVerfGE 74, 257; BGHZ 118, 201, 206; BGHZ 95, 10, 19; and BGHZ 74, 9, 17; *see also* BGHZ 36, 18, 21 et seq.
577. BGHZ 118, 201, 206 et seq.

Chapter 3. Contributory Fault

193. The contributory fault defence, codified in section 254 BGB, is a specific expression of the general principle of good faith.[578] According to section 254(1) BGB, the tortfeasor's liability will be reduced to the extent the victim's own negligence contributed to the damage. Moreover, section 254(2) sentence 1 BGB also states the victim's duty to avert or mitigate the damage. Section 254 BGB adheres to the concept of comparative liability. Contributory fault principally does not exclude the victim's claim as a whole; in most cases, responsibility is proportionally distributed among the parties according to the individual circumstances.

194. In the context of section 254 BGB, the term 'fault' does not refer to the culpable and unlawful violation of a legal duty since the victim is under no such duty to the tortfeasor. It rather refers to the victim's careless behaviour with respect to his own interests and belongings.[579] It, therefore, can be described as 'culpable conduct against oneself'.[580] Section 254 BGB requires, however, that the victim is capable of fault in terms of sections 827 and 828 BGB.[581] The victim must have the basic understanding that self-protection is necessary.[582] Nevertheless, section 829 BGB is also applicable by analogy.[583]

195. Culpable conduct has to be taken into account, regardless of the degree of the victim's carelessness. In order to determine the reduction of a claim, the judge has to weigh the extent of the wrongdoer's culpable conduct with the degree of carelessness attributable to the tort victim.[584] The specific circumstances of an individual case may, however, indicate a reduction of the victim's claim to zero (e.g., if the victim consciously acted to his own detriment). However, the victim's carelessness may be found insignificant if the wrongdoer has wilfully caused the damage.[585]

196. The victim's contributory fault may result from an act as well as from an omission. It may occur either before or after the damaging event. Section 254(2)

---

578. Cf. BGH, *NJW* 2014, 2493, 2494; BGH, *NJW* 1982, 168; and Grüneberg, in: Grüneberg, BGB, § 254 No. 1 (82nd ed., 2023).
579. Cf. BGH, *NJW* 2014, 2493, 2494; BGH, *NJW* 2009, 582, 585; Grüneberg, in: Grüneberg, BGB, § 254 No. 1 (82nd ed., 2023); and Oetker, in: Münchener Kommentar zum BGB, § 254 Nos 3 et seq. (9th ed., 2022).
580. *See* BGHZ 3, 46, 49; BGHZ 57, 137, 145; BGH, *NJW* 1970, 944, 946; BGH, *NJW* 2009, 582, 585; BGH, *NJW* 2014, 2493, 2494; and Oetker, in: Münchener Kommentar zum BGB, § 254 Nos 3 et seq. (9th ed., 2022).
581. RGZ 108, 87, 89; BGHZ 9, 316, 317; BGHZ 24, 325, 327; OLG Saarbrücken, *NJW* 2007, 1888, 1889; and OLG Stuttgart, *VersR* 2009, 206, 209.
582. OLG Celle, *NJW* 1968, 2146.
583. BGHZ 37, 102, 107; BGH, *NJW* 1973, 1795; and Grüneberg, in: Grüneberg, BGB, § 254 No. 9 (82nd ed., 2023).
584. Cf. BGH, *NJW* 2009, 582, 586.
585. *See* BGHZ 98, 148, 158; BGH, *NJW* 1980, 1518, 1519; and Grüneberg, in: Grüneberg, BGB, § 254 No. 65 (82nd ed., 2023).

sentence 1 BGB describes two cases of culpable omissions. In the first case, the victim has omitted to notify the wrongdoer with respect to the risk of exceptionally extensive damage, provided the latter did not and should not know of the risk.[586] In the other case, the victim has culpably omitted to avert or mitigate the damage. The tort victim has to apply all the care a reasonable person would consider necessary in light of the specific circumstances in order to prevent an impending danger.[587] For instance, a cyclist or a pedestrian has to slow down if he realizes that the driver of a motor vehicle does not intend to afford him his lawful right of way,[588] the passenger of a car has to fasten the safety belt,[589] and the rider of a motorcycle has to wear a helmet.[590] However, the tort victim is usually not obligated to raise a credit in order to provide interim financing with respect to the adjustment of the damage.[591]

197. Although section 254 BGB principally presupposes the careless conduct of the tort victim, the rule also applies to operational risks or hazards emanating from an object, provided they are attributable to the victim under considerations of strict liability.[592] For instance, if a cyclist negligently causes an accident resulting in the injury of the driver of a motor vehicle, the latter's claim will be reduced with respect to the vehicle's operational hazard, regardless of whether the driver also acted culpably.[593] Contributory negligence may further lead to a reduction of the victim's claim if the claim is based on one of the numerous strict liability provisions. The respective statutes, as a rule, explicitly refer to section 254 BGB.[594] If both parties are merely responsible for an operational hazard, liability is also proportionally distributed. Some of the strict liability statutes include specific provisions which order a division of liability.[595] The Federal Supreme Court also applies section 254 BGB if the victim acts at his own risk. Someone consciously exposing himself to danger has to accept a reduction of his claim.[596]

198. Section 254 BGB is also applicable to the victim's detriment if the careless conduct of his legal representatives or assistants has contributed to the damage. According to section 254(2) sentence 2 BGB, the rules of section 278 BGB are applicable *mutatis mutandis*. Although this reference seems to apply only with respect to the omissions described in section 254(2) sentence 1 BGB, it is generally accepted that it also applies to contributory fault regarding the causation of the damage as described in section 254(1) BGB.[597] The reference to section 278 BGB

586. *See* BGH, *NJW-RR* 2010, 909, 910.
587. BGHZ 3, 46, 49; and BGHZ 9, 316, 318.
588. Cf. Grüneberg, in: Grüneberg, BGB, § 254 No. 19 (82nd ed., 2023).
589. *See* BGHZ 74, 25 et seq.
590. BGH, *NJW* 1965, 1075.
591. *See* BGH, *NJW* 1989, 290, 291.
592. Cf. BGHZ 6, 319, 320; BGHZ 12, 124, 128; BGH, *VersR* 1981, 354, 355; and BGH, *NJW* 2013, 3235, 3237.
593. Cf. Grüneberg, in: Grüneberg, BGB, § 254 No. 10 (82nd ed., 2023).
594. *See*, e.g., s. 9 StVG, s. 4 HPflG, s. 6(1) ProdHaftG.
595. *See*, e.g., s. 17 StVG.
596. Cf. BGHZ 34, 355.
597. Constant case law since RGZ 62, 106, 108; *see also* BGH, *NJW* 2009, 582, 586.

shows, however, that an existing relationship under the law of obligations is required for the applicability of section 254 BGB with respect to the attribution of a representative's or an assistant's fault. Without such an existing obligation, the victim is responsible for his helpers only under the conditions of section 831 BGB.[598]

598. *See* BGHZ 1, 248, 249; BGHZ 73, 190, 192; BGHZ 103, 338, 342; and BGH, *NJW* 1980, 2573, 2575.

Chapter 4. Exemption Clauses

199. Exemption clauses are common in the area of contract law. Principally, tort liability may also be excluded by contractual agreements.[599] The parties must, however, explicitly (or, in case of a tacit agreement, at least sufficiently clearly) agree upon the extension of a contractual exclusion of liability to tort law claims.[600] Certain restrictions apply if an exemption clause is included in a standard form contract. According to section 309 No. 7b BGB, exclusions or limitations of liability for damages caused by a grossly negligent breach of duty by the user of a standard form contract or by a wilful or grossly negligent breach of duty by a statutory agent or servant of the user, are null and void if included in a consumer contract. Section 309 No. 7a BGB states further restrictions with respect to bodily injury. The user of a standard form contract may not exclude or limit his liability for negligently caused injury to life, body, or health. The same rules apply with respect to the wilful or negligent causation of such an injury by a statutory agent or servant of the user.

599. *See* Spindler, in: BeckOGK, BGB, § 823 No. 37 (version 01.02.2023).

600. Cf. BGH, *NJW* 1979, 2148; for a detailed description *see* Thyssen, *Die Haftungsfreizeichnung im Deliktsrecht und in der Gefährdungshaftung* (1997).

Part V. Causation

200. Causation is a crucial element of all tort law claims. The term 'causation' refers to a causal connection between the tortfeasor's conduct and the damage. German law basically distinguishes the causal connection between the tortfeasor's actions (or omissions) and the infringement of a legally protected interest, i.e., the causation that gives rise to liability (*haftungsbegründende Kausalität*) and the causal connection between the infringement and the resulting damage (*haftungsausfüllende Kausalität*).[601]

201. In a technical sense, causation means that an event is the necessary consequence of another event. Thus, the wrongdoer's conduct has to be a *conditio sine qua non* of the victim's injury. The test is whether the injury would have occurred but for the tortfeasor's conduct ('but-for' test).[602] In this context, all human conduct can be a cause, regardless of whether it is an action or an omission. In contrast to positive actions, omissions cannot start a causal chain. Therefore, the 'but-for' test of the *conditio sine qua non* formula must be slightly modified; an omission has caused the infringement of a legally protected interest if the omitted action could not be (hypothetically) added without the infringement being lost.[603] The mere possibility that the infringement would not have happened had the wrongdoer carried out the activity is not enough.[604]

202. Difficulties with respect to the 'but-for' test may arise in cases of multiple causation, especially mass tort cases, in which the damage was caused by more than one tortfeasor or at least could have been caused in various ways. No problems arise, however, when several persons jointly commit a tort. Each tortfeasor is responsible for the damage.[605] If the damage is caused by two independent events, each of which would alone be suitable to cause the harm, they are both considered

601. *See* Grüneberg, in: Grüneberg, BGB, Vorb v § 249 No. 24 (82nd ed., 2023); Oetker, in: Münchener Kommentar, BGB, § 249 No. 105 (9th ed., 2022); and Teichmann, in: Jauernig, BGB, Vor §§ 249–253 No. 24 (18th ed., 2021).
602. *See* Spindler, *AcP* 208 (2008), 283, 285 et seq.; Grüneberg, in: Grüneberg, BGB, Vorb v § 249 No. 25 (82nd ed., 2023); Markesinis, Bell and Janssen, *Markesinis's German Law of Torts* 61 (5th ed., 2019); Teichmann, in: Jauernig, BGB, Vor §§ 249–253 No. 26 (18th ed., 2021); and BGH, *NJW* 2011, 2690, 2963.
603. Constant case law of the Federal Supreme Court: cf. BGH, *NJW* 1961, 868, 870; BGH, *NJW* 1973, 1688; and BGH, *NJW* 2003, 295, 296.
604. *See* BGHZ 64, 46, 51; and BGH, *NJW* 1984, 432, 434.
605. *See* s. 830(1) sentence 1 BGB.

to be causal in a legal sense (*Doppelkausalität*).[606] However, if each of the two events only partially caused the damage, the judge has to determine the shares of liability according to section 287 ZPO.[607] Whenever it remains doubtful who of two or more persons participating in a tortious conduct actually caused the damage, they are jointly and severally liable according to section 830(1) sentence 2 BGB (*alternative Kausalität*). A precondition is that two or more persons independently acted in a tortious way that was generally suitable to cause harm. It must be certain that one of them initiated the cause for the damage.[608] If, however, at least the causal involvement of one of two or more wrongdoers is certain, the others, who only possibly also set a cause, are not liable under section 830(1) sentence 2 BGB.[609] Abettors and assistants are liable to the same extent the tortfeasor is liable.[610]

203. Since the *conditio sine qua non* principle leaves a multitude of activities as causes for the violation of legally protected interests, it is generally viewed as insufficient. To limit the extensive scope of liability left after the application of the *conditio sine qua non* formula, German scholars and courts have developed a concept of legal cause, which is described as 'adequate causation' (*adäquate Kausalität*).[611] According to the theory of adequate causation, an action or omission is a relevant cause only if it is not just under particularly exceptional and extremely unlikely circumstances but generally suitable to produce a certain result.[612] The wrongdoer's point of view is irrelevant for the determination of adequacy; the test rather is an objective *ex post* analysis. All circumstances that could be recognized by an 'optimal observer' at the time of the wrongdoer's conduct have to be taken into account.[613] The optimal observer is virtually omniscient. The entire available know-how has to be considered.[614] Consequences, which are covered by the wrongdoer's intent, are always adequately caused.[615] Furthermore, adequacy is not excluded if a noticeable risk materializes in a completely unusual manner.[616]

204. As a result of the optimal observer approach, the theory of adequate causation also reduces the multitude of relevant causes only slightly. Another way to limit liability is a reference to the scope of the violated rule (*Schutzzweck der Norm*). According to this theory, the infringement of a legally protected interest (or

606. *See* BGH, *VersR* 1971, 818, 819; BGH, *VersR* 1983, 731, 732; BGH, *NJW* 1992, 2691, 2692; BGH, *NJW-RR* 2012, 728, 730; BGH, *NJW* 2013, 2018, 2019; and BGH, *WM* 2014, 1447, 1449.
607. *See* BGH, *LM* BGB § 276 (Ca) No. 11; BGH, *LM* BGB § 823 (C) No. 4; and BGH, *VersR* 1964, 49, 51.
608. BGHZ 25, 271.
609. BGHZ 67, 14; and BGH, *NJW* 1999, 2895.
610. *See* s. 830(2) BGB.
611. *See* RGZ 50, 219, 222; cf. BGH, *NJW* 2011, 2690, 2964; BAG, *NJW* 2009, 251, 255; and Spindler, *AcP* 208 (2008), 283, 286.
612. *See* RGZ 133, 126, 127; BGH, *NJW* 2002, 2232, 2233; BAG, *NJW* 2009, 251, 255; BGH, *NJW* 2011, 2690, 2964; and OLG Hamm, *NJW-RR* 2013, 349, 350.
613. Cf. BGHZ 3, 261, 266; OLG München, *VersR* 1991, 1391; and OLG Hamm, *NJW-RR* 2013, 349, 350.
614. BGH, *VersR* 1972, 67, 69.
615. BGHZ 79, 259, 262.
616. BGH, *VersR* 1961, 465.

the damage) must fall within the protective ambit of the contractual or statutory duty breached by the wrongdoer. In other words, the wrongdoer's conduct must be the kind of mischief the violated rule was designed to prevent.[617] The theory of the violated rule's scope had first been elaborated for contractual claims.[618] However, today, it is generally recognized by German courts that it also applies to tort law claims.[619] An example of damages that are not covered by the protective purpose of the violated rule is a decrease in earnings attributable to an early retirement following the discovery of arteriosclerosis after the victim of an accident was admitted to the hospital.[620] Likewise, the victim of a traffic accident cannot obtain recovery of his litigation costs for criminal proceedings that were instituted in connection with the accident.[621]

205. Specific problems arise with respect to the so-called hypothetical causation (hypothetische *Kausalität*). In a case of hypothetical causation, the damage caused by the tortfeasor would have been caused by another person if the tortfeasor had refrained from his conduct. German courts and commentators disagree upon the relevance of such a 'reserve cause' (*Reserveursache*).[622] In a factual sense, the actual cause is a *conditio sine qua non*, notwithstanding a potential alternative cause. Hence, all reserve causes would be immaterial.[623] However, today, it is agreed upon that hypothetical reserve causes may be relevant in a legal sense. Hypothetical causes are usually taken into account whenever an injured person or a damaged object already had the disposition for the damage. In such a situation, the wrongdoer only has to compensate the tort victim for the object's value in consideration of the disposition. This may, under certain circumstances, lead to a reduction of the claim to zero.[624] It has to be kept in mind, however, that the tortfeasor has to prove the disposition of the damage.[625] In most cases, this amounts to an insuperable barrier. In contrast to the cases of imminent damage, reserve causes are generally irrelevant if they occur after the tortfeasor's liability has already arisen.[626] Otherwise, the tort victim would be left with no claim at all: The wrongdoer could refer to the hypothetical cause, and the reserve cause did not actually cause the damage. An exception is made, however, for consequential damages (*Folgeschäden*), such as

617. Cf. BGHZ 27, 137, 140; BGHZ 35, 311, 315; BGHZ 57, 245, 256; BGH, *NJW* 1999, 3203; BGH, *NJW* 2011, 2690, 2964; BGH, *NJW* 2013, 1679, 1680; BGH, *NJW* 2014, 2190, 2191; and Spindler, *AcP* 208 (2008), 283, 287.
618. The theory has been developed by Rabel, *Das Recht des Warenkaufs* 495 et seq. (1936).
619. *See,* e.g., BGHZ 27, 137, 138; BGH NJW 1958, 1041 (for claims based on s. 823(1) BGB); BGHZ 96, 231, 236 (for claims based on s. 826 BGB); BGHZ 39, 358, 365; BGHZ 90, 310, 312 (for claims based on s. 839 BGB); BGH, *NJW* 2013, 1679, 1680 (for claims based on s. 823(2) BGB and s. 7 StVG); and BGH, *NJW* 2014, 2190, 2191.
620. Cf. BGH, *NJW* 1968, 2287.
621. Cf. BGHZ 27, 137, 140 et seq.
622. *See* Grüneberg, in: Grüneberg, BGB, Vorb v § 249 Nos 55 et seq. (82nd ed., 2023); and Oetker, in: Münchener Kommentar, BGB, § 249 Nos 207 et seq. (9th ed., 2022).
623. This used to bet the position of the Supreme Court of the German Reich, *see* RGZ 141, 365, 367; RGZ 144, 80, 84; and RGZ 169, 117, 120.
624. Cf. BGHZ 20, 275; and BGHZ 29, 207, 215.
625. *See* BGHZ 8, 288; and BGH, *VersR* 1969, 43, 44.
626. *See* BGHZ 29, 207, 215.

continuing reductions in earning capacity, provided the reserve cause would not have resulted in a claim against a third party.[627]

206. In some cases, the damage is caused merely by inducing another person to inflict damage upon himself or upon a third person. The actual injurious conduct is a reaction to the inducement. If the person setting the incentive would always be responsible for any kind of 'psychic causation' (*psychische Kausalität*), the risk of liability would be immense. Therefore, German courts restrict accountability by evaluating the specific circumstances of each individual case. The Federal Supreme Court principally asks if the tortfeasor's conduct has provoked the victim's or a third party's decision to act and if the person actually causing the damage legitimately felt provoked to act.[628] A provocation (*Herausforderung*) that is suitable to attribute the damage to the person setting the inducement is usually affirmed by the Federal Supreme Court if the acting person had a basically acceptable motivation for his conduct.[629] Hence, the tortfeasor is only liable if he creates an increased risk;[630] he is not liable for the general risk to life.

627. *See* BGH, *DB* 1979, 352; and Grüneberg, in: Grüneberg, BGB, Vorb v § 249 No. 62 (82nd ed., 2023).
628. *See* BGH, *ZIP* 2001, 338, 339 et seq.
629. Cf. BGH, *NJW* 2012, 1951, 1952; BGH, *NJW* 2002, 2232, 2233; BGH, *NJW* 1987, 2925, 2926; and BGH, *NJW* 1978, 421, 422.
630. Cf. BGH, *NJW* 1997, 865, 866; BGH, *NJW* 2012, 1951, 1952; and OLG Hamm, *NJW-RR* 2013, 349, 351.

Part VI. Remedies

Chapter 1. General Principles

207. The German Civil Code includes a number of general provisions on remedies in sections 249–254 BGB. Specific provisions for tort law claims are codified in sections 842–851 BGB. Furthermore, the general rules of the Civil Code are also supplemented by the numerous strict liability laws, which also include rules on the assessment of damages.[631]

208. The regular remedy under German tort law is compensation for the loss suffered by the victim. The basic aim of the Civil Code's provisions on remedies is to put the victim in the same position he would be in without the injury. Section 249(1) BGB principally orders a priority of restitution in kind (*Naturalrestitution*) over monetary compensation; a person obligated to make compensation shall restore the situation that would have existed if the circumstances invoking liability had not occurred. Hence, the victim can require the tortfeasor to take the necessary measures to restore the *status quo ante*. Since an exact restoration is usually not possible, section 249(1) BGB has to be read to the effect that it simply demands the restoration of an economically comparable situation.[632]

209. In case of bodily injury or property damage, however, the victim may choose monetary compensation.[633] Moreover, the victim may also demand compensation in money if the liable tortfeasor does not provide restitution in kind within a reasonable period set by the victim, provided the victim has declared that he will not accept restitution in kind after the period's expiration.[634] Finally, only monetary compensation can be claimed if restitution in kind is impossible or insufficient to compensate the victim.[635] According to section 251(2) BGB, the tortfeasor may opt for compensation in money if compensation in kind would require disproportionate efforts. In this case, the tortfeasor has to bear the burden of proof.[636] Expenditures

631. *See.* e.g., ss 7–11 ProdHaftG, ss 5–10 HPflG, ss 9–13 StVG, and ss 12–16 UmweltHG.
632. Cf. RGZ 76, 146.
633. *See* s. 249(2) sentence 1 BGB.
634. *See* s. 250 BGB.
635. *See* s. 251(1) BGB.
636. BGH, *NJW* 2011, 1145, 1146; BGH, *NJW* 2010, 1068, 1070; BGH, *NJW* 2009, 1066, 1067; and Oetker, in: Münchener Kommentar, BGB, § 251 No. 75 (9th ed., 2022).

incurred in healing an animal, however, are not disproportionate for the single reason that they exceed the animal's value.[637] Conversely, the recovery of sensitive data deleted from a laptop computer provided by the employer could constitute such a disproportionate effort within the meaning of section 251(2) BGB.[638]

210. The compensation owed by the tortfeasor also includes lost profit.[639] As a rule, the victim has to prove the damage. However, section 252 sentence 2 BGB states that profit is deemed to have been lost if, in the ordinary course of events or in the particular circumstances of the individual case, especially with respect to the preparations and provisions made, it could have been expected with probability. Additionally, section 287 ZPO allows the judge to estimate occurrence as well as the scope of the damage if it is in dispute. Section 253(1) BGB limits compensation in money for non-pecuniary harm to the cases specified by law. According to section 253(2) BGB, the injured party may demand fair compensation in money for non-pecuniary damages in case of injury to his body or health, the deprivation of freedom, or a violation of the right to sexual self-determination.

211. The term 'damage' is usually defined as any detriment that has been caused to a person with respect to the person's rights or legally protected interests.[640] Pecuniary damage is commonly determined by an assessment of the difference between the victim's actual wealth and the hypothetical wealth the victim would have without the damaging event (*Differenzhypothese*).[641] Thus, the damage consists of a decrease in assets and lost profit. However, if the tort victim also receives benefits from the damaging event, the compensation may be adjusted by these benefits (*Vorteilsausgleichung*), resulting in a reduction of the victim's claim,[642] provided that the reduction does not run counter to the purposes of compensation and, additionally, does not unreasonably favour the tortfeasor.[643]

637. *See* s. 251(1) sentence 2 BGB.
638. Cf. BGH, *NJW* 2009, 1066, 1067 et seq.
639. *See* s. 252 BGB.
640. Cf. Grüneberg, in: Grüneberg, BGB, Vorb v § 249 No. 9 (82nd ed., 2023).
641. BGH, *NJW* 1958, 1085; BGHZ 99, 182, 196 et seq.; BGH, *NJW* 1994, 2357, 2359; BGH, *NJW-RR* 2005, 611, 612; BGH, *NJW* 2012, 675, 676; *see* Grüneberg, in: Grüneberg, BGB, Vorb v § 249 No. 10 (82nd ed., 2023); and Oetker, in: Münchener Kommentar, BGB, § 249 Nos 16 et seq. (9th ed., 2022).
642. Cf. BGH, *NJW* 2012, 675, 676; BGH, *NJW* 2009, 1870, 1871; BGH, *NJW* 2007, 3130, 3132; BGH, *NJW* 2006, 499; Grüneberg, in: Grüneberg, BGB, Vorb v § 249 Nos 67 et seq. (82nd ed., 2023); and Teichmann, in: Jauernig, BGB, Vor §§ 249–253 Nos 40 et seq. (18th ed., 2021); *see also* Part VI, Ch. 3, §4.
643. BGH, *NJW* 2012, 675, 676; BGH, *NJW* 2009, 1870, 1871; BGH, *NJW* 2007, 3130, 3132; BGH, *NJW* 2006, 499; BGH, *NJW* 1990, 1360; and Oetker, in: Münchener Kommentar, BGB, § 249 Nos 235 et seq. (9th ed., 2022).

Chapter 2. Kinds of Damages

§1. Individual and Collective Damage

212. Unlike other legal systems, German tort law makes no distinction between individual and collective damage. It adheres to a strictly individualistic approach. Hence, even in a mass tort situation with multiple victims, the individual damage of each particular victim has to be allocated. The German Code of Civil Procedure does not provide rules for any kind of class action comparable to the US model.

§2. Direct and Indirect Damage

213. As discussed above, damage principally is defined as any detriment caused to a person with respect to his rights or legally protected interests. Liability under the rules of German civil law encompasses direct damage (*unmittelbarer Schaden*), i.e., the deterioration of the infringed right or interest, as well as indirect damage (*mittelbarer Schaden*), i.e., further damage resulting from the initial infringement. Among the items falling under direct damage are the replacement costs in case of the loss or destruction of an object, the costs of repair and, in case of injury to body or health, the medical costs and nursing expenses.[644] According to German courts, the loss in value upon resale regarding a damaged automobile or a damaged building is also direct damage.[645] The other impairments caused by the damaging event, such as lost profit[646] or loss of use, are indirect damages.[647] Although compensation for indirect damage is not excluded in principle, the distinction is of relevance with respect to the scope of the compensation owed by the tortfeasor in cases of hypothetical causation.[648]

§3. Pecuniary and Non-pecuniary Loss

214. The tort victim has suffered pecuniary loss (*Vermögensschaden*) if his actual present wealth is less than the wealth he would have without the damaging event. In principle, pecuniary loss may be compensated in money or kind. A person's wealth consists of all goods that can be measured in terms of money. Non-pecuniary loss (*Nichtvermögensschaden*) is an impairment of a person's rights or legally protected interests that does not result in a reduction of wealth. As seen above, monetary compensation for non-pecuniary harm is limited by section 253(1) BGB to the cases specified by law. Such a case specified by law is compensation for pain and suffering in case of injury to body, health, freedom, or the right to

644. *See* Grüneberg, in: Grüneberg, BGB, Vorb v § 249 No. 15 (82nd ed., 2023).
645. Cf. BGH, *VersR* 1969, 473, 474; and OLG Frankfurt, *BB* 1991, 503.
646. *See* s. 252 BGB.
647. *See* Grüneberg, in: Grüneberg, BGB, Vorb v § 249 No. 15 (82nd ed., 2023).
648. *See* Part V.

sexual self-determination.[649] Although not explicitly specified by the law, it is generally recognized by German courts and commentators that the victim may also demand compensation for pain and suffering in case of infringements of the right to one's personality.[650]

215. Section 253(1) BGB only affects compensation in money. The tort victim's claim for compensation in kind pursuant to section 249(1) is not excluded by section 253(1) BGB. However, in case of non-pecuniary harm, restitution in kind is often impossible and, therefore, only of limited significance. An example of restitution in kind in case of non-pecuniary harm would be the retraction of defamatory statements.[651]

216. In order to determine the nature of the damage, it has to be ascertained whether the victim's wealth has decreased. Although the definition of 'wealth' appears to be straightforward at first glance, the classification of damage as pecuniary or non-pecuniary loss may bring about difficult demarcation problems, especially with respect to temporary limitations of the ability to use an object. The case law on the question of whether a mere restriction of use amounts to pecuniary harm is extremely rich. On the one hand, German courts consider the temporary unavailability of an automobile a pecuniary loss and, thereby, an item of damage for which recovery can be obtained (even if the victim does not rent a replacement vehicle)[652] unless the victim would not or could not have used it anyway.[653] On the other hand, temporary use restrictions are viewed as non-pecuniary harm if they concern the ability to use a caravan,[654] a swimming pool,[655] a fur coat,[656] a speedboat,[657] or a garage.[658] In a more recent decision, the Federal Supreme Court was confronted with the question of whether the restriction of means of modern communication, i.e., the connection to the internet, amounts to pecuniary harm within the meaning of section 253(1) BGB. By virtue of the increasing importance of internet connectivity as an economic commodity and the role thereof in daily life, the Court rightfully concluded that the deprivation of internet access is comparable to the temporary unavailability of an automobile and, therefore, constitutes a loss position within the meaning of section 253(1) BGB.[659]

217. According to a widely criticized decision of the Federal Supreme Court, the award of damages in these cases depends on whether the respective objects play a

649. *See* s. 253(2) BGB.
650. Cf. BVerfG, *NJW* 2000, 2187; and BGH, *NJW* 2000, 2195, 2197.
651. Cf. Grüneberg, in: Grüneberg, BGB, § 253 No. 3 (82nd ed., 2023).
652. *See* BGHZ 40, 345; BGHZ 45, 212; BGHZ 88, 11; and BGH, *NJW* 1985, 2471.
653. Cf. BGH, *NJW* 1968, 1778.
654. *See* BGHZ 86, 128.
655. *See* BGHZ 76, 179, 180.
656. *See* BGHZ 63, 393, 394.
657. *See* BGHZ 89, 60.
658. *See* BGH, *NJW* 1993, 1793.
659. *See* BGH, *VersR* 2013, 587; and Spindler, *JZ* 2013, 897, 898.

vital and fundamental role in everyday life.[660] The term 'fundamental role' is construed rather narrowly: While a fundamental role in everyday life is attributed to the matrimonial home,[661] parts of an apartment that are merely of marginal importance, such as an internal flat that is used only occasionally, do not meet the criterion.[662] The view of the Federal Supreme Court is based on the notion that the use of an object as such already represents an economic value (*Kommerzialisierungsgedanke*). Another theory to achieve the recoverability of actual immaterial harm is the so-called frustration approach (*Frustrationstheorie*). According to this theory, frustrated expenditures (i.e., expenditures invested by the victim to use an object that became futile because of the damaging event) are generally seen as a pecuniary loss. The Federal Supreme Court, however, rejected a general frustration approach.[663]

218. Another problem related to the commercialization of non-pecuniary interests is the question of whether a tort victim may claim compensation for the lost enjoyment of a holiday (i.e., the loss of leisure and recreation). In its famous 'Cruise' case, the Federal Supreme Court held that the delight of a holiday may represent a pecuniary interest that can give rise to pecuniary loss if partially or wholly ruined.[664] Other decisions also showed a tendency to accept the idea of commercialization with respect to 'lost holiday'.[665] Since 10 October 1979, however, the legislator adopted this view solely in the area of contract law: According to section 651n(2) BGB, a traveller is entitled to reasonable compensation in money regarding the uselessly spent holiday time, whenever his voyage is thwarted or significantly spoiled. Consequently, the Federal Supreme Court held in a leading case that compensation for the loss of leisure and recreation in case of a ruined vacation could no longer be claimed under the rules of tort law.[666]

219. Even under the commercialization approach, the tort victim cannot claim recovery for the infringement of a mere affection interest (*Affektionsinteresse*). Hence, German courts have, *inter alia*, denied compensation for a film with Antarctic photographs that was lost in the mail.[667]

§4. Pure Economic Loss

220. Pure economic loss (*reiner Vermögensschaden*) is fully recoverable under the rules of contract law. In case of a contractual relation, the close bond between

660. Cf. BGHZ 98, 212, 220.
661. Cf. BGHZ 98, 212, 224.
662. Cf. BGHZ 117, 260, 262.
663. *See*, e.g., BGHZ 55, 146, 151; BGHZ 71, 234, 237; BGHZ 99, 182, 197; BGHZ 114, 196; BGH, *NJW* 1991, 2708; and BGH, *NJW* 2000, 2342.
664. *See* BGH, *NJW* 1956, 1234, 1235.
665. Cf. BGHZ 63, 98; BGHZ 77, 116, 124; BGHZ 80, 366; BGHZ 82, 219; and BGHZ 85, 50.
666. *See* BGHZ 86, 212; *see also* OLG Düsseldorf, *NJW-RR* 2007, 854, 855.
667. *See* LG Hamburg, *NJW-RR* 2000, 653.

the contracting parties justifies the far-reaching liability: the required privity of contract ensures that liability is not limitless. In contrast to the rules of contractual liability, German tort law does not generally allow compensation for pure economic loss. Pure economic interests are protected as such only by certain provisions. Moreover, the rules of the Civil Code providing compensation for pure economic loss usually presuppose a 'qualified' tortious conduct.

221. While section 823(1) BGB, the most important provision of German tort law, allows recovery for economic loss only if one of the enumerated rights or interests is violated, pure economic loss is fully recoverable under section 826 BGB in case of wilful damage contrary to public policy. According to section 826 BGB, the tortfeasor shall be responsible not only for bodily injury, damage to property, or the violation of other absolute rights but also for pure economic loss resulting from such conduct. Furthermore, a person infringing a statute intended for the protection of others is also liable for pure economic loss under section 823(2) BGB, provided the statute was designed to protect economic interests.

222. As described above, in addition to the differences regarding vicarious liability, the restricted recoverability of pure economic loss under the rules of tort law is one of the main reasons for the extensive application of contractual liability by German courts (e.g., pre-contractual liability or contracts with protective effects for a third party).[668]

§5. Actual and Future Damage

223. Pursuant to section 249(1) BGB, a person obligated to make compensation shall restore the situation that would have existed if the circumstances invoking liability had not occurred. This paraphrase undoubtedly implies compensation for actual damage. Under the terms of section 252 sentence 1 BGB, the tort victim may also claim lost profit. However, this provision has a mere descriptive function. Compensation for lost profit can already be claimed as restitution in kind under the general rule of section 249(1) BGB.[669] The term 'lost profit' relates to all advantages not attributable to the tort victim's assets at the time of the damaging act that would have become part of his assets devoid of the damaging act.[670] Hence, section 252 BGB is also applicable if, because of the tortious conduct, the victim forfeits a gratuitous benefit or a claim to unemployment benefit.[671] Lost profits from prohibited activities, however, are not compensable.[672] Thus, the tort victim cannot, e.g., claim

668. *See* General Introduction, § 5.
669. *See* BGH, *NJW* 1987, 50, 52.
670. Cf. BGH, *WM* 2009, 1145, 1147; BGH, *NJW* 2000, 2669, 2670; and Grüneberg, in: Grüneberg, BGB, § 252 No. 1 (82nd ed., 2023).
671. Grüneberg, in: Grüneberg, BGB, § 252 No. 1 (82nd ed., 2023).
672. BGH, *NJW* 1980, 775.

lost profits deriving from unlawful advertising efforts.[673] With respect to illegal contracts, lost profit is not compensable if the contract's content violates a statutory prohibition in terms of section 134 BGB.[674] As a consequence, there is no duty to compensate the tort victim for lost earnings deriving from illicit employment.[675]

224. Section 252 sentence 1 BGB is complemented by section 252 sentence 2 BGB, which codifies an exception from the general rule that the tort victim has to prove his damages in order to claim compensation. The provision states that potential earnings are deemed to be lost profit if, in the ordinary course of events or in the particular conditions of the individual case, especially with respect to the preparations and provisions made, such earnings could have been expected with a high degree of probability. The tort victim only has to prove the circumstances that give rise to the probability of future earnings in the ordinary course of events or the specific situation of the case.[676] The Federal Supreme Court is anxious not to overstrain the tort victim's ability to supply such evidence.[677] The thwarting of a mere chance of earning, however, does not justify a claim for lost profit.[678] Since section 252 sentence 2 BGB refers to the ordinary course of events, the rule permits an abstract assessment of damages.[679]

§6. Other Costs

225. The tort victim may also claim compensation for costs spent on the assessment of damages. Hence, the wrongdoer is liable, e.g., for the victim's expenditures for an expert opinion as long as they are necessary for the appropriate prosecution of an action.[680] Moreover, the recoverable damage may also include expenses for the discovery and return of an abducted child,[681] costs of private investigators,[682] costs of interpreters,[683] or even a reward for the return of stolen items.[684] Although a tort victim is not entitled to monetary compensation for the time spent for the extrajudicial settlement of a claim, he may nevertheless claim recovery for the costs of obtaining judicial or extrajudicial payment.[685] This claim for reimbursement of

673. *See* BGH, *NJW* 1964, 1181, 1183; and Grüneberg, in: Grüneberg, BGB, § 252 No. 2 (82nd ed., 2023).
674. BGH, *NJW* 1980, 775; *see also* LG Düsseldorf, *NJW-RR* 2012, 1401, 1403.
675. LG Karlsruhe, *NJW* 1975, 1420; and LG Oldenburg, *NJW-RR* 1988, 1496.
676. BGH, *NJW* 1964, 661, 662; BGH, *NJW* 1970, 1411, 1412; BGH, *NJW* 2011, 1145, 1146; and BGH, *NJW* 2012, 2266.
677. Cf. BGH, *NJW* 1959, 1079; BGH, *NJW* 1987, 1703, 1707; BGH, *NJW* 1993, 1989, 1990; BGH, *NJW* 2000, 3287, 3288; and BGH, *NJW* 2011, 1145, 1146; *see also* BAG, *NJW* 2013, 331, 332.
678. BGH, *NJW* 1983, 442, 443; and BGH, *NJW* 2012, 2266.
679. *See* BGH, *NJW* 1959, 1079; BGH, *NJW* 1974, 895; BGH, *NJW* 1988, 2234, 2236; and BAG, *NJW* 2013, 331, 332.
680. BGH, *NJW* 1974, 34, 35; BGH, *NJW-RR* 1989, 956; and Oetker, in: Münchener Kommentar, BGB, § 249 Nos 180 et seq. (9th ed., 2022).
681. *See* OLG Koblenz, *NJW-RR* 1994, 899.
682. *See* BGH, *NJW* 1990, 2060, 2061; and BAG, *NZA-RR* 2011, 231, 232.
683. *See* AG Osnabrück, *VersR* 1989, 1277.
684. *See* BGH, *VersR* 1967, 1168, 1169.
685. Cf. Grüneberg, in: Grüneberg, BGB, § 249 Nos 56 et seq. (82nd ed., 2023).

the costs and expenses relating to substantive law is independent of the entitlement to costs under the rules of civil procedure.[686]

226. Under the provisions of the German Code of Civil Procedure, the party winning a lawsuit does not have to contribute to the costs of the proceedings and may recover from the other party the expenses for his attorney. According to section 91(1) ZPO, the party losing a lawsuit in its entirety has to bear all costs of the proceedings and the other parties' costs of legal counsel. Whenever a party is only partially successful in a lawsuit, the court has to either proportionally distribute the costs among the parties or offset the costs of each party according to section 92(1) ZPO. Despite being successful in a lawsuit, a party causing additional (unnecessary) costs, e.g., in case of unsuccessful offensive or defensive means or an interlocutory judgment by default, has to bear part of the costs.[687] Moreover, a party who has unnecessarily initiated a lawsuit has to bear the costs of the proceedings if the defendant immediately admits the claim unless the defendant's conduct gave the plaintiff reason to file a civil action.[688]

§7. Mitigation of Damages

227. According to section 254(2) sentence 1 BGB, the tort victim is obligated to avert or mitigate the damage. The provision does not stipulate an enforceable legal duty but rather an obligation the tort victim should observe in his own interest. The Civil Code does not explicitly state the actions to be implemented by the tort victim in order to comply with this obligation. To act in accordance with section 254(2) sentence 1 BGB, the tort victim has to take all necessary measures a conscientious and understanding person would take.[689] A concretion of this formula has to take into account the specific circumstances of each individual case.[690] The victim's expenditures for averting or mitigating the damage are part of the compensation owed by the tortfeasor,[691] regardless of whether his measures were successful.[692]

686. *See* BGHZ 66, 112, 114.
687. *See* s. 95 Zivilprozessordnung (ZPO) (interlocutory judgment by default) and s. 96 ZPO (unsuccessful offensive or defensive means).
688. *See* s. 93 ZPO; instructive: OLG München, *NJW-RR* 2012, 42, 43.
689. BGH, *NJW* 1952, 299, 300; and Grüneberg, in: Grüneberg, BGB, § 254 No. 36 (82nd ed., 2023).
690. For an instructive compilation of the Federal Supreme Court's jurisdiction, *see* Looschelders, in: BeckOGK, BGB, § 254 Nos 256 et seq. (version 01.02.2023); and Grüneberg, in: Grüneberg, BGB, § 254 Nos 38 et seq. (82nd ed., 2023).
691. BGH, *NJW* 1993, 2685, 2687.
692. BGH, *NJW* 1959, 933, 934; and Grüneberg, in: Grüneberg, BGB, § 254 No. 36 (82nd ed., 2023).

Chapter 3. Assessment and Compensation of Damages

§1. Objective Versus Subjective

228. In case of injury to property, the creditor of a claim for damages is usually entitled to compensation amounting to the damaged object's common value (*gemeiner Wert*). The ordinary or common value of an object is the value it has for anybody. It is determined by an objective test. Usually, the common value is indicated by the market price. Under the objective method, the specific worth the item might have for the tort victim is irrelevant. The assessment is to be accomplished without considering the framework of personal relations within which the damaged object has been placed.

229. However, under the rules of German tort law, the specific value an item subjectively bears for the tort victim is also recoverable. The subjective method of assessment complies with the basic aim of the Civil Code's provisions on remedies, which is to put the victim in the same position he would be in without the injury. The specific value an item may have for the victim usually exceeds the market value. If a piece of the victim's collection is destroyed, the damage consists not only of the single object's loss but also of the decrease in value of the collection as a whole.

230. Nonetheless, the tort victim may not claim recovery for the infringement of a mere affection interest.[693] The main reason for this limitation is the missing calculability of such immaterial damages.

§2. Concrete Versus Abstract

231. Under German tort law, the damage may be assessed either concretely or abstractly. Principally, the compensable damage must be assessed concretely.[694] Decisive factors are the actual decrease in wealth as well as a failing materialization of an increase in wealth. The victim may claim recovery for his whole economic interest.[695]

232. An abstract calculation of damages, however, takes into account the usual course of events. Pursuant to section 252 sentence 2 BGB, an abstract assessment of damages is permissible with respect to lost profits:[696] profit is deemed to have been lost if it could have been expected with probability according to the particular

693. *See* Part VI, Ch. 2, §3.
694. *See* Grüneberg, in: Grüneberg, BGB, Vorb v § 249 No. 21 (82nd ed., 2023); and Teichmann, in: Jauernig, BGB, Vor §§ 249–253 No. 58 (18th ed., 2021).
695. *See* Grüneberg, in: Grüneberg, BGB, Vorb v § 249 No. 21 (82nd ed., 2023).
696. *See* Part VI, Ch. 3, §5.

circumstances or the ordinary course of events. However, the tortfeasor is free to furnish proof that the actual damage is less than the abstract damage under section 252 BGB.[697]

233. The tort victim may claim the market price of a damaged object as minimum compensation (*Mindestschaden*). With respect to the damaging of an object, this follows directly from section 249(2) sentence 1 BGB, which states that the victim, in case of damage to an object, may demand the amount of money necessary to effect an object's restitution instead of restitution in kind. Regarding the destruction or deprivation of an object, it follows from the general principle that pecuniary damage is calculated by an assessment of the difference between the victim's actual wealth and the hypothetical wealth he would have without the damaging event.

§3. Methods of Assessing Damages

234. As a rule, German tort law requires a concrete assessment of damages. An abstract assessment is, however, permissible with respect to lost profit.[698]

§4. Equitable Limitation of Damages

235. Usually, there is no equitable limitation of damages under German tort law. However, as in all areas of private law, tort law claims have to be viewed against the background of the principle of good faith. A specific expression of this principle is section 254 BGB, according to which claims can be reduced in case of contributory fault.[699]

236. Another example is the adjustment of damages by benefits received (*Vorteilsausgleichung*). If the victim gains pecuniary advantages from the damaging event, such benefits may result in a reduction of the victim's claim in order to compensate for the advantages.[700] Mitigation of damages by benefits received requires a causal connection between the damaging event and the benefits.[701] Furthermore, the adjustment of damages has to be in accordance with the compensation's purpose, i.e., the adjustment shall not be unreasonably burdensome for the victim and not inequitably disencumbering for the tortfeasor.[702]

---

697. Cf. BGHZ 29, 393, 398; BGHZ 74, 221, 224; and BGH, *NJW* 1983, 758.
698. *See* Part VI, Ch. 3, §2.
699. *See* Part IV, Ch. 3.
700. Cf. Grüneberg, in: Grüneberg, BGB, Vorb v § 249 Nos 67 et seq. (82nd ed., 2023); and Teichmann, in: Jauernig, BGB, Vor §§ 249–253 Nos 40 et seq. (18th ed., 2021).
701. BGH, *NJW* 1984, 2457, 2458; and BGH, *NJW* 1997, 2378.
702. BGH, *NJW* 1968, 491; BGH, *NJW* 1982, 32, 33; and BGH, *NJW* 1990, 1360.

§5. METHODS OF PAYMENT

I. Lump Sum

237. According to section 249 BGB, damage to property usually has to be compensated in kind, although the victim may opt for compensation in money. Moreover, the victim may also demand monetary compensation if the tortfeasor does not provide restitution in kind within a reasonable period of time set by the victim, provided the latter has declared that he will not accept restitution in kind after the period's expiration. Further, monetary compensation is the only available reparation if restitution in kind is unfeasible or insufficient to compensate the victim. The tortfeasor may opt for compensation in money according to section 251(2) BGB if compensation in kind would require disproportionate efforts. Whenever the true scope of the damage remains doubtful, section 287 ZPO empowers the judge to determine the amount of compensation, provided the victim can at least prove the occurrence of pecuniary loss. Hence, the victim bears the burden of proof. If the victim is entitled to monetary compensation for immaterial damage, the judge has to estimate a reasonable amount according to the circumstances of the individual case.

238. In case of bodily injury, the tortfeasor usually has to compensate the victim for his medical expenses. Additionally, the victim may claim compensation for earnings that were lost as a result of the damaging event.[703] The tort victim's loss is determined without taking into account the continuation of wage payment by his employer or social security benefits.[704] If the victim is in receipt of such benefits, however, his claim is regularly transferred by law to the employer or social insurance institution granting the benefits.[705] A person who is made incapable of earning a livelihood as a result of bodily injury may demand compensation for the reduced chances of future earnings in the form of a lump sum instead of annuities only under special circumstances. Section 843(3) BGB requests a serious cause for a lump sum settlement. A serious cause in this context may exist, *inter alia*, if the tortfeasor lives abroad, and thus, the enforcement of the claim for annuities would be exceptionally burdensome for the victim.[706]

II. Annuities

239. As seen above, compensation by way of money annuities is the regular remedy if, in consequence of injury to body or health, the earning capacity of the injured person is destroyed or impaired.[707] Only under exceptional circumstances may the tort victim claim a lump sum payment.[708] Compensation by payment of a

703. *See* s. 842 BGB.
704. *See* BGHZ 7, 30; BGHZ 21, 112; and BGHZ 90, 334, 338.
705. For further references *see* Grüneberg, in: Grüneberg, BGB, Vorb v § 249 Nos 113 et seq. (82nd ed., 2023).
706. Cf. Sprau, in: Grüneberg, BGB, § 843 No. 18 (82nd ed., 2023).
707. *See* s. 843(1) BGB.
708. *See* Part VI, Ch. 3, §5, I.

money annuity has the advantage that the annuity may be adapted to changing circumstances, thereby facilitating the assessment. Annuities are fixed in the particular judgment until the prospective time of retirement. The amount and duration are dependent on the kind of occupational disability as well as on the physical and mental condition of the tort victim.[709] If the underlying circumstances significantly change, adaptation of the annuities to the victim's real needs may be claimed with an action under section 323 ZPO.

240. Whenever a tortious conduct results in the victim's death, according to section 844(2) BGB, the tortfeasor shall compensate a third party, to whom the deceased at the time of injury stood in a relationship by virtue of which he was legally bound to furnish maintenance, by the payment of a money annuity, insofar as the deceased would have been bound to furnish maintenance during the presumable duration of his life, provided the third party is deprived of the right to claim maintenance in consequence of the victim's death. The assessment of annuities requires a future-orientated prognosis.[710] In order to determine the amount of compensation according to section 287 ZPO, the judge, therefore, needs to exhaustively evaluate all factors decisive for a future-orientated prognosis, such as the financial ability and the life expectancy of the deceased person and the neediness of the entitled person.[711] The obligation to make compensation arises even if, at the time of the injury, the third party was conceived but not yet born.[712] The widow of the deceased may claim annuities even in case of a remarriage, provided the support she receives from her new husband falls short of previous maintenance.[713]

241. Similar to the general tort law provisions of the Civil Code, numerous special, strict liability laws also include express provisions on compensation by way of money annuities for a reduced earning capacity resulting from injury to the body or health.[714] However, these statutes, as a rule, also state that the tort victim may request payment of a lump sum in exceptional situations (usually by simply referring to section 843(2) BGB).[715]

III. Others

242. As seen above, the principal remedy under the German Civil Code is restitution in kind, i.e., a restoration of the former state,[716] which is, however, not

709. Sprau, in: Grüneberg, BGB, § 843 No. 4 (82nd ed., 2023).
710. Sprau, in: Grüneberg, BGB, § 843 No. 4 (82nd ed., 2023).
711. BGH, *VersR* 2012, 1048, 1049; BGH, *NJW* 2004, 358, 360; and Sprau, in: Grüneberg, BGB, § 843 No. 4 (82nd ed., 2023); *see also* Diederichsen, *NJW* 2013, 641, 644.
712. *See* s. 844(2) sentence 2 BGB.
713. Sprau, in: Grüneberg, BGB, § 843 No. 20 (82nd ed., 2023).
714. *See*, e.g., s. 9 ProdHaftG, s. 8 HPflG, s. 14 UmweltHG and s. 13 StVG.
715. *See*, e.g., s. 9(2) ProdHaftG, s. 8(2) HPflG, s. 14(2) UmweltHG, and s. 13(2) StVG.
716. *See* Part VI, Ch. 1.

always feasible. In case of certain bodily injuries or the death of a person, restitution of the former state is impossible. As far as property damage is concerned, restitution in kind is often practicable. Instead of paying a certain amount of money, the tortfeasor may restore the situation as it was before the damaging event, provided the victim does not opt for monetary compensation under section 249(2) sentence 1 BGB. Alternatively, the tort victim may himself provide for such restitution of the former state. If the victim does so, he may claim the necessary amount of money for the restoration. Necessary in this context is the amount a reasonable, economically thinking person would have spent in the specific situation.[717] Furthermore, the monetary compensation shall not lead to an unjust enrichment; the tort victim may justly seek complete and comprehensive compensation but shall not gain profit from the damaging event.[718]

717. *See* BGHZ 54, 82, 85; BGHZ 61, 346, 349; BGH, *NJW* 1992, 1618, 1619; BGH, *NJW* 2009, 3022, 3023; and BGH, *NJW* 2012, 50, 51.
718. Constant case law: cf. BGH, *NJW* 2012, 50, 51; BGH, *NJW* 2009, 3022, 3023; BGH, *NJW* 2007, 67, 68;and BGH, *NJW* 2006, 2176, 2180.

Chapter 4. Personal Injury and Death

§1. PECUNIARY LOSSES

243. The primary remedy in case of personal (bodily) injury is compensation for the tort victim's medical expenses and lost earnings. Section 842 BGB states that the tortfeasor's obligation to make compensation on account of a tort, which was directed against another person's body or health, extends to the detriment the act causes to the victim's earnings or prosperity. The damage resulting from lost earnings principally has to be compensated by money annuities.[719] In Germany, a victim suffering bodily injury is usually already compensated for his medical expenses by a social security institution. Likewise, the social security system also provides basic protection for persons who are no longer able to secure their livelihood by their own labour. Therefore, section 116 of the 10th book of the Social Security Code (*Sozialgesetzbuch – Zehntes Buch* (SGB X)) transfers the victim's claim against the tortfeasor to the social security institution providing the compensation. This assignment by operation of law puts the social security institution in a position to reclaim the expenses from the wrongdoer.

244. If the victim is killed by the tortious conduct, the person bound to make compensation shall make good the funeral expenses to the person who has the obligation of bearing such expenses.[720] The recoverable expenses under section 844(1) BGB correspond with the costs the heir has to bear according to section 1968 BGB.[721] They do not include the costs for the maintenance of the burial place[722] and, as a rule, the travel expenses a family member had to spend in order to attend the funeral.[723] In addition to the funeral expenses, all persons who had a legal title to be maintained by the deceased may claim money annuities insofar as they are deprived of the right to claim maintenance as a result of the victim's death.[724] Apart from these annuities, surviving dependants who stood in a particularly close relationship with the killed person at the time of the infringement are entitled to claim appropriate compensation in money for their emotional suffering according to section 844(3) sentence 1 BGB. Such a relationship is presumed if the surviving dependant was the spouse, life partner, parent, or child of the killed person. The actual amount depends on the intensity of the relationship, the personal conditions of the surviving dependant, including the mental capacity, and the circumstances of the infringing act insofar as they affect the surviving dependant.[725]

---

719. *See* Part VI, Ch. 3, §5, II.
720. *See* s. 844(1) BGB.
721. Cf. OLG Hamm, *NJW-RR* 1994, 155.
722. *See* BGHZ 61, 238.
723. *See* BGHZ 32, 72.
724. *See* Part VI, Ch. 3, §5, II.
725. *See* Sprau, in: Grüneberg, BGB, § 844 No. 25 (82nd ed., 2023).

§2. Non-pecuniary Losses

245. In case of injury to body or health, the victim may demand fair compensation in money for non-pecuniary damages (*Schmerzensgeld*), i.e., for pain and suffering, according to section 253(2) BGB. Before the amendment of section 253(2) BGB, in the course of the recent tort law reform, compensation for pain and suffering was limited to claims that were based on the general tort law rules of the Civil Code. The main reason for the narrow field of application was the notion that immaterial damage, especially the feeling of pain, cannot easily be determined in terms of money. Since 1 August 2002, however, it may also be claimed under the various special laws providing strict liability for certain dangerous activities.[726]

246. According to the Federal Supreme Court, the award of immaterial damages under section 253(2) BGB has two basic functions: it achieves the purpose of reimbursing the victim for the pain he had to endure (*Ausgleichsfunktion*), and it grants the victim satisfaction or retribution (*Genugtuungsfunktion*).[727] A third function that plays an important role in recent decisions of the Federal Supreme Court is the prevention of future infringements (*Präventionsfunktion*). However, the latter function predominantly concerns violations of the right to one's personality.[728] It has to be pointed out that the claim for immaterial damage may not be divided into its separate functions since it is a single unitary claim.[729]

247. The award of compensation for pain and suffering requires that one of the interests enumerated in section 253(2) BGB is violated (i.e., body, health, freedom, or the right of sexual self-determination). Hence, compensation for purely mental pain, which is not a direct result of injury to body or health, cannot be awarded. This restriction is of particular significance in cases where a person's health is impaired because of the killing of a close relative: Compensation for pain and suffering may only be claimed if the shock is of such severity that it amounts to bodily injury; the individual grief is not compensable under section 253(2) BGB.[730] Consequently, the Federal Supreme Court refused to grant compensation for the individual grief suffered due to the loss of a pet.[731] However, German courts consider even an unwanted pregnancy an injury to body in terms of section 253(2) BGB.[732]

248. The compensation that is awarded for the victim's pain and suffering is calculated from the point of equity. The underlying thought is that similar injuries

726. *See*, e.g., s. 8 ProdHaftG, s. 6 HPflG, s. 13 UmweltHG, and s. 11 StVG.
727. *See* BGHZ 128, 117, 119 et seq.; OLG Saarbrücken, *NJW* 2008, 1166, 1168; and Grüneberg, in: Grüneberg, BGB, § 253 No. 4 (82nd ed., 2023).
728. Cf. BGHZ 128, 1, 15 et seq.; BGH, *NJW* 1995, 861, 865.
729. Cf. BGHZ 128, 117; and Spindler, in: BeckOK, BGB, § 253 No. 14 (65th ed., 2023).
730. Cf. OLG Nürnberg, *NJW* 1998, 2293; *see also* OLG Hamm, *VersR* 1998, 730, 731; OLG Nürnberg, *VersR* 1997, 328; OLG Düsseldorf, *NJW-RR* 1996, 214; and Diederichsen, *NJW* 2013, 641, 647.
731. BGH, *NJW* 2012, 1730, 1731; *see also* Diederichsen, *NJW* 2013, 641, 647.
732. Cf. BGH, *NJW* 1995, 2407, 2408; BGH, *NJW* 1980, 1452; OLG Düsseldorf, *NJW* 1995, 788, 789; and OLG Oldenburg, *NJW* 1996, 2432, 2433.

should result in comparable damage awards, irrespective of the foundation of the claim.[733] Relevant factors for determining the scope of the compensation primarily are the kind and duration of the injury and the resulting pain,[734] as well as the tortious intent of the tortfeasor.[735] Other aspects include the victim's age and personal circumstances, the length of a hospital stay, the degree of impairment of the victim's life or personal dignity,[736] the causation of permanent deformations, and even the impairment or cancellation of a planned holiday.[737] However, it is irrelevant whether the person claiming compensation comes from a legal system with extraordinarily high awards for pain and suffering (especially in the US).[738] The victim's contributory fault is merely one factor among others for the determination of the recoverable amount.[739]

249. In practice, important aids regarding the determination of the compensation's scope are the various schedules reporting the courts' decisions on immaterial damage.[740] These schedules are regularly updated and list the different awards of compensation for pain and suffering, basically sorted by the various types of injuries and the amount of damages. All in all, the sums awarded for pain and suffering are rather modest, especially when compared with US verdicts. For example, a severe brain trauma, which resulted in organic brain damage with permanent emotional, physical, motor, and cognitive consequences, may lead to the award of EUR 112,500.[741] In specific cases of serious injuries that result in permanent paralysis where the victim is conscious, however, the award of an amount of up to EUR 500,000 may be justified.[742]

---

733. *See* BGH, *VersR* 1970, 281, 282; and OLG Frankfurt, *DAR* 1994, 21, 23.
734. Cf. BGH, *VersR* 1988, 943; and OLG Oldenburg, *VersR* 1996, 726, 727.
735. Cf. OLG Saarbrücken, *NJW* 2008, 1166, 1168.
736. Cf. OLG Hamm, *NJW-RR* 2009, 959, 960.
737. For further references, *see* Grüneberg, in: Grüneberg, BGB, § 253 Nos 15 et seq. (82nd ed., 2023).
738. *See* OLG Koblenz, *NJW-RR* 2002, 1030.
739. Grüneberg, in: Grüneberg, BGB, § 253 No. 20 (82nd ed., 2023); and Spindler, in: BeckOK, BGB, § 253 No. 68 (65th ed., 2023).
740. *See* Hacks, Wellner, Häcker and Offenlock, *SchmerzensgeldBeträge 2023* (41th ed., 2022); and Slizyk, *Schmerzensgeld 2023* (19th ed., 2023).
741. LG Dortmund, *NJW-RR* 2000, 402.
742. *See* LG München I, *NJW-RR* 2001, 1246, 1247.

Chapter 5. Various Damages

250. In a case of damage to property, the tort victim may claim restitution in kind under section 249(1) BGB. If the tort victim chooses restitution in kind, the tortfeasor has to restore the state that would have existed without the damaging act. The tortfeasor may, however, choose the way he renders restitution in kind. Hence, the victim has no right, e.g., to choose a specific repair shop. The tortfeasor even is allowed to repair the damaged property himself if he is sufficiently skilled.[743] Since the tortfeasor's right to choose a certain manner to render restitution in kind may be unacceptable to the tort victim, section 249(2) sentence 1 BGB allows the victim to opt for monetary compensation instead if the tortfeasor caused property damage.[744] The tort victim may claim the amount of money necessary to effect the damaged property's restitution. Necessary in these terms is the amount a reasonable, understanding and economically thinking person would consider essential to ensure adequate restoration.[745] If an object is lost or fully destroyed, the amount will be determined in view of the current replacement value. With respect to cars, the replacement value will be approximately 12%–25% above the current market value due to the dealer's margin.[746] Should the car still have been in mint condition (i.e., with a mileage of less than 1,000 kilometres), the damage is assessed in consideration of the original price.[747]

251. In case an object is not fully destroyed but merely damaged, the tort victim may choose between the amount of money necessary to repair the object and the difference between the object's current replacement value and its salvage value.[748] The cost of repair has to be determined objectively. Usually, the amount actually spent indicates the appropriate value. However, the tort victim may opt for a fictive assessment of damages. He may, on the basis of an expert opinion, claim the amount of money a professional repair shop would charge for an accurately executed repair.[749] In such a case, it is irrelevant whether the damaged object is repaired by the tort victim himself, by an illicit worker, or not at all.[750] If the tort victim opts for a repair of the damaged object, he may also claim the loss in value upon resale (*merkantiler Minderwert*), i.e., the loss in value a damaged object has despite a professionally executed repair.[751]

743. Brand, in: BeckOGK, BGB, § 249 No. 112 (version 01.03.2023).
744. The same rule applies with respect to bodily injury, *see* s. 249(2) sentence 1 BGB.
745. *See* BGH, *NJW* 1970, 1454, 1454; BGH, NJW 1974, 34, 35; BGH, *NJW* 1992, 1618, 1619; BGH, *NJW* 2012, 50, 51; Brand, in: BeckOGK, BGB, § 249 No. 128 (version 01.03.2023); and Grüneberg, in: Grüneberg, BGB, § 249 No. 12 (82nd ed., 2023).
746. Brand, in: BeckOGK, BGB, § 249 No. 190 (version 01.03.2023).
747. BGH, *NJW* 1982, 433; BGH, *NJW* 1983, 2694; and Brand, in: BeckOGK, BGB, § 249 No. 136 (version 01.03.2023).
748. BGH, *NJW* 1972, 1800, 1801; and Brand, in: BeckOGK, BGB, § 249 No. 125 (version 01.03.2023).
749. Grüneberg, in: Grüneberg, BGB, § 249 No. 14 (82nd ed., 2023).
750. *See* BGH, *NJW* 1973, 1647, 1648; BGH, *NJW* 1975, 160; BGH, *NJW* 1976, 1396; BGH, *NJW* 1985, 1222; and BGH, *NJW* 2003, 2085.
751. Grüneberg, in: Grüneberg, BGB, § 251 No. 14 (82nd ed., 2023); and Oetker, in: Münchener Kommentar, BGB, § 249 Nos 53 et seq. (9th ed., 2022).

252. The tortfeasor's duty to compensate also extends to consequential loss. Hence, the tort victim may claim compensation for tax disadvantages,[752] increased insurance rates,[753] lawyer's and court fees in connection with the enforcement of his claim,[754] and expenses for an expert opinion.[755] He is, however, not entitled to compensation for the expenditure of time in connection with the settlement of the claim.[756]

752. Oetker, in: Münchener Kommentar, BGB, § 249 Nos 506 et seq. (9th ed., 2022).
753. BGH, *NJW* 1984, 2627.
754. Brand, in: BeckOGK, BGB, § 249 Nos 172 et seq. (version 01.03.2023); and Grüneberg, in: Grüneberg, BGB, § 249 Nos 56 et seq. (82nd ed., 2023).
755. BGH, *NJW* 1974, 34, 35; and BGH, *NJW* 2004, 3042.
756. BGH, *NJW* 1976, 1256; BGH, *NJW* 1977, 35; BGH, *NJW* 1980, 119; and Grüneberg, in: Grüneberg, BGB, § 249 No. 59 (82nd ed., 2023).

Chapter 6. Interference with Collateral Benefits

§1. Insurance

253. Insurance coverage is widespread in Germany, as either indemnity insurance or third-party insurance. A common form of indemnity insurance is a householder's comprehensive insurance (*Hausratversicherung*), which covers damage to the house's contents. Often, such householder's comprehensive insurance is combined with personal liability insurance (*Privathaftpflichtversicherung*), covering damage caused by one of the family members living in a household. Insurance coverage is common not only in the private sector but also in the industrial sector. Business enterprises usually insure against certain hazards, such as liability risks, fire or theft, and consequential loss resulting from a temporary interruption of business.

254. These voluntary insurances are supplemented by mandatory insurance (*Pflichtversicherung*) for certain hazardous activities, especially the operation of a motor vehicle, under the rules of the Obligatory Insurance Act. According to section 1 PflVG, the keeper of a motor vehicle has the duty to conclude an insurance contract providing sufficient coverage as required by the appendix to the Obligatory Insurance Act. The Obligatory Insurance Act has the aim that the victim of a traffic accident shall not be faced with an insolvent tortfeasor. This goal is also furthered by granting the victim a direct claim against the insurer according to section 3 No. 1 PflVG. Hence, it is not necessary for the victim to sue the tortfeasor primarily in order to bring a claim for insurance coverage into existence.

255. Whenever an insurance company indemnifies a tort victim, the victim's claim against the tortfeasor or any other person that initiated a cause for the injury or contributed to its causation is assigned to the insurer by operation of law according to section 86 of the Insurance Act (VVG). As a consequence of this assignment, the insurance company is in a position enabling it to shift the loss to the truly responsible person.

§2. Social Security

256. Akin to private insurance, social security has a significant impact on tortious liability. The far-reaching German system of mandatory social insurance guarantees that most victims suffering bodily injury are indemnified for their medical expenses, lost earnings, and increased necessities by social health insurance (*Gesetzliche Krankenversicherung*). Moreover, compensation for damages resulting from accidents at work is provided by mandatory occupational accident insurance (*Gesetzliche Unfallversicherung*). The respective social insurance premiums are distributed among the workers and their employers.

257. As described above, section 116 SGB X assigns the victim's claim against the tortfeasor to the social security institution providing the compensation by operation of law. The social security institution may seek indemnification by bringing a subrogation claim for the sum it has paid to the victim against the primarily responsible wrongdoer. The assignment by operation of law includes not only claims based on the general tort law provisions of the Civil Code but also claims under the various strict liability laws and even contractual claims of the victim.

258. Of particular importance with respect to the mandatory occupational accident insurance is the so-called liability privilege for the employer (*Arbeitgeberprivileg*) according to section 104 of the 7th book of the Social Security Code (*Sozialgesetzbuch – Siebtes Buch* (SGB VII)). The employer is only liable to his employees for personal injury resulting from accidents at work if he wilfully caused the damage or if the damage was caused 'en route' (i.e., in particular, on the way to or from the workplace).[757] According to section 105(1) SGB VII, the same rules apply to persons employed by the same enterprise if they cause bodily injury to a co-worker in the course of their employment. The often problematic distinction of whether damage was caused 'en route' or at work (leading to the application of sections 104, 105 SGB VII) has given rise to a vast case law. Courts usually ask if the employee was injured in the employer's organizational sphere or if the injury only had a loose connection with that sphere.[758] A shuttle service between the employee's home and the workplace can be attributed to the employer's sphere if the transportation is job-related and conducted with a company vehicle.[759]

§3. Others

259. In connection with the damaging event, the tort victim may receive not only insurance and social security benefits but also monetary benefits deriving from other sources. If this is the case, such benefits may result in a reduction of the victim's claim in order to compensate for the benefits received.[760]

757. *See* s. 104(1) Sozialgesetzbuch, Siebtes Buch.
758. Cf. BGH, *NZA* 2004, 1165, 1166 et seq.; and BAG, *DB* 2004, 656, 657 et seq.
759. BGHZ 157, 159, 162 et seq.; and BAG, *DB* 2004, 656, 657 et seq.; *see also* BGHZ 145, 311, 313 et seq.
760. *See* Part VI, Ch. 3, §4.

Chapter 7. Other Remedies

§1. Restitution for Unjust Enrichment

260. The German Civil Code provides a number of actions for persons who are deprived of their property or other benefits without justification by law.[761] The rules on unjust enrichment (*ungerechtfertigte Bereicherung*) are based on the notion that unjustified asset transfers should be compensated. An unjust enrichment may be caused either by the conveyance of an asset from one person to another or by an intrusion upon another person's rights or interests that causes an asset transfer, provided a legal ground (*rechtlicher Grund*) for the transfer is not available. The most important basis for an unjust enrichment action is section 812(1) sentence 1 BGB, which reflects the ancient Roman *condictiones indebiti et sine causa*, and states that a person who obtains something by the performance of another person or in any other way at the expense of such person, in the absence of legal ground, is bound to return it to him.

261. Unlike most tort law claims regarding compensation for damages, claims based on the Civil Code's rules on unjust enrichment are not based on the principle of fault. An action based on section 812 BGB may be brought against the person who enriched himself at the plaintiff's expense, even if he did not act culpably. Another important difference between tort law and the law of unjust enrichment has recently been eliminated by the German legislator. Prior to 1 January 2002, the limitation period for unjust enrichment claims was thirty years, while the respective period for tort law claims was considerably shorter (three years). This had the effect that an action based on section 812 BGB was still possible, even if a tort law claim had already been barred by the expiration of the limitation period. However, in the course of the recent reform of the law of obligations, the legislator set the regular statutory limitation period, which applies to unjust enrichment claims as well as to tort law claims, to three years.[762]

§2. Injunctive Relief

262. Injunctive relief is provided by the rules of German civil law in a number of cases where a claim for damages is available. However, contrary to such claims for compensation, injunctive relief may be obtained independent of the defendant's fault; the mere infringement of one of the plaintiff's rights or legally protected interests is sufficient.

263. The Civil Code's predominant provision for injunctive relief is section 1004 BGB. Although from its wording, the rule appears to be applicable only in cases of interference with property, it is generally recognized that injunctive relief under section 1004 BGB may also be obtained if one of the other rights or legally

761. *See* ss 812–822 BGB.
762. *See* s. 195 BGB.

protected interests enumerated by section 823(1) BGB is violated. Section 1004 BGB requires the actual and imminent threat of an infringement, i.e., a serious concern that the right or legally protected interest will be violated, but for injunctive relief. Another precondition of section 1004 BGB is the unlawfulness of the threatening infringement.[763]

264. Other claims for injunctive relief are provided, *inter alia*, by section 12 BGB for infringements of the right to one's name, section 862 BGB for interferences with possession, and in several special laws, such as section 139 of the Patent Act (*Patentgesetz* or *PatG*) or section 97 of the Copyright Act (*Urheberrechtsgesetz* or *UrhG*) for infringements of intellectual property.

§3. Punitive Damages

265. Under the rules of German tort law, damages have a compensatory character only. The aim of tortious liability is to put the victim in the same position he would be in, devoid of the injurious act. Thus, there is no possibility for the tort victim to claim punitive damages.

763. Cf. Herrler, in: Grüneberg, BGB, § 1004 No. 12 (82nd ed., 2023).

Selected Bibliography

§1. Tort Law in General

Andreas Spickhoff, Die Grundstruktur der deliktischen Verschuldenshaftung, JuS 2016, 865.

Basil S. Markesinis, John Bell & André Janssen, *Markesinis's German Law of Torts* (5th ed., 2019).

Christian Förster, Verschuldensvermutung bei der Amtshaftung – Aufsichtspflicht von Kindergartenpersonal, NJW 2013, 1201.

Christian v. Bar, Gemeineuropäisches Deliktsrecht, Vol. I (1996), Vol. II (1999).

Claus-Wilhelm Canaris, Grundstrukturen des deutschen Deliktsrechts, *VersR* 2005, 577.

Eduard Picker, Das Deliktsrecht im Zivilrechtssystem, ZfPW 2015, 385.

Erwin Deutsch, *Allgemeines Haftungsrecht* (2nd ed., 1996).

Erwin Deutsch & Hans-Jürgen Ahrens, *Deliktsrecht* (6th ed., 2014).

Gert Brüggemeier, *Deliktsrecht* (1986).

Gert Brüggemeier, *Prinzipien des Haftungsrechts* (1999).

Gert Brüggemeier, *Haftungsrecht: Struktur, Prinzipien, Schutzbereich* (2006).

Hein Kötz & Gerhard Wagner, *Deliktsrecht* (13th ed., 2016).

Jan D. Lüttringhaus, Deutsches Delikts- und Schadensrecht unter unionsrechtlichem Einfluss, VersR 2014, 653.

Jan Oster, Das allgemeine Persönlichkeitsrecht ist aufzugeben – eine neue Deliktsrechtsdogmatik für Verletzungen von Persönlichkeitsrechtsgütern, ZfPW 2021, 434.

Jörg Neuner, Die Einwilligung im Deliktsrecht, JuS 2021, 617.

Klaus Vieweg, *The Law of Torts*, Introduction to German Law 197–226 (Ebke & Finkin eds. 1996).

Manfred Wandt, *Gesetzliche Schuldverhältnisse* (9th ed., 2018).

Mathias Rohe, Gründe und Grenzen deliktischer Haftung, 201 *AcP* 117–164 (2001).

Maximilian Fuchs, Werner Pauker & Alex Baumgärtner, Deliktsrecht (9th ed., 2016).

Thomas Riehm, 'Dieselgate' und das Deliktsrecht, DAR 2016, 12.

§2. Damages

Andreas Cahn, *Einführung in das neue Schadensersatzrecht* (2003).

Selected Bibliography

Angela Diederichsen, Ansprüche naher Angehöriger von Unfallopfern, *NJW* 2013, 641.

Christian Förster. Schadensrecht – Systematik und neuste Rechtsprechung, JA 2015, 801.

Dieter Medicus, Ansprüche auf Schadensersatz, *JuS* 1986, 665.

Eduard Picker, Vertragliche und deliktische Schadenshaftung, *JZ* 1987, 1041.

Gerald Spindler, Anmerkung zu BGH, Urteil vom 24.01.2013 – III ZR 98/12, *JZ* 2013, 897.

Gerhard Wagner, *Neue Perspektiven im Schadensersatzrecht – Kommerzialisierung, Strafschadensersatz,* Kollektivschaden, Gutachten A für den 66. Deutsche Juristentag, in: Verhandlungen des sechsundsechzigsten Deutschen Juristentages (2006).

Gerhard Wagner, Das zweite Schadensersatzrechtsänderungsgesetz, *NJW* 2002, 2049.

Hans Stoll, *Neuere Entwicklungen auf dem Gebiete des deutschen Schadensrechtes* (1976).

Heinrich Honsell & Friedrich Harrer, Entwicklungstendenzen im Schadensersatzrecht, *JuS* 1985, 161.

Heinrich Honsell & Friedrich Harrer, Schaden und Schadensberechnung, *JuS* 1981, 441.

Herman Lange & Gottfried Schiemann, *Schadensersatz* (3rd ed., 2003).

Klaus Budewig & Markus Gehrlein, *Das Haftpflichtrecht nach der Reform* (2003).

Markus Gehrlein, Grundlagen des Schadensrechts, *JA* 1995, 69.

Nils Jansen, Konturen eines europäischen Schadensrechts, *JZ* 2005, 160.

Stefan Homann, Typische Probleme des Schadensersatzrechts und ihre Einordnung, *JuS* 2002, 554.

Wolfgang Däubler, Die Reform des Schadensersatzrechts, *JuS* 2002, 625.

§3. Causation

Constantin Kruse, *Alternative Kausalität im Deliktsrecht: eine historische und vergleichende Untersuchung* (2006).

Egon Lorenz, *Grundsatz und Grenzen der Folgenzurechnung im Schadensersatzrecht*, Festschrift für Deutsch, 251 (1999).

Erwin Deutsch, *Zurechnungszusammenhang, Rechtswidrigkeit und Verschulden*, Festschrift für Medicus, 77 (1999).

Hans Stoll, *Kausalzusammanhang und Normzweck im Deliktsrecht* (1968).

Hans-Joachim Musielak, Kausalität und Schadenszurechnung im Zivilrecht, JA 2013, 241.

Hermann Lange, Adäquanztheorie, Rechtswidrigkeitszusammenhang, Schutzzwec klehre und selbständige Zurechnungsmomente, *JZ* 1976, 198.

Peter Hanau, *Die Kausalität der Pflichtwidrigkeit* (1971).

§4. Unlawfulness/Fault

Erwin Deutsch, *Fahrlässigkeit und erforderliche Sorgfalt* (2d ed. 1995).

Erwin Deutsch, Der Begriff der Fahrlässigkeit im Zivilrecht, *Jura* 1987, 505.

Gerhard Wagner, *Öffentlich-rechtliche Genehmigung und zivilrechtliche Rechtswidrigkeit* (1989).
Hans Carl Nipperdey, Rechtswidrigkeit und Schuld im Zivilrecht, *Karlsruher Forum* 1959, 3.
Karl Larenz, Möglichkeiten einer Begrenzung der Haftung über Kausalität, Rechtswidrigkeit, Verschulden, *Karlsruher Forum* 1959, 10.
Karl Larenz, *Rechtswidrigkeit und Handlungsbegriff im Zivilrecht*, Festschrift für Dölle 169 (1963).
Nils Jansen, Das Problem der Rechtswidrigkeit bei § 823 Abs. 1 BGB, 202 *AcP* 517 (2002).
Olaf Deinert, Unfallversicherungsregress und innerbetrieblicher Schadensausgleich, *RdA* 2013, 146.
Reinhold Zippelius, Die Rechtswidrigkeit von Handlung und Erfolg, 157 *AcP* 390 (1957).
Ronny Hauck, Der Schutz von Minderjährigen bei Eingriffen in höchstpersönliche Rechte und Rechtsgüter, *NJW* 2012, 2398.

§5. Duties to Ensure Public Safety

Andreas Fuchs, Arbeitsteilung und Haftung, *JZ* 1994, 533.
Christian Förster, Verkehrssicherungspflichten, JA 2017, 721.
Christian v. Bar, *Verkehrspflichten* (1980).
Christian v. Bar, Entwicklungen und Entwicklungstendenzen im Recht der Verkehrs(sicherungs)pflichten, *JuS* 1988, 169.
Claus-Wilhelm Canaris, *Schutzgesetze – Verkehrspflichten – Schutzpflichten*, Festschrift für Larenz 27 (1983).
Detlef Kleindiek, *Deliktshaftung und juristische Person* (1997).
Erich Steffen, Verkehrspflichten im Spannungsfeld von Bestandsschutz und Handlungsfreiheit, *VersR* 1980, 409.
Georg Patzelt, *Verkehrssicherungspflichten* (4th ed., 2006).
Gerald Spindler, *Unternehmensorganisationspflichten* (2nd ed., 2011).
Hans Stoll, *Richterliche Fortbildung und gesetzliche Überarbeitung des Deliktsrechts* (1984).
Jan Schröder, Verkehrssicherungspflicht gegenüber Unbefugten, 179 *AcP* 567 (1979).
Karsten Schmidt, Haftung und Zurechnung im Unternehmensbereich, *Karlsruher Forum* 1993, 4.
Lothar Vollmer, Haftungsbefreiende Übertragung von Verkehrssicherungspflichten, *JZ* 1977, 371.
Peter Ulmer, Die deliktische Haftung aus der Übernahme von Handlungspflichten, *JZ* 1969, 163.
Thomas M.J. Möllers, *Rechtsgüterschutz im Umwelt-* und *Haftungsrecht* (1996).
Thomas M.J. Möllers, Verkehrspflichten gegenüber Kindern, *VersR* 1996, 153.
Thomas Raab, Die Bedeutung der Verkehrspflicht und ihre systematische Stellung im Deliktsrecht, *JuS* 2002, 1041.

§6. Liability for Acts of Others

Anne Strohbach, *Der Dritte im Schadensersatzrecht* (2006).
Dieter Medicus, *Zur deliktischen Eigenhaftung von Organpersonen*, Festschrift für W. Lorenz 155 (1991).
Dieter Medicus, *Zum Anwendungsbereich der Übernehmerhaftung nach § 831 Abs. 2 BGB*, Festschrift für Deutsch 291 (1999).
Ernst v. Caemmerer, Reformprobleme der Haftung für Hilfspersonen, *ZfRV* 1973, 241.
Frank Walter Schmitz, *Die deliktische Haftung für Arbeitnehmer* (1994).
Gerhard Hassold, Die Lehre vom Organisationsverschulden, *JuS* 1982, 583.
Gert Brüggemeier, Organisationshaftung – Deliktsrechtliche Aspekte innerorganisatorischer Funktionsdifferenzierung, 191 *AcP* 33 (1991).
Gunther Teubner, Verbund, Verband oder Verkehr – zur Außenhaftung von Franchising-Systemen, 154 *ZHR* 295 (1990).
Nicolas Eilers, Haftung des Verrichtungsgehilfen gemäß § 831 BGB, ZFS 2013, 124.
Rupert Kiser, Die Haftung des Fuhrparkhalters nach § 831 BGB hinsichtlich Auswahl und Beaufsichtigung des Fahrers, *VersR* 1984, 213.
Theodor Baums, *Haftung für Verrichtungsgehilfen nach deutschem und schweizerischem Recht*, Festschrift für Lukes 623 (1989).
Uwe Diederichsen, Zum Entlastungsbeweis für Verrichtungsgehilfen, *ZRP* 1968, 60.

§7. Liability of Parents, Teachers, Instructors, and Auditors

Albrecht Fuchs, *Studien zur elterlichen Aufsichtspflicht* (1995).
Bernhardt Großfeld & Birgit Mund, Die Haftung der Eltern nach § 832 I BGB, *FamRZ* 1994, 1504.
Christian Hartmann, Unmittelbare und mittelbare Aufsichtspflicht in § 832 BGB – pflichtbeschränkende Übertragung der Verkehrssicherung auf Dritte?, *VersR* 1998, 22.
Christoph H. Seibt and Bernward Wollenschläger, Dritthaftung des Abschlussp rüfers kapitalmarktorientierter Unternehmen, *DB* 2011, 1378.
Erwin Quambusch, *Das Recht der geistig Behinderten* (3d ed. 1995).
Hans-Joachim Albilt, *Haften Eltern für ihre Kinder?* (1987).
Menno Aden, Die Beweislast des Klägers im § 832 BGB, *MDR* 1974, 9.
Michael J. Schmidt, Aufsichtspflicht nach § 832 BGB, *VersR* 1982, 822.
Oliver Brand, Die Haftung des Aufsichtspflichtigen nach § 832 BGB, JuS 2012, 673.
Tessa Schoof, *Die Aufsichtspflicht der Eltern über ihre Kinder im Sinne des § 832 Abs. 1 BGB* (1999).

§8. Liability for Buildings and Animals

Christina Eberl-Borges, Die Tierhalterhaftung des Diebes, des Erben und des Minderjährigen, *VersR* 1996, 1070.

Erwin Deutsch, Gefährdungshaftung für laborgezüchtete Mikroorganismen, *NJW* 1976, 1137.
Erwin Deutsch, Der Reiter auf dem Pferd und der Fußgänger unter dem Pferd, *NJW* 1978, 1998.
Erwin Deutsch, Die Haftung des Tierhalters, *JuS* 1987, 673.
Friedrich Kreft, *Die Haftungsvoraussetzung durch ein Tier*, 25 Jahre Karlsruher Forum 153 (1983).
Gordian N. Hasselblatt, Reiten auf eigene Gefahr, aber fremde Rechnung?, *NJW* 1993, 2577.
Gottfried Baumgärtel, *Neue Tendenzen der Beweislastverteilung bei der Tierhalterhaftung*, 25 Jahre Karlsruher Forum 85 (1983).
Hans Hermann Seiler, *Tierhalterhaftung, Tiergefahr und Rechtswidrigkeit*, Festschrift für Albrecht Zeuner 279 (1994).
Hans Reinold Horst, Ausgewählte Fragen zum Schadensersatz wegen des Grundstückszustands, *MDR* 1998, 570.
Harald Hoffmann, Tierhalter- und Tierhüterhaftung, *ZFS* 2000, 181.
Jörg Petershagen, *Die Gebäudehaftung* (2000).
Michael Terbille, Der Schutzbereich der Tierhalterhaftung nach § 833 S. 1 BGB, *VersR* 1994, 1151.
Michael Terbille, Die Beweislastverteilung bei der Tierhalterhaftung nach § 833 S. 1 BGB, *VersR* 1995, 129.
Simone Hensen, Die Haftung des Nutztierhalters, NJW-Spezial 2017, 265.
Walter Dunz, Reiter wider Pferd, *JZ* 1987, 63.
Werner Lorenz, *Die Gefährdungshaftung des Tierhalters nach § 833 Satz 1 BGB* (1992).

§9. Strict Liability

Andreas Blaschczok, *Gefährdungshaftung und Risikozuweisung* (1993).
Anne Röthel, Gefährdungshaftung, Jura 2012, 244.
Dagmar Coester-Waltjen, Beweiserleichterungen und Gefährdungshaftungen, *Jura* 1996, 608.
Dieter Medicus, Gefährdungshaftung im Zivilrecht, *Jura* 1996, 561.
Erwin Deutsch, Das neue System der Gefährdungshaftungen: Gefährdungshaftung, erweiterte Gefährdungshaftung und Kausal-Vermutungshaftung, *NJW* 1992, 73.
Hans Stoll, Adäquanz und normative Zurechnung bei der Gefährdungshaftung, *Karlsruher Forum* 1983, 184.
Michael R. Will, *Quellen erhöhter Gefahr* (1980).
Susanne Hehl, *Das Verhältnis von Verschuldens- und Gefährdungshaftung* (1999).

§10. Road Traffic Act

Alexander Neumann, Die Haftung bei Verkehrsunfällen – eine Einführung, JA 2016, 167.
Rüdiger Martis, Die Haftung des Fahrzeugführers nach §§ 7, 18 StVG, *JA* 1997, 45.
Rüdiger Martis, Mitverursachung und Mitverschulden beim Straßenverkehrsunfall mit einzelnen Haftungsquoten, *JA* 1997, 141.

Selected Bibliography

§11. Medical Malpractice

Adolf Laufs, Bernd-Rüdiger Kern & Rehborn, *Handbuch des Arztrechts* (5th ed., 2019).

Alexander P.F. Ehlers & Maximilian Broglie, *Arzthaftungsrecht* (5th ed., 2014).

Christian Katzenmeier, *Arzthaftungsrecht* (2002).

Christoph Schärtl, Die Beweislastverteilung im Arzthaftungsprozess, NJW 2014, 3601.

Erich Steffen & Wolf-Dieter Dressler, *Arzthaftungsrecht* (9th ed., 2002).

Erwin Deutsch & Andreas Spickhoff, *Medizinrecht* (7th ed., 2014).

Gerald Mäsch, Demokratisches Schamanentum in Wahlkampfzeiten – Risiken und Nebenwirkungen des Patientenrechtegesetzes, *NJW* 2013, 1354.

Gerald Spindler & Oliver Rieckers, Auswirkungen der Schuld- und Schadensrechtsreform auf die Arzthaftung, *JuS* 2004, 272.

Karlmann Geiß & Hans-Peter Greiner, *Arzthaftpflichtrecht* (5th ed. 2006).

Markus Gehrlein, *Leitfaden zur Arzthaftpflicht* (2000).

Wolfgang Frahm, Wolfgang Nixdorf & Alexander Walter, *Arzthaftungsrecht* (4th ed., 2009).

§12. Product Liability

Christian Katzenmeier, Entwicklungen des Produkthaftungsrechts, *JuS* 2003, 943.

Detlef Koch, *Produkthaftung: Zur Konkurrenz von Kaufrecht und Deliktsrecht* (1995).

Friedrich Graf v. Westphalen, *Produkthaftungs-Handbuch* (2nd ed., 1997/1999).

Gerhard Wagner, Produktvigilanz und Haftung, *VersR* 2014, 905.

Hans Josef Kullmann, Bernhard Pfister, Karlheinz Stöhr & Gerald Spindler, *Produzentenhaftung* (loose-leaf compilation, 2021).

Joachim Schmidt-Salzer, *Produkthaftungsrecht* (2nd ed., 1988/1990).

Jürgen Oechsler, Die Haftung des Niederspannungsnetzbetreibers nach dem Produkthaftungsgesetz, *NJW* 2014, 2080.

Justus Meyer, *Instruktionshaftung* (1992).

Maximilian Fuchs & Alex Baumgärtner, Ansprüche aus Produzentenhaftung und Produkthaftung, JuS 2011, 1057.

Michael Molitoris & Thomas Klindt, Aktuelle Entwicklungen im Produktsic herheits- und Produkthaftungsrecht, NJW 2017, 1582.

Walter Rolland, *Produkthaftungsrecht* (1990).

§13. Environmental Liability

Fritz Nicklisch, Umweltschutz und Haftungsrisiken, *VersR* 1991, 1093.

Lothar Knopp, Hagen Lohmann & Jochen Schumacher, Das Umweltschadensgesetz in der Rechtsprechungspraxis, NuR 2017, 741.

Lutz Michalski, Das Umwelthaftungsgesetz, *Jura* 1995, 617.

Matthias Ruffert, Verantwortung und Haftung für Umweltschäden, *NVwZ* 2010, 117.

Michael Kloepfer, *Umweltrecht* (3rd ed., 2004).

Peter Salje, Die Entscheidungspraxis zum UmweltHG, *VersR* 1998, 797.

Peter Salje & Jörg Peter, *Umwelthaftungsgesetz* (2nd ed., 2005).

§14. Liability of Public Authorities

Boas Kümper, zur Drittgerichtetheit von Amtspflichten bei der Verletzung staatlicher Kontroll- und Überwachungspflichten – zugleich Anmerkung zu BGH, Urt. v. 08.11.2012 – III ZR 151/12 -, *DVBl* 2013, 1022.
Friedrich Schoch, Amtshaftung, *Jura* 1988, 585 & 648.
Fritz Ossenbühl, *Staatshaftungsrecht* (5th ed. 1998).
Ingo Saenger, Staatshaftung wegen Verletzung europäischen Gemeinschaftsrechts, *JuS* 1997, 865.
Michael Wurm, Drittgerichtetheit und Schutzzweck der Amtspflicht als Voraussetzung für die Amtshaftung, *JA* 1992, 1.
Wolfgang Schlick, Die Rechtsprechung des BGH zur Amtshaftung, NJW 2014, 2915.

§15. Contributory Fault

Albrecht Zeuner, *Zum Verhältnis zwischen Fremd- und Eigenverantwortlichkeit im Haftungsrecht*, Festschrift für Medicus 693 (1999).
Alexander Barde & Markus Gentzsch, Die Haftung von Beteiligten – Grundwissen zu § 830 I 2 BGB, JA 2016, 895.
Horst-Eberhard Henke, Die Versäumnisse Dritter und die Zurechnung als Mitverschulden des Geschädigten, *JuS* 1990, 30.
Horst-Eberhard Henke, Die Bewältigung des Mitverschuldens – eine anspruchsvolle juristische Technik, *JuS* 1991, 265.
Johannes Hager, Das Mitverschulden von Hilfspersonen und gesetzlichen Vertretern des Geschädigten, *NJW* 1989, 1640.
Thomas Honsell, *Die Quotenteilung im Schadensersatzrecht* (1977).
Walter Dunz, 'Eigenes Mitverschulden' und Selbstwiderspruch, *NJW* 1986, 2234.

§16. Injunctive Relief

Barbara Stickelbrock, Angleichung zivilrechtlicher und öffentlichrechtlicher Haftungsmaßstäbe beim Störerbegriff des § 1004 BGB, 197 *AcP* 456 (1997).
Egon Schneider, Der Widerruf von Werturteilen, *MDR* 1978, 613.
Elke Herrmann, *Der Störer nach § 1004 BGB (1987).*
Elke Herrmann, Haftungsvoraussetzungen nach § 1004 BGB – Neuere Entwicklung und Lösungsvorschlag, *JuS* 1994, 273.
Stephan Buchholz & Wolfram Radke, Negatorische Haftung und Billigkeit, *Jura* 1997, 454.

Selected Bibliography

Index

The numbers here refer to paragraph numbers.

Index

www.ingramcontent.com/pod-product-compliance
Lightning Source LLC
Chambersburg PA
CBHW071347230926
51846CB00002B/474
9789403500287